Palgrave Macmillan Studies in Banking and Financial Institutions

Series Editor: **Professor Philip Molyneux**

The Palgrave Macmillan Studies in Banking and Financial Institutions are international in orientation and include studies of banking within particular countries or regions, and studies of particular themes such as Corporate Banking, Risk Management, Mergers and Acquisitions, etc. The books' focus is on research and practice, and they include up-to-date and innovative studies on contemporary topics in banking that will have global impact and influence.

Titles include:

Yener Altunbaş, Blaise Gadanecz and Alper Kara
SYNDICATED LOANS
A Hybrid of Relationship Lending and Publicly Traded Debt

Yener Altunbaş, Alper Kara and Öslem Olgu
TURKISH BANKING
Banking under Political Instability and Chronic High Inflation

Elena Beccalli
IT AND EUROPEAN BANK PERFORMANCE

Paola Bongini, Stefano Chiarlone and Giovanni Ferri *(editors)*
EMERGING BANKING SYSTEMS

Vittorio Boscia, Alessandro Carretta and Paola Schwizer
COOPERATIVE BANKING: INNOVATIONS AND DEVELOPMENTS
COOPERATIVE BANKING IN EUROPE: CASE STUDIES

Roberto Bottiglia, Elisabetta Gualandri and Gian Nereo Mazzocco *(editors)*
CONSOLIDATION IN THE EUROPEAN FINANCIAL INDUSTRY

Alessandro Carretta, Franco Fiordelisi and Gianluca Mattarocci *(editors)*
NEW DRIVERS OF PERFORMANCE IN A CHANGING FINANCIAL WORLD

Dimitris N. Chorafas
CAPITALISM WITHOUT CAPITAL

Dimitris N. Chorafas
FINANCIAL BOOM AND GLOOM
The Credit and Banking Crisis of 2007–2009 and Beyond

Violaine Cousin
BANKING IN CHINA

Vincenzo D'Apice and Giovanni Ferri
FINANCIAL INSTABILITY
Toolkit for Interpreting Boom and Bust Cycles

Peter Falush and Robert L. Carter OBE
THE BRITISH INSURANCE INDUSTRY SINCE 1900
The Era of Transformation

Franco Fiordelisi
MERGERS AND ACQUISITIONS IN EUROPEAN BANKING

Franco Fiordelisi, Philip Molyneux and Daniele Previati *(editors)*
NEW ISSUES IN FINANCIAL AND CREDIT MARKETS

Franco Fiordelisi, Philip Molyneux and Daniele Previati *(editors)*
NEW ISSUES IN FINANCIAL INSTITUTIONS MANAGEMENT

Franco Fiordelisi and Philip Molyneux
SHAREHOLDER VALUE IN BANKING

Hans Genberg and Cho-Hoi Hui
THE BANKING CENTRE IN HONG KONG
Competition, Efficiency, Performance and Risk

Carlo Gola and Alessandro Roselli
THE UK BANKING SYSTEM AND ITS REGULATORY AND SUPERVISORY FRAMEWORK

Elisabetta Gualandri and Valeria Venturelli *(editors)*
BRIDGING THE EQUITY GAP FOR INNOVATIVE SMEs

Kim Hawtrey
AFFORDABLE HOUSING FINANCE

Otto Hieronymi (editor)
GLOBALIZATION AND THE REFORM OF THE INTERNATIONAL BANKING AND MONETARY
SYSTEM

Munawar Iqbal and Philip Molyneux
THIRTY YEARS OF ISLAMIC BANKING
History, Performance and Prospects

Sven Janssen
BRITISH AND GERMAN BANKING STRATEGIES

Kimio Kase and Tanguy Jacopin
CEOs AS LEADERS AND STRATEGY DESIGNERS
Explaining the Success of Spanish Banks

Alexandros-Andreas Kyrtsis (editor)
FINANCIAL MARKETS AND ORGANIZATIONAL TECHNOLOGIES
System Architectures, Practices and Risks in the Era of Deregulation

M. Mansoor Khan and M. Ishaq Bhatti
DEVELOPMENTS IN ISLAMIC BANKING
The Case of Pakistan

Mario La Torre and Gianfranco A. Vento
MICROFINANCE

Philip Molyneux and Eleuterio Vallelado (editors)
FRONTIERS OF BANKS IN A GLOBAL WORLD

Imad A. Moosa
THE MYTH OF TOO BIG TO FAIL

Simon Mouatt and Carl Adams (editors)
CORPORATE AND SOCIAL TRANSFORMATION OF MONEY AND BANKING
Breaking the Serfdom

Anastasia Nesvetailova
FRAGILE FINANCE
Debt, Speculation and Crisis in the Age of Global Credit

Anders Ögren (editor)
THE SWEDISH FINANCIAL REVOLUTION

Dominique Rambure and Alec Nacamuli
PAYMENT SYSTEMS
From the Salt Mines to the Board Room

Catherine Schenk (editor)
HONG KONG SAR's MONETARY AND EXCHANGE RATE CHALLENGES
Historical Perspectives

Noël K. Tshiani
BUILDING CREDIBLE CENTRAL BANKS
Policy Lessons for Emerging Economies

Ruth Wandhöfer
EU PAYMENTS INTEGRATION
The Tale of SEPA, PSD and Other Milestones Along the Road

The full list of titles available is on the website:
www.palgrave.com/finance/sbfi.asp

Palgrave Macmillan Studies in Banking and Financial Institutions
Series Standing Order ISBN 978-1-4039-4872-4

You can receive future titles in this series as they are published by placing a standing order. Please contact your bookseller or, in case of difficulty, write to us at the address below with your name and address, the title of the series and the ISBN quoted above.

Customer Services Department, Macmillan Distribution Ltd, Houndmills, Basingstoke, Hampshire RG21 6XS, England

The Myth of Too Big to Fail

Imad A. Moosa
Professor of Finance, RMIT, Australia

palgrave
macmillan

First published 2010 by
PALGRAVE MACMILLAN

Palgrave Macmillan in the UK is an imprint of Macmillan Publishers Limited, registered in England, company number 785998, of Houndmills, Basingstoke, Hampshire RG21 6XS.

Palgrave Macmillan in the US is a division of St Martin's Press LLC, 175 Fifth Avenue, New York, NY 10010.

Palgrave Macmillan is the global academic imprint of the above companies and has companies and representatives throughout the world.

Palgrave® and Macmillan® are registered trademarks in the United States, the United Kingdom, Europe and other countries

ISBN 978-1-349-32567-2   ISBN 978-0-230-29505-6 (eBook)
DOI 10.1057/9780230295056

This book is printed on paper suitable for recycling and made from fully managed and sustained forest sources. Logging, pulping and manufacturing processes are expected to conform to the environmental regulations of the country of origin.

A catalogue record for this book is available from the British Library.

A catalogue record for this book is available from the Library of Congress.

10 9 8 7 6 5 4 3 2 1
19 18 17 16 15 14 13 12 11 10

To Nisreen and Danny

This page intentionally left blank

Contents

List of Figures

Preface

Too big to fail (TBTF)—the notion that failing big firms must be saved by the government because their failure represents unacceptable systemic risk—has become a household concept and a popular topic for bloggers. Like most people, I became interested in the topic as a result of the heated debate following the rescue, among others, of Citigroup and AIG in the U.S. and Northern Rock and the Royal Bank of Scotland in the U.K. The global financial crisis has brought the TBTF debate back to centre stage, where it once was following the rescue of Continental Illinois in 1984 and Long-Term Capital Management in 1998. The difference on this occasion lies in the amount of taxpayers' money that has been put into the rescue operations. Some people, including myself, question TBTF rescues not only on economic, but also on ethical and moral grounds. The motivation for writing this book was the desire to explain why most people feel outraged about the TBTF doctrine and the consequent bailouts of financial institutions.

This book is highly (but fairly) critical of the TBTF doctrine and related issues such as *laissez faire* finance, the trend towards massive deregulation, and the undeserved status of the financial sector in the economy. It is critical of not only the practice but also the ideas that drive the practice, some (or most) of which are the products of academic work. Some economists, politicians and policy makers think—or at least thought—that the TBTF problem does not exist or that it exists but it is not serious enough to warrant a diversion of resources to solve the problem. Others believe that it exists and that it is serious but we have to live with it and keep on salvaging financial institutions deemed too big to fail, no matter how much it costs. I will argue that the TBTF problem exists, that it is serious, and that it should (and can) be solved. Most of the discussion in this book pertains to developments in the U.S., where deposit insurance was invented and the term "too big to fail" was coined. Similar developments and issues will also be discussed from a U.K. perspective.

I have had the manuscript (or parts of it) read by some people, including academics (trained in economics and otherwise) and an ordinary tax-paying citizen. The comments I received from academics were driven by what seemed to be ideology. While those on the left of the political spectrum applauded what I wrote, those on the right were rather critical. They thought that I used unnecessarily strong language and that I was excessively harsh on financiers and the academics who stood behind them. They claimed that the discussion was "polemic". They also objected to use of such words and expressions as "parasitic operations", "horrendously unsound", "bewildered", "junk food", and "love affair". Interestingly, most of these words and expressions appear in the book because I quoted the people who had used them in the first place.

My response to these claims is that this issue has a moral dimension that has brought about outrage from ordinary people. It is a normative issue that you cannot be neutral about, and any discussion is bound to be highly opinionated. The ordinary tax-paying citizen who read the whole of the manuscript commented on the tone of the language used in the book by saying that "really it's mild considering the sense of moral outrage any sane person like yourself feels these days about those behind the global financial crisis". She added: "it's good to hear someone logically and methodically pick to pieces what is so sick, and deeply wrong with this world of high finance that has got itself into such a mess". This book has been written to explain, by using economic analysis as well as empirical and historical evidence, the popular outrage about TBTF and the taxpayers-funded bailouts of failing financial institutions. There are no ideological drives or a hidden agenda.

Following an introductory chapter in which the concept of TBTF is explained, Chapter 2 presents a history of financial deregulation and how it is related to the emergence of the TBTF doctrine. A discussion is also presented of bailouts that took place during the global financial crisis (in 2008, to be precise). In Chapter 3 there is a description of some highly-publicized and notorious rescue operations involving, among others, Continental Illinois, Long-Term Capital Management, American International Group and the Royal Bank of Scotland. Chapter 4 is devoted to a discussion of why financial institutions pursue growth policies, reaching the conclusion that the primary motive for growing big is the privilege of the TBTF status. Chapter 5 presents an argument that in most countries the financial sector is far too big relative to the size of the economy. It is also argued that academia has contributed, in more than one way, to the "stardom" of the financial sector. Chapter 6 covers a discussion that leads to the conclusion that size does matter but political connection is the key to obtaining the TBTF status. Arguments are presented in Chapter 7 against the TBTF doctrine and the rescue operations that the doctrine justifies. Chapter 8 puts forward suggestions to solve the TBTF problem, including the breaking up of big financial institutions, appropriate regulation, and the enhancing of the credibility of regulators by refusing to bail out failing institutions. Chapter 9 is devoted to a discussion of the Basel II Accord, where it is demonstrated that Basel II provides inadequate regulation and that it could not have dealt adequately with the global financial crisis, let alone have prevented it. Some concluding remarks are presented in Chapter 10, ending with the final thought that the TBTF doctrine must perish.

Writing this book would not have been possible if it was not for the help and encouragement I received from family, friends and colleagues. My utmost gratitude must go to my wife and children who had to bear the opportunity cost of writing this book. My gratitude also goes to Lee Smith who is my source of due diligence. She read the whole manuscript word for word and came up with numerous suggestions that have made the book more readable. I would also like to thank my colleagues and friends, including John Vaz, Andrew Sanford, Michael Dempsey, Petko Kalev, Param Silvapulle and Mervyn Silvapulle. I should not forget the friends I socialize with, including Liam Lenten, Theo Gazos, Brien McDonald, Steffen Joeris, Larry Li and Tony Naughton. In preparing the manuscript, I benefited from an exchange of ideas with members of the Table 14 Discussion Group, and for this reason I would like to thank Bob Parsons, Greg O'Brien, Greg Bailey, Bill Breen, Rodney Adams and Paul Rule. Greg Bailey, who is as opposed to TBTF rescues as I am, was particularly helpful as he read parts of the manuscript and made some good suggestions.

My thanks go to friends and former colleagues who live far away but provide help via means of telecommunication, including Kevin Dowd (whom I owe an intellectual debt), Razzaque Bhatti, Ron Ripple, Bob Sedgwick, Sean Holly, Dave Chappell, Dan Hemmings and Ian Baxter. With his rather strong intuition, Ron Ripple made some insightful comments on parts of the manuscript, and for that I am grateful to him. In particular, he brought my attention to an important point that I had previously overlooked, that taxing financial institutions and using the proceeds to salvage failed ones will not solve the moral hazard problem associated with TBTF protection.

This book was mostly written in Kuwait when I was visiting Kuwait University. I therefore acknowledge the help and encouragement I received from Sulaiman Al-Jassar, Nabeel Al-Loughani, Khalid Al-Saad, Yasir Al-Kulaib, Abdulla Al-Obaidan, Mohammed Al-Abduljalil, Husain Al-Muraikhi and Sulaiman Al-Abduljader. Last, but not least, I would like to thank the crew at Palgrave Macmillan, my favourite publisher, particularly Lisa von Fircks who was highly supportive of the idea of writing a book on the TBTF doctrine.

Naturally, I am the only one responsible for any errors and omissions in this book. It is dedicated to my beloved children, Nisreen and Danny, who believe that McDonald's and KFC are too big to fail.

Imad A. Moosa

List of Abbreviations

ABS	Asset-Backed Securities
AIG	American International Group
AMA	Advanced Measurement Approach
ANST	Asymmetric Nonlinear Smooth Transition
ARCH	Autoregressive Conditional Heteroscedasticity
ARFIMA	Autoregressive Fractionally Integrated Moving Average
ARIMA	Autoregressive Integrated Moving Average
ARMA	Autoregressive Moving Average
ATM	Automated Telling Machines
BBC	British Broadcasting Corporation
BCBS	Basel Committee on Banking Supervision
BIA	Basic Indicators Approach
BIS	Bank for International Settlements
BOA	Bank of America
CAVIAR	Conditional Autoregressive Value at Risk
CD	Certificate of Deposit
CDO	Collateralized Debt Obligation
CDS	Credit Default Swap
CEO	Chief Executive Officer
CFO	Chief Financial Officer
CFPA	Consumer Financial Protection Agency
CFTC	Commodity Futures Trading Commission
CIA	Central Intelligence Agency
DEA	Drug Enforcement Agency
DIDMCA	Depository Institutions Deregulation and Monetary Control Act
DSGE	Dynamic Stochastic General Equilibrium (model)
EGARCH	Exponential Autoregressive Conditional Heteroscedasticity
EMH	Efficient Market Hypothesis
EU	European Union
FDIC	Federal Deposit Insurance Corporation
FDICIA	Federal Deposit Insurance Corporation Improvement Act
FIRREA	Financial Institutions Reform, Recovery and Enforcement Act
FPU	Financial Products Unit
FRBNY	Federal Reserve Bank of New York
FSA	Financial Services Authority

FTSE	Financial Times Stock Exchange (100 stock price index)
GARCH	Generalized Autoregressive Conditional Heteroscedasticity
GDP	Gross Domestic Product
HSBC	Hong Kong and Shanghai Banking Corporation
IMF	International Monetary Fund
IPO	Initial Public Offering
LTCM	Long-Term Capital Management
MBS	Mortgage-Backed Securities
NASA	National Aeronautics and Space Administration
NBFI	Non-Bank Financial Institution (or Intermediary)
NTBTF	Not Too Big to Fail
OTC	Over the Counter
RAF	Royal Air Force
RBS	Royal Bank of Scotland
SEC	Securities and Exchange Commission
SETAR	Self-Exciting Threshold Autoregressive (model)
SF	Swiss Franc
SIFI	Systemically Important Financial Institution
SIV	Structured (or Special) Investment Vehicle
TAR	Threshold Autoregressive
TARP	Troubled Assets Relief Program
TBTE	Too Big to Exist
TBTF	Too Big to Fail
TBTS	Too Big to Save
TCTF1	Too Contagious to Fail
TCTF2	Too Correlated to Fail
TCTF3	Too Concentrated to Fail
TIUSCTF	Too Important under Specific Conditions to Fail
TPCTF	Too Politically Connected to Fail
TPTBDT	Too Powerful to be Dedicated to
TSITF	Too Systemically Important to Fail
UBS	United Bank of Switzerland
UN	United Nations
VAR	Value at Risk
WOBO	Worthy of Bail Out

1
The Too Big to Fail Doctrine

1.1 The meaning and origin of TBTF

Too big to fail (TBTF) is a doctrine postulating that the government cannot allow very big firms (particularly major banks and financial institutions) to fail, for the very reason that they are big. Dabos (2004) argues that TBTF policy is adopted by the authorities in many countries, but it is rarely admitted in public. This doctrine is justified on the basis of systemic risk, the risk of adverse consequences of the failure of one firm for the underlying sector or the economy at large. The concept of TBTF is relevant to financial institutions in particular because it is in the financial sector where we find large and extremely interconnected institutions. For example, some 82 per cent of foreign exchange transactions are conducted by banks with other banks and non-bank financial institutions (Bank for International Settlements, 2007). This is why the failure of one financial institution is bad news for its competitors. In other industries, the failure of a firm is typically good news for other firms in the same industry because it means the demise of a competitor and the inheritance of its market share by existing firms. As we are going to see, size and interconnectedness determine systemic risk, but that is not all. Financial institutions are also politically powerful, which gives them a comparative advantage in the "race" to obtain the TBTF status.

Another interpretation

Sometimes, another interpretation is given to the TBTF doctrine—that a big firm cannot (or is unlikely to) fail, simply because it is big (see, for example, Seeling, 2004 who also suggests the term "too public to fail"). The underlying reasoning is that big firms benefit from economies of

1

scale and scope (the cost reductions resulting from size and diversity, respectively) which make them more efficient than small firms. A big firm is typically more diversified than a small firm, which puts the big firm in a superior competitive position and reduces its exposure to the risk of structural changes in the economy. A big firm also enjoys significant market power and a lower cost of capital. It is in this sense that Murray (2009) describes the American International Group (AIG) by saying that "although it was too big to fail, it failed". By the same token, the Soviet Union was labelled TBTF by the Central Intelligence Agency (CIA) in the 1960s and 1970s. The same has been said of the Roman Empire, the Byzantine Empire and the British Empire (and they all failed).

Likewise, the U.S. has been described as being too big to fail due to its economic size and financial muscle, although it has lost most of its manufacturing base and has an economy that is based on the consumption of mainly imported goods. The underlying idea here is that the U.S. is TBTF as long as the Chinese and Saudis are willing to finance the twin deficit, which would be the case because these countries hold so much dollar-denominated assets that they cannot afford to allow the U.S. to fail. In this sense, Greece may also be described as TBTF as it was languishing in its debt crisis in early 2010. It has been suggested that Greece has some 6000 beautiful islands that can be sold. After all, Greece got itself into a messy situation by using income from its airports as collateral against some shabby derivatives that allowed the government to borrow on a massive scale while escaping scrutiny by the European Union.

Too big to be allowed to fail

In what follows, however, TBTF is taken to mean "too big to be allowed [by the government] to fail". Thus, TBTF policy refers to the possibility of bailing out a large financial institution to prevent its failure or limit the losses caused by the failure (Ennis and Malek, 2005). Alternatively, Hetzel (1991) defines TBTF as "the practice followed by bank regulators of protecting creditors (uninsured as well as insured depositors and debt holders) of large banks from loss in the event of failure". This concept may apply to entities other than companies. For example, the announcement in late November 2009 that Dubai was seeking to restructure its massive debt sent shivers into regional and other stock markets. Dubai is deemed to be too big and too interconnected (financially) to fail, which means that the sister state of Abu Dhabi would not allow Dubai's failure by tapping into its oil-generated financial reserves to finance the bailout of Dubai. That course of events came true when Abu Dhabi put in $10 billion to help Dubai pay off its debt. Greece also obtained TBTF recognition in the conventional sense, receiving billions of dollars (or euros) from the European Union to pay off its debt. Yet the word going around is that the possibility of default has not been discarded completely.

Beyond cities like Dubai and countries like Greece, football clubs have started to develop a taste for TBTF. In early 2010 the issue of debt in the English Premium League was a hot topic as Portsmouth went into receivership. Big English football clubs, with debt totalling £3.5 billion, may start to demand bailout by claiming the TBTF status. Claiming TBTF rescue works like a snowball: once it is granted to one firm, others start factoring the possibility of obtaining the privilege in their decisions.

There is no agreement on what makes a particular institution TBTF and another institution NTBTF (not too big to fail). This is an issue that we will come back to in Chapter 6. A TBTF firm can be described as a "financial firm whose liabilities are implicitly guaranteed by all of us, free of charge". This is a great arrangement for financial institutions because, as a commentator puts it, "they get to borrow from the Federal Reserve at zero percent and make whatever bets they like". He also argues that "they [financial institutions] get the profits and saddle taxpayers with losses", and that "through cognitive capture and campaign donations, they effectively control our regulatory apparatus and our Congress". TBTF, the commentator concludes, is "about the financiers versus everybody else, and we are losing badly" (https://self-evident.org/?p=720).

Ambiguity

Seeling (2004) points out that the concept of too big to fail can be ambiguous, in the sense that there is no consensus view on what is meant by "too big" and "to fail". As far as "too big" is concerned, Seeling suggests two interpretations: big relative to some objective standard and big in absolute terms, which means that size can be either absolute or relative.

Then what does "failure" mean in the context of TBTF? In general terms, business failure means that the business ceases to exist, implying that common shareholders suffer the first loss, followed by preferred shareholders, subordinated creditors, and general creditors. The management also suffers from the loss of employment. But this is not necessarily what happens under a TBTF bailout. For example, when Continental Illinois was rescued under the TBTF doctrine in 1984, it was recapitalized and the U.S. government—represented by the Federal

Deposit Insurance Corporation (FDIC)—took an ownership position. Shareholders were wiped out, but the interests of creditors (including uninsured creditors) were protected. Senior management was removed and members of the board of directors were replaced. Seeling (2004) considers TBTF as the justification for government intervention to "protect some but not all of the claimants who would be adversely affected in a bankruptcy". Likewise, Gup (1998) points out that "the TBTF doctrine means that the organization may continue to exist, and insured depositors will be protected; but stockholders, subordinated debt holders, managers, and some general creditors may suffer losses". The process is therefore discretionary or, as van Rixtel *et al* (2004) describe it, a "supervisory ad hoc pragmatism".

Sprague (1986) distinguishes amongst three basic choices that the FDIC has: (i) pay off a failed bank—that is, give the insured depositors their money; (ii) sell it to a new owner with FDIC assistance; or (iii) prevent it from failing—that is, bail it out. In a pay off, insured depositors receive their money promptly, cheques in process bounce, the bank disappears, while uninsured depositors and creditors await the liquidation proceeds. When a failed bank is sold, all depositors and creditors (insured and uninsured) are fully protected, and a new bank replaces the old one with no interruption of services. In a bailout, the bank does not close, depositors and creditors are fully protected, but the management is fired while shareholders suffer a loss of value.

TBTF and the global financial crisis

The global financial crisis has brought the TBTF debate back to centre stage. Moss (2009) concludes that "the dramatic federal response to the current financial crisis has created a new reality, in which virtually all systemically significant financial institutions now enjoy an implicit guarantee from the government that they will continue to exist (and continue to generate moral hazard) long after the immediate crisis passes". The crisis has made it clear that the TBTF doctrine amounts to saving banks from their own mistakes by using taxpayers' money (hence, the issue has a moral dimension). I have recently come across a rather interesting cartoon on the morality of using taxpayers' money to bail out failed financial institutions during the global financial crisis. In the cartoon a man says: "I am contributing to efforts aimed at putting an end to the global financial crisis". A woman asks: "are you some sort of a financial wizard?". The man answers: "no, I am a taxpayer". This cartoon encompasses the spirit of the view that government bailout of failed financial institutions is painfully ludicrous. Most people also believe that bailouts amount to funnelling funds into "parasitic operations" at the cost of starving the productive base and infrastructure of resources and that the only beneficiary of bailouts is the financial elite who boost their already immense personal fortunes.

The crisis has also given rise to parallel notions, some of which are rather cynical. One of these notions is that of "too politically connected to fail", as there is widespread belief that the decision whether or not to bail out a financial institution depends on how politically connected it is. This is probably why Lehman Brothers was allowed to fail but not AIG. Some critics of selective bailouts believe that AIG was saved because its failure would have caused the failure of Goldman Sachs, which is probably the most politically connected financial institution. It was Hank Paulson, the former U.S. Treasury Secretary (and the former boss at Goldman), who insisted on saving AIG in his last days as Treasury Secretary under President Bush. Goldman Sachs received a big chunk of the taxpayers' money that was paid by the Treasury to AIG. Lewis (2009a) is sarcastic about a "rumour" that "when the U.S. government bailed out AIG and paid off its gambling debt, it saved not AIG but Goldman Sachs".

A big problem?

Bailing out financial institutions on the basis of the TBTF doctrine is a big problem, not in the least because it is expensive to the extent that it imposes a heavy financial burden on future generations. Instead of allocating scarce financial resources to health and education, these resources are used to revive the failed institutions' balance sheets. It also gives rise to a significant moral hazard, a term used to describe the tendency of financial institutions to take excessive risk (with other people's money, be it deposits, loans or funds under management) because they know that they will be rescued if things go wrong. In other words, the doctrine is a direct inducement for large institutions to act irresponsibly.

Stern (2008) believes that "the too-big-to-fail problem now rests at the very top of the ills elected officials, policymakers and bank supervisors must address". Stern also believes that TBTF represents greater risk and should be assigned higher priority than many would think. But Mishkin (2006) argues that Stern and Feldman (2004) "overstate the importance of the too-big-to-fail problem and do not give enough credit to the FDICIA [Federal Deposit Insurance Corporation Improvement Act] legislation of 1991 for improving bank regulation and supervision". He even argues that "the evidence does not support a worsening of the too-big-to-fail problem" and that "the evidence seems to support that there has been substantial improvement on this score". Some economists go as far as denying the existence of a TBTF problem. Stern (2008) believes that one reason for playing down the seriousness of the TBTF problem is that "some may have viewed TBTF reforms as a poor use of scarce resources". If Stern's reasoning is valid, then there is a fallacy here: it is TBTF rescues, rather than TBTF reform, that represent a poor use of scarce resources. Those who see TBTF reform as representing a poor use of scarce resources seem to be oblivious to the fact that prevention is invariably cheaper and more effective than treating symptoms (let alone the disease).

In the aftermath of the global financial crisis, and the massive bailouts of badly-managed financial institutions, we know that Mishkin was wrong while Feldman was right. However, Mishkin thinks that we have to live with the TBTF problem, arguing that "there could be no turning back on too big to fail" and that "you can't put the genie in the bottle again" (Dash, 2009). This is inconsistent with the suggestion put forward by Mishkin (2001) to eliminate too big to fail in the corporate sector as part of a set of financial policies that can help make financial crises less likely in emerging market countries. But Mishkin seems to be ambivalent about TBTF. For example, Mishkin (1992) argued that giving regulators the discretion to engage in a TBTF policy creates incentives for large banks to take on too much risk, thus exposing the deposit insurance fund and taxpayers to large potential losses. Yet, he does not advocate giving up the discretionary use of TBTF policy under "special circumstances". Instead he recommends the use of other means to curb the tendency of banks to take on risk.

TBTF: To ignore or not to ignore?

Typically, politicians and regulators either ignore the problem or give the impression that it is not such a big deal. Even worse, the TBTF issue is used to justify bailing out failed financial institutions because of the power these institutions have over legislators and the government. When the TBTF problem resurfaced during initial stages of the global financial crisis, only Mervyn King, the governor of the Bank of England, rang the alarm bell. King made it clear that TBTF is at the heart of the current financial crisis and that it would be at the heart of the next financial crisis. On 20 October 2009, King called for banks to split up so that their retail arms are separated from riskier investment banking operations, and he also criticized the finance industry's failure to reform despite "breathtaking levels of taxpayer support".

As popular outrage mounted we started to notice a change of heart on the part of politicians and regulators. In his speech to the G20 finance ministers in St Andrews (Scotland) on 7 November 2009, the former British Prime Minister, Gordon Brown, surprised everyone by saying that banking cannot go back to "business as usual", backed by government guarantees that banks would be rescued in the event of a crisis and leaving taxpayers to pick up the bill. That was a radical change (or a pleasant flip-flop) from his earlier stance. One possible explanation for the change of heart is that Mr Brown feared being seen as too soft on bankers, which was the case when he was Chancellor of the Exchequer (*The Economist*, 2009a). The views expressed by Brown are not shared by the hierarchy of the British Treasury, nor (of course) by the British Bankers' Association, and they were taken with a big pinch of salt by the U.S. Treasury Secretary, Tim Geithner. The mayor of London, Boris Johnson, is adamant that no one should dare touch the City (the nickname for the London finance industry). Subsequently, Geithner himself started to become tougher on the issue when his boss, President Obama, took a confrontational stance against big financial institutions and proposed to impose some restrictions on what they can do. Even Alan Greenspan, who advocated deregulation and always denied the existence of the TBTF problem, started to complain about bailouts when he said: "at one point, no bank was too big to fail" (McKee and Lanman, 2009).

One explanation why politicians and regulators tend to overlook the TBTF issue is the very proposition that some financial institutions are so large that they pose systemic risk, in the sense that the failure of one of these institutions may cause systemic failure (the failure of the entire financial system). This sounds terrible, even apocalyptic, and it is intended to. How can an elected official vote in such a way as to create systemic risk that could cause the failure of the whole financial system? Instead, this official must vote to approve the bailout of a failed institution (it is "patriotic" to vote this way). In their classic book on the TBTF issue, Stern and Feldman (2004) argue that bank bailouts are motivated by the desire to prevent the economy-wide consequences of big bank failure. Would-be bailed out institutions in turn endeavour to portray themselves as posing systemic risk, arguing with politicians along the lines that "if you do not bail us out, the dire consequences of our failure will be catastrophic for all, including the government". Naturally, the acceptance of this message by policymakers, regulators and their bosses (the politicians) is facilitated by knowing who is who in the government. Even better, this message can be transmitted more smoothly if former or future staff members are or will be in the government. Hence, we have the notion of "too politically connected to fail".

Stern and Feldman (2004) also suggest other factors as providing motivation for regulators to indulge in TBTF behaviour. Regulators could be motivated by personal rewards, such as the prospect of lucrative banking jobs, or because of fear of having banking failures under their watch. The third factor they suggest is that when the government rescues a bank it can then direct credit the way it desires. While I find the second factor extremely plausible and the underlying argument convincing, the third factor looks trivial, particularly in a country like the U.S.

Cynical notions

Cynical notions that crop up in discussion of the TBTF doctrine include "too big to survive", "so big that it had to fail", "too big to succeed", "too big to unwind", "too big to discipline adequately" and "too big to rescue". These notions imply that size could be detrimental to the survival of an institution and that economies of scale and scope may not materialize. This issue is dealt with in detail in Chapter 4, showing how some financial institutions have failed or incurred significant losses because of the desire to be big. Hence the reason why a TBTF institution is saved following failure is the very reason that caused failure in the first place: size. When size is replaced with complexity, the notion becomes "too complex to fail". It is, however, the case that size and complexity go together.

Likewise, there are the notions of "too big to fail is too big", "too big to save" and "too big for their boots", implying that an institution that is TBTF must not be allowed to be that big because it becomes either difficult or expensive to save. These notions provide the rationale for one way to deal with the TBTF problem: preventing financial institutions from growing too big. Although not related to finance, the Israelis have recently argued that some of the settlements in the occupied West Bank are "too big to evacuate".

TBTF and deregulation

There is no doubt that the TBTF problem has arisen (at least in part) because of deregulation. At one time regulatory measures were in place to stop banks from growing too big. For example, the Glass-Steagall Act of 1933 prevented commercial banks from growing big by indulging in securities underwriting, and prevented investment banks from growing big by undertaking commercial banking activities. Measures were also put in place to prevent banks from growing big by branching out into insurance, brokerage services and fund management.

Over the past decades, these measures have been dismantled in the name of economic freedom and the power of the market (which is always right!). It is deregulation (starting with the Reagan deregulation) that has allowed financial institutions to grow without limits to become eligible for the TBTF status. This is indeed a problem because an implicit guarantee by the government that a TBTF institution will not be allowed to go down can only encourage the management of these institutions to take excessive risk, particularly because of a pay structure that is dominated by bonuses. The TBTF doctrine and the moral hazard it creates have contributed significantly to the global financial crisis.

1.2 Rewarding recklessness: An anecdote

I have come across an anecdote about banks that are rewarded for big mistakes arising from greed and incompetence. When we consider real-life stories of financial institutions deemed TBTF, we realize that these stories resemble this hypothetical anecdote. The following is my version of the anecdote, which involves a bank that indulges in commercial banking (loans and deposits) as well as investment banking (issuing securities).

The proprietor of a bar realizes that most of his customers are unemployed alcoholics. Having no regular income, these customers stop coming to the bar, opting instead for the more economical option of sniffing glue or petrol. To attract these customers back to the bar, the proprietor comes up with an ingenious idea, the idea of "drink now and pay later". When the word gets around about the availability of a drink-now-and-pay-later facility, drinkers who have no regular income become patrons of this bar, and as a result the business flourishes. With huge demand for drinks at this bar, the proprietor boosts sales further by increasing prices regularly, which patrons do not mind (inelastic demand under the drink-now-and-pay-later arrangement). By using the future cash flows (payments for consumed drinks when they become due) as collateral, the bar receives generous loans (financed by retail deposits) from the bank.

An imaginative financial engineer working for the investment banking division of our bank comes up with a plan to securitize the cash flows to be received from patrons by issuing bonds against them. These bonds are called Booze bonds (Bozo bonds is also an appropriate name). Since diversification reduces risk, the financial engineer recommends that Booze bonds are to be issued in two tranches, the most risky of which is backed by cash flows from unemployed alcoholics, whereas the other tranche is backed by cash flows from employed moderate drinkers who are also allowed to use the drink-now-and-pay-later facility (which they accept because they are heavily indebted).

A particular rating agency grants Booze bonds an AAA rating because the bank offered the highest fee for the highest rating. Investors rush to buy Booze bonds because the return on these bonds is four percentage points higher than the yield on U.S. Treasury bonds—what a deal! Booze bond prices continue to rise, and demand for these bonds financed by bank (the same bank) loans grows rapidly. The bank keeps a big chunk of the risky tranche for itself because it is the high-return tranche. The inventor of Booze bonds, the imaginative financial engineer, gets a hefty bonus.

When it is time to pay Booze bondholders, the bank demands payment from the bar. The bar demands payment from the drink-now-and-pay-later patrons, but very little is received from the employed moderate drinkers and nothing from the unemployed alcoholics. Since the bar cannot fulfil its obligations to the bank, the business is forced into bankruptcy. The bar closes down and the employees lose their jobs.

Overnight, Booze bonds drop in price by 90 per cent, and the bank finds itself stuck with non-performing loan and securities portfolios. As a result, the bank refrains from extending new loans, thus freezing credit and economic activity. The bank endures extensive losses particularly because of its involvement in both commercial and investment banking. The suppliers of the bar get into trouble because they provided the proprietor with generous payment extensions and invested their firms' pension funds in Booze bonds. They find themselves in a position where they have to write off bad debt, while losing over 90 per cent of the presumed value of the bonds.

Fortunately for the bank, one of its executives used to be in government while a current cabinet minister used to be on the board of the bank. Both of them convince the government to bail out the bank by a no-strings-attached cash infusion. The funds required for this bailout are obtained from new taxes levied mostly on employed, middle-class, non-drinkers. Does this not sound familiar?

1.3   TBTF: A privilege of banks and other financial institutions

The TBTF status is typically granted to big banks and other financial institutions, which means that financial institutions command special importance. While this is certainly true, the importance of financial institutions should be taken to imply the need to regulate them or prevent them from growing big so that they would not pose systemic risk. Unfortunately, the importance of financial institutions is taken to imply their entitlement to the TBTF status and therefore the privilege of protection by taxpayers' money. So, what is special about banks and other financial institutions?

The special importance of banks

Banks are special. Palia and Porter (2003) describe banks as "unique economic entities, primarily due to their ability to create money and the impact that bank information production and liquidity services have on the real economy". Mishkin (2006) argues that banks are special because "banking institutions are especially well suited to minimizing transaction costs and adverse selection and moral hazard problems". When banks fail, he adds, "the information capital they have developed may disappear and, as a result, many borrowers will not have access to funds to pursue productive investment opportunities".

In general, banks are important for a number of reasons, the first of which is the difference between the degrees of liquidity of their assets and liabilities, which makes them highly vulnerable to depositor withdrawal and, in extreme cases, bank runs. This characteristic is described by *The Economist* (2008a) as the "inherent fragility of their business model". In this respect, the argument goes, "even the strongest bank cannot survive a severe loss of confidence, because the money it owes can usually be called more quickly than the money it is owed". A bank does not keep sufficient liquidity to pay back all depositors at the same time, which exposes the bank to the risk of a run when depositors start to doubt the soundness of its financial position and rush to withdraw their money. Bank runs are contagious and may generate systemic instability. What makes this characteristic of banks even more crucial is that they take deposits from "mums and dads" (or, as banks call them, retail depositors). It is, of course, in the interest of the smooth running of the whole system that this money is put into banks rather than hidden under the mattress.

Banks are important because they lie at the heart of the payment system (they are the creators of money, the medium of exchange), providing the lubricant for the whole economy. Almost all financial transactions are facilitated through commercial banks, including credit card payments, cheques, direct salary deposits and online payments. Failure of the payment system is conducive to economic disaster. If the failure of one bank can cause the failure of the entire payment system, then this is solid justification for TBTF protection. However, it is not clear how to determine whether the failure of Bank X can cause the failure of the entire payment system (hence, it is TBTF), while the failure of Bank Y will not be that serious (hence, it is NTBTF). Actually, history provides conjectural evidence indicating that the payment system can fail because of hyperinflation (as in Germany in the early 1920s), but there is no evidence for the proposition that the failure of one bank can cause a failure of the payment system. Some 5000 U.S. banks failed in the Great Depression of the 1930s but the payment system survived. There was no incidence of settling transactions through barter.

The other reason for the special importance of banks, according to *The Economist* (2008a), is the role they play in allocating financial resources among various sectors of the economy. The failure of banks leads to a reduction in credit flows to the rest of the economy, and hence adverse economic consequences. This point is expressed succinctly by *The Economist* (2008a) as follows: "if banks suffer, we all suffer". There is, of course, a significant element of truth in this proposition but the question that arises here is whether or not bailing out a failed bank will put it back in the business of lending money. The answer to this question is "no", as indicated by the observation that there has been an outcry about the reluctance of bailed out banks to extend credit during the global financial crisis while they were busy distributing bonuses. For example, the Royal Bank of Scotland (RBS) received massive amounts of funds from the British government but failed to assist economic recovery by extending credit to small businesses. However, the RBS kept on paying bonuses to its senior staff even while incurring significant losses. Both President Obama and former Prime Minister Brown have criticized banks for this kind of behaviour. One may wonder why a failed bank is bailed out in the hope that it will be back in the business of extending credit rather than using the bailout money to extend credit to the productive sectors of the economy via a special government agency (for example, the domestic equivalent of USAID).

Commercial banks versus other financial institutions

There are characteristics that distinguish commercial banks from other financial institutions. For example, investment banks are different because they operate wholly in financial markets, they do not take retail deposits, and they are not a direct part of the payment system. Non-bank financial institutions (NBFIs) do not pose an equal threat to financial stability, since their liabilities are not redeemable on demand at par. They are not exposed to the risk of customer runs since their liabilities are market-priced like their assets. When financial institutions that raise money from capital markets (by issuing securities) make wrong investment decisions, their investors will lose their money without further repercussions for the financial system at large. This is why it has been argued that commercial banks require special attention. And this is why commercial banks are the sole subject of the capital-based regulation under Basel II, not that the Basel II capital-based regulation is effective or appropriate (see Chapter 9). However, this should not be taken to imply that NBFIs ought to be exempted from regulation as some would argue. For one thing, these institutions (particularly hedge funds) are heavy borrowers from commercial banks, which means that their failure may bring about the failure of some banks (which has been rather conspicuous during the global financial crisis). Moreover, major commercial banks typically have investment banking arms and they indulge in other financial services and products (such as insurance), which means that improperly-run non-commercial banking activity could have adverse effects on commercial banks. During the global financial crisis, most of the damage was caused not by the failure of a commercial bank, but by the failure of an insurance company, American International Group (AIG), which was indulged in the unregulated activity of selling insurance policies known as credit default swaps (CDSs).

It is also argued that banks are special because they face an asymmetric loss function, which is a consequence of handling other people's money. An asymmetric loss function means that banks reap the financial gains from risk taking but only assume a fraction of the ensuing losses. At the 2008 *International Financing Review* conference in London, a joke went round that bankers had lost a lot of money but "the good news was that it was other people's money" (*The Economist*, 2008b). Having an asymmetric loss function, however, is also a feature of other financial institutions, particularly hedge funds, some of which are owned and operated by investment banks. As a matter of fact, hedge funds are even worse in this respect because they are highly leveraged. In his speech to the G20 finance ministers held in November 2009 in St Andrews, the former British Prime Minister talked about the asymmetric loss function of the financial sector at large, pointing out that "it cannot be accepted that the benefits of success in this [financial] sector are reaped by the few but the costs of its failure are borne by all of us" (Cordon and Quinn, 2009).

Another reason why banks are regarded as special is the sheer size of the interbank market, resulting from the fact that banks deal with each other on a massive scale. This is the characteristic of interconnectedness, which is equally applicable to other financial institutions. We cannot distinguish banks from other financial institutions on the grounds that banks are more connected among themselves than with other financial institutions and that other institutions are less connected among themselves than banks. For example, the 2007 survey of the global foreign exchange market, which is conducted by the Bank for International Settlements every three years, shows that 42 per cent of foreign exchange transactions are conducted among banks and 40 per cent are conducted between banks and other financial institutions (Bank for International Settlements, 2007). The percentage of foreign exchange transactions conducted with other financial institutions has been on the increase. In the 2004 survey, banks conducted 53 per cent of the transactions among themselves and 33 per cent with other financial institutions (Bank for International Settlements, 2005).

The argument that banks are different from, and more important than, other financial institutions is typically used to justify the proposition that regulation should be directed at banks while other financial institutions should be left alone so that they can "innovate". But banks and other financial institutions share some characteristics that make them susceptible to failure. For example, they share the characteristic that they are particularly exposed to the failure of governance, because they are opaque and their business is to take risk. Yet another problematic feature of financial institutions in general is that the levels of turnover and product development are high, making it unlikely that staff would experience full business and product cycles (which weakens the institutional memory of the last crisis). They all share an executive compensation system that rewards short-term performance, thus encouraging risk taking. They all share the bonus culture and the unwarranted award of stardom to dealers who happen to do well in one year (by taking excessive risk), only to bring the institution to its knees another year. But then if banks are more important than other financial institutions, why is it that the TBTF status is granted to investment banks, insurance companies and hedge funds? As a matter of fact, the bulk of bail-out money used to save failed financial institutions during the global financial crisis was spent on investment banks (and their hedge funds) and a particular giant insurance company that blew up the world financial system (AIG).

1.4   The pros and cons of financial regulation

Financial institutions typically demand less regulation and supervision in the name of the economic efficiency resulting from the operations of free markets. Yet, when things go wrong (because of the lack of regulation, amongst other things) the same institutions cry "help" or threaten "bail us out or it will be a financial doomsday". Financial regulation has been a controversial issue, but I am flabbergasted by the observation that even in the post-global financial crisis era, deregulation is still supported by the proponents of *laissez faire* finance despite the damage inflicted on the world economy and financial system by the lack of regulation (among other factors).

Justifying regulation

There are two issues of controversy when it comes to regulation. The first is whether or not financial regulation in general is useful, while the second is whether or not banks are special and should be subject to more regulation.

As far as general regulation is concerned, the justification is simple: consumer protection and financial stability. However, the opponents of financial regulation argue that deregulation boosts competition and therefore efficiency, which is beneficial for customers. For example, it is argued that the removal of the interest ceiling in the U.S. (Regulation Q), the abolition of restrictions on interstate banking expansion, and the removal of obstacles that allowed the creation of financial supermarkets are deregulatory measures that have led to increased competition and therefore efficiency. While the argument against Regulation Q is plausible, it is counterintuitive to argue that allowing financial institutions to grow big without limits is conducive to increased competition. Anyone with knowledge of introductory microeconomics will tell us that consolidation leads to oligopoly, which (by definition) implies less competition. The argument that consumers are better off with financial conglomerates (as they can do all of their transactions with the same institution) is flawed, because a big institution has oligopolistic power that it uses to its advantage, not to the advantage of customers. Deregulation has indeed led to more concentrated market power, as we are going to see in Chapter 4. Apart from consumer protection and the achievement of financial stability, regulation is necessary to get rid of the menace of too big to fail.

We now move to the second point that the special importance of banks (relative to non-financial firms and non-bank financial institutions) provides justification for the proposition that regulation should be directed at banks. There is no question that banks are more important than other financial institutions, but this does not mean that non-bank financial institutions should be left alone (hedge funds, for example, have been totally unregulated). The problems endured by Bear Stearns in the early stages of the global financial crisis came as a result of the difficulties encountered by two of its hedge funds.

Banking regulation can be justified on the basis of market failure such as externalities, market power, and asymmetry of information between buyers and sellers (Santos, 2001). A primary objective of banking regulation is to curtail the negative externalities arising from bank failure that could result in a systemic crisis. In the absence of regulation, banks could create violent swings in the amount of money and have real effects on business activity and prices. Banks' provision of liquidity services leaves them exposed to runs (and therefore failure) which is what happened to Northern Rock in 2007. This is because banks operate with a balance sheet that combines a large portion of liabilities in the form of demand deposits and a large portion of assets in the form of long-term illiquid loans. Deposit insurance may be the solution but the opponents of regulation argue that it creates moral hazard and adverse selection.

The second justification for bank regulation is the inability of depositors to monitor banks. The "representation hypothesis" has been put forward to justify banking regulation on the basis of the governance problems created by the separation of ownership from management and the inability of depositors to monitor banks. While it is important for investors to monitor banks because they are exposed to adverse selection and moral hazard, the task is costly and requires access to information. The process is further complicated by the fact that this activity will be wasteful when duplicated by several parties and the fact that deposits are held by unsophisticated depositors who may not have the incentive to monitor their banks because they hold insignificant deposits. Hence there is a need for a monitoring representative of depositors, which can be provided by regulation.

Arguments against regulation

Disagreement is widespread on whether banks should be regulated and, if so, how they should be regulated. This disagreement reflects the lack of consensus on the nature of market failure that makes free banking suboptimal. Some economists dispute the arguments typically presented in favour of banking regulation, arguing that regulatory actions have been double-edged, if not counterproductive (for example, Kaufman and Scott, 2000). Others suggest that regulation does not necessarily accomplish the declared objective of reducing the probability of bank failure and that a case could be argued that the opposite result can be expected (for example, Koehn and Santomero, 1980). Benston and Kaufman (1996) assert that (i) most of the arguments that are used frequently to support special regulation for banks are not supported by either theory or empirical evidence, (ii) an unregulated system of enterprise tends to achieve an optimal allocation of resources, and (iii) one reason for bank regulation is the provision of revenue and power for government officials. There is a significant volume of literature on free banking, which is the ultra-extreme view of banking regulation sceptics (for example, Dowd, 1993, 1996a, 1996b).

Doerig (2003) argues that regulators do not take into account the fact that risk creates value and that profits come from risk taking. His reasoning goes as follows: by attempting to avoid systemic risk (which arises from the effect of the failure of a single financial institution on the whole financial sector and the economy at large) in the name of creditors and investors, regulators end up making the financial system more unstable. Lack of profitability, the argument goes, represents a supervisory problem even if the underlying institution is compliant with regulation, hence "sustained, sound and diversified profitability is THE precondition for protecting creditors and avoiding systemic risks".

No one would argue against the need for financial institutions to be profitable and that there is a positive risk-return trade-off. Regulation should not deprive financial institutions from a reasonable rate of return above the risk-free market rate, which is achievable only through risk taking. At the same time, regulation should hinder attempts to take excessive risk with other people's money just to maximize one's own bonuses in the short run. Why is it that a rogue trader who takes excessive risk to maximize his or her own bonus and fails is accused of "internal fraud" (in the form of unauthorized trading) while it is fine for a hedge fund manager to leverage 100:1 and lose other people's money because of excessive risk taking? It is not reasonable risk taking that I am talking about, it is greed-motivated excessive risk taking. This is probably what Mr Doerig was talking about when he wrote his report back in 2003 (when things were rosy and excessive risk taking was the norm). If not, I hope that he has changed his mind after witnessing the devastation inflicted on the world economy by attempts to be excessively profitable.

1.5   TBTF as an extension of the banking safety net

The provision by the government of a (financial) safety net for banks has arisen out of concern about the economy-wide effect of financial crises. Deposit insurance is the most common form of safety net. In the U.S. the Federal Deposit Insurance Corporation (FDIC) was created in the 1930s to provide deposit insurance, a guarantee of repayment of deposits up to a certain limit. The idea was that by protecting small depositors, banking panics and runs could be avoided. By the late 1960s, only six other countries had adopted deposit insurance, but a large number of countries embraced the scheme in the 1990s. The global financial crisis has reinforced this tendency.

Another form of banking safety net is the provision by the government (central bank, etc) of direct support to banks. This support may take the form of lending from the central bank to financial institutions experiencing difficulties, which lies within the central bank function of being a lender of last resort. Otherwise it could be a direct infusion of cash into these institutions, which is what happened in the U.K. in the midst of the global financial crisis. This injection of funds could be the outcome of TBTF policy, which is the ultimate safety net. Under this policy, there is no limit on the compensation of depositors and other creditors.

The presence of a banking safety net is a double-edged sword. The positive side is that it can prevent banking panics, but the negative side is that it creates moral hazard, the tendency of banks to take on excessive risk. This is even more so under TBTF protection whereby depositors and creditors are fully covered. In this case banks will not be subject to discipline from depositors, which encourages them to take risk with impunity in the spirit of the risk-return trade-off. As a result, the probability of bank failures rises.

It is for this reason that Stern and Feldman (2004) believe that TBTF is a contributory factor to the onset of financial crises. Honohan and Klingebiel (2000) agree with this view, arguing that "unlimited deposit guarantees, open-ended support, repeated capitalization, debtor bailout, and regulatory forbearance are associated with a tenfold increase in the fiscal cost of banking crises". While Mishikin (2006) agrees with this statement, he argues that "it is more accurate to attribute banking crises not to too-big-to-fail but rather to too-politically-important-to-fail", which includes almost all banks. While I agree with the notion of too politically important to fail and find it more realistic than that of too big to fail, I disagree with Mishkin that all banks are too politically important to fail. In Chapter 7, it will be argued that to be worthy of bailout a bank must be too politically connected to fail, for which size is a necessary but not a sufficient condition.

2
The History of TBTF

2.1 Financial crises and regulation

Looking at the historical record, we can see that regulation has worked in the past by reducing risk and boosting consumer confidence. The historical record is depicted in Figure 2.1, which shows the number of bank failures in the U.S. over the period 1864–2000. Until 1933, the U.S. experienced banking panics roughly every 15 to 20 years. In the 1930s the Great Depression struck and the banking system nearly collapsed. In response to a dire situation, the Roosevelt administration engineered sweeping regulatory measures, including the introduction of federal deposit insurance, securities regulation, banking supervision, and the separation of commercial and investment banking under the Glass-Steagall Act. The regulatory measures resulted in the stability of the U.S. financial system over much of the 20th century. For some 50 years, the country experienced no major financial crises, the longest such period on record.

The turning point

Significant financial failures re-emerged in the 1980s, and with that came the notion of TBTF as the government became a "rescuer of last resort". In *Liar's Poker*, Michael Lewis (1989) portrays the 1980s as "an era where government deregulation allowed less-than-scrupulous people on Wall Street to take advantage of others' ignorance, and thus grow extremely wealthy". In the 1980s the U.S. experienced the collapse of Continental Illinois, the first major bank to be offered the TBTF status. According to Sprague (1986), "the combined 200 failures in 1984 and 1985 exceeded the forty-year total from the beginning of World War II to the onset of the 1980s". Then there was the savings and loan crisis, followed by the bank failures of the early 1990s that forced the government to recapitalize the FDIC's Bank Insurance Fund. Long-Term Capital Management (LTCM), a largely unregulated hedge fund, collapsed in 1998 but it was saved from bankruptcy by a Fed-initiated plan, on the grounds that it was posing systemic risk. That event marked the perilous action of granting the TBTF status to shadowy, risky and mysterious creatures known as hedge funds. In the first decade of the 21st century we have already witnessed the bursting of the tech bubble in 2001, the accounting scandals that destroyed Enron in 2001 and WorldCom in 2002, and the worst crisis since the 1930s, the global financial crisis (and its predecessor the subprime crisis).

The rise of *laissez faire* finance

It is no coincidence that all these financial crises followed a concerted push by bankers, right-wing economists, and *laissez faire* policymakers to deregulate financial markets and institutions. Although a deregulatory agenda was embraced by congressional Democrats and Republicans alike, President Reagan set the philosophical tone in his 1981 inaugural address when he declared that "government is not the solution to our problem; government is the problem". Ironically, these were the words of a president under whose watch the TBTF title was granted to a major bank, Continental Illinois. If the government cannot provide solution to economic and financial problems, then it is rather strange that the Reagan administration used taxpayers' money to solve the big problem Continental Illinois found itself in as a result of horrendously unsound decisions and strategies put in place by its incompetent management. Thereafter, regulatory minimalism and a "market knows best" mindset took hold and dominated decision-making for nearly three decades. Spaventa (2009) argues on similar grounds, pointing out that regulators were caught by the crisis with their eyes wide shut, having resisted attempts to allow regulation to keep pace with financial innovation. He explains his view as follows:

> This was coherent with the prevailing creed: that markets were self-regulating and only required the lightest possible public touch; that self-interest would lead to proper risk assessment; that capital deepening was always good for growth, no matter how.

Free marketeers have been in charge, calling the shots since the early 1980s. Economics has been dominated by the free-market ideology, which led economists and regulators alike to overlook concerns about market failure, hence financial markets have endured considerable deregulation. Posner (2009) contends that "most economists, and the kind of officials who tend to be appointed by Republican presidents, are heavily invested in the ideology of free markets, which teaches them that competitive markets are on the whole self-correcting". But he adds that it is not just the Republicans, describing President Clinton as the "consolidator of the Reagan revolution". Posner argues that "his [Clinton's] economic policies were shaped by establishment Wall Street figures now in disrepute, such as Robert Rubin, along with economists like Alan Greenspan... and Lawrence Summers". And despite the meltdown of 2007–08, free marketeers are still around. Old habits die hard, it seems, but there are encouraging signs. On 16 December 2008, George Bush said: "to make sure that the economy doesn't collapse, I've abandoned free market principles to save the free market system" (Taylor, 2009).

Deregulation and bank failure

Some may argue that the pattern of bank failure exhibited in Figure 2.1 may provide no more than circumstantial evidence against deregulation. However, Wilmarth (2004) presents convincing arguments

Figure 2.1 Bank Failures in the U.S. (1864–2000)

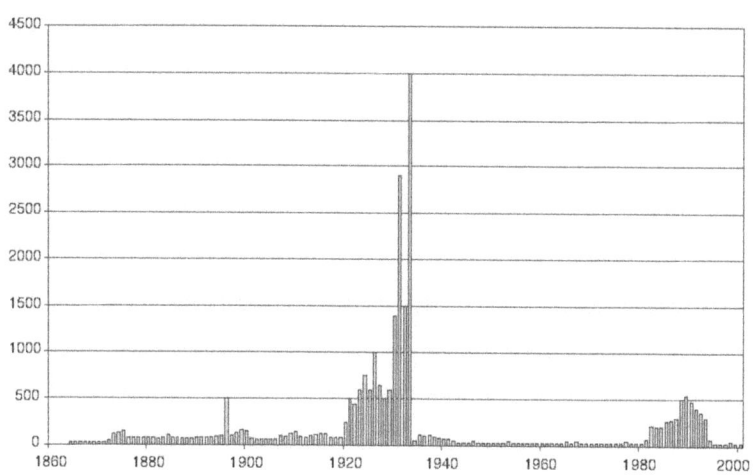

Data Source: Historical Data of the United States: Colonial Times to 1970 (Government Printing Office, 1970); FDIC.

for the linkage between deregulation and banking crises that may trigger government bailout of failing institutions. He puts forward the following sequence of events as an explanation for this linkage:

1. Deregulation broadens lending powers and permissible investment outlets while enhancing competitive pressure. Under these conditions, banks have the incentive to boost their profits by expanding lending and investments into unconventional areas.
2. The expanded availability of debt and equity financing produces an economic boom.
3. Asset markets overshoot their fundamental or fair values, creating an asset price bubble.
4. The bubble bursts and the boom becomes a bust. Market participants rush to the safety of liquid assets, selling long-term assets.
5. The bursting of the bubble produces adverse macroeconomic effects as creditors become more restrained and cautious.
6. The continuing fall in asset prices and rising number of defaults inflict losses on banks and other financial institutions. These losses impair depositors and creditors confidence and threaten a systemic crisis.
7. To prevent such a crisis the TBTF doctrine is invoked. The government comes in to rescue failing financial institutions.

Thus, the causal relation between deregulation and financial crises is not only supported by evidence from financial history, it can also be substantiated by simple intuition. The incidence of bank failure depicted in Figure 2.1 is not just circumstantial evidence.

2.2 The history of deregulation

The 1980s witnessed at least three important acts of deregulation in the U.S. The Depository Institutions Deregulation and Monetary Control Act (DIDMCA) of 1980 removed restrictions on the operations of financial institutions. The Garn-St Germain Act of 1982 allowed depository institutions to acquire failing institutions across geographic boundaries. And the Financial Institutions Reform, Recovery and Enforcement Act (FIRREA) of 1989 allowed commercial banks to acquire either healthy or failing savings and loans associations. When President Reagan signed into law the Garn-St Germain Act, he stated "all in all, I think that we hit the jackpot" (Krugman, 2009). But who are "we"?

Deregulation in the 1990s

More followed in the 1990s. The McFadden Act of 1927 prevented banks from establishing branches across state lines. The Douglas Amendment to the Bank Holding Company Act of 1956 complemented the McFadden Act by preventing interstate acquisitions of banks by bank holding companies. The effect was that no single bank could control the entire market for bank deposits. Geographic restrictions effectively limited the concentration of any bank in obtaining deposits and loans. By 1994 most U.S. states had approved nationwide interstate banking, propelling interstate expansion via mergers and acquisitions. The Reigle-Neal Interstate Banking and Branching Efficiency Act of 1994 eliminated most of the restrictions on interstate mergers and allowed commercial banks to open branches nationwide. The weakening of regulatory restrictions against interstate banking was a significant factor leading to the growth of mergers activity in banking.

The Banking Act of 1933, known as the Glass-Steagal Act, was prompted by problems that arose in 1929 when some banks sold some of their poor quality securities to the trust accounts established for individuals. Some banks also engaged in insider trading, buying or selling corporate securities based on confidential information provided by firms that had requested loans. The Act prevented any depository institution from underwriting corporate securities. The separation of commercial banking from investment banking was intended to prevent potential conflict of interest. Banks argued against the Act, stating that any conflict of interest could be resolved by regulators and that participating in the securities business enables them to have easy access to marketing, technological, and managerial resources, which would reduce the prices of securities-related services to consumers. As we have seen, the period between the advent of the Glass-Steagal Act in 1933 and the start of wholesale deregulation in the 1980s was rather tranquil, witnessing very few bank failures. Some critics warned that the Act would cripple the U.S. financial sector, but they have been proved to be wrong.

The Financial Services Modernization Act, also called the Gramm-Leach-Bailey Act, was passed in 1999 to replace the Glass-Steagal Act. A commentator describes the repeal of the Glass-Steagall Act as follows (Washington's Blog, 2009):

> When Glass Steagall was revoked and the giants started doing both types of banking, it was like a single crop cannibalizing another crop and becoming a new super-organism. Instead of having

diversity, you've now got a monoculture of the new super-crop, susceptible to being wiped out by a pest.

Scheer (2010) argues that the seeds of the repeal of the Glass-Steagal Act were sown in 1987 when President Reagan chose Alan Greenspan to replace Paul Volcker as the head of the Fed. Greenspan was chosen by Reagan because he shared affection for free markets. Scheer sees the repeal of the Glass-Steagall Act as coming when Greenspan, Robert Rubin and Larry Summers joined forces with the Wall Street lobby to obtain Bill Clinton's signature on the law that eliminated Glass-Steagall.

The deregulatory measures of the 1990s also covered insurance, a line of business that banks had been engaged in to a limited extent. In 1995 the U.S. Supreme Court ruled that commercial banks could sell annuities (paying a premium now for a future stream of annual payments). Since annuities had previously been sold by insurance companies, this ruling paved the way for banks to penetrate the insurance market. In 1998 regulators allowed a merger between Citicorp and Traveler's Insurance Group, encouraging more consolidation. The Financial Services Modernization Act of 1999 confirmed that mergers between banks and insurance companies would be allowed. The Act permitted bank holding companies to engage in any financial activity through their subsidiaries. As a result, consolidation in the financial sector gathered tremendous momentum.

Deregulation continued in the first decade of the 21st century. In 2004, the Securities and Exchange Commission (SEC) relaxed the net capital rule, which enabled investment banks to increase significantly the level of debt they were taking on, fuelling the growth in mortgage-backed securities. The SEC has admitted that self-regulation of investment banks contributed to the global financial crisis (*New York Times*, 27 September 2008).

Regulatory failure

Regulators have failed to enact new regulations to keep up with the development of new financial products. Over time, a huge amount of financial activity migrated away from regulated and transparent markets and institutions to the lightly regulated or unregulated shadow markets encompassing mortgage brokers, hedge funds, private-equity funds, off-balance sheet structured-investment vehicles, and a booming market in opaque (and useless) derivatives, particularly collateralized debt obligations (CDOs) and credit default swaps (CDSs). As early as 1997, the then

Fed Chairman, Alan Greenspan, fought to keep the derivatives market unregulated. With the advice of the President's Working Group on Financial Markets, the Congress and President allowed the self-regulation of the over-the-counter (OTC) derivatives market when they enacted the Commodity Futures Modernization Act of 2000 (Summers *et al*, 1999).

Lynn Turner (2009) makes the interesting comment that she disagrees when "people like President Obama say our problem is that we had an outdated regulatory system" because "it was a regulatory system that in the past two decades had not become out of date, but rather had been almost entirely dismantled by Congress and the various administrations". She lists the following measures of deregulation (some of which have already been mentioned) and aspects of regulatory failure:

1. Passing the Gramm-Leach-Bailey Act, which guaranteed large financial "supermarkets" that can only be too big to fail, while prohibiting the SEC from being able to require regulation of investment bank holding companies.
2. Cutting the budgets of the SEC and the Commodity Futures Trading Commission (CFTC) and effectively dismantling these agencies.
3. Failure of Congress and the administrations to take regulatory measures against new financial products such as credit derivatives.
4. Exempting from regulatory oversight hedge funds and private equity funds.
5. Allowing banks to engage in unsound lending practices as regulators became "prudential supervisors".
6. Failure of Congress to provide authority, tools and resources for the Office of Federal Housing Enterprise Oversight.
7. Failure to scrutinize credit rating agencies.
8. Failure by Congress to bring greater transparency to the financial reporting of equity compensation (stock options).
9. Preventing investors from getting justice through legitimate legal action.
10. Denial by the SEC of shareholders' right to have the same access as the managers who work for them to the proxy of the companies they owned.
11. Pressure by Congress to undo transparent accounting practices.
12. Putting people who did not believe in regulation in charge of regulatory agencies (Greenspan, to name just one).

Moss (2009) makes the interesting point that the success of the 1930s regulatory measures led to deregulation. As a result of some 50 years of financial calm following the advent of the Glass-Steagal Act, financial stability was taken for granted and regulation looked burdensome and unnecessary. He makes the analogy that "it was as if, after sharply reducing deadly epidemics through public health measures, policy-makers concluded that these measures weren't really necessary, since major epidemics were not much of a threat anymore". Likewise Posner (2009) points out that "excessive deregulation of the financial industry was a government failure abetted by the political and ideological commitments of mainstream economists, who overlooked the possibility that the financial markets seemed robust because regulation had prevented financial crises".

2.3   Evolution of the TBTF doctrine

There are precursors to the TBTF doctrine: the "essentiality doctrine" and the "domino theory of banking". The essentiality doctrine authorized the FDIC to provide assistance to a failing insured bank if its continued operations were deemed "essential to provide adequate banking services in the community" (however, there was no clear-cut definitions of "essential" and "community"). The doctrine was used for the first time in 1971 to bail out Unity Bank, a small minority-owned bank in Boston. The domino theory of banking was put forward in 1980 in relation to First Pennsylvania Bank. A former chairman of the FDIC, Irving Sprague, quotes several officials making statements in the spirit of the domino theory, such as "any solution but failure"; and "if First Pennsylvania went down, its business connections with other banks would entangle them also and touch off a crisis in confidence that would snowball into other bank failures" (Sprague, 1986). Todd and Thomson (1990) make it clear that the FDIC was not the sole originator of the TBTF doctrine as it evolved out of the essentiality doctrine. Other "culprits" include the Fed, the Comptroller of the Currency, large U.S. and foreign banks, and politicians. It was a truly collective effort that led to the birth of the monster called TBTF.

A new era

The era of too big to fail began in earnest in July 1984 when the Reagan administration nationalized Continental Illinois with the FDIC taking 80 per cent ownership and the responsibility for its bad loans. Hetzel (1991) described the bailout of Continental Illinois as exemplifying "most clearly the transformation of the FDIC into a modern Reconstruction Finance Corporation". The break from normal practice divided the administration. Treasury Secretary Donald Regan found the intervention outrageous, calling it "bad public policy" and arguing that "it represents an unauthorized and unlegislated expansion of federal guarantees in contradiction of executive branch policy" (Gelinas, 2009). But the White House accepted the argument put forward by the Fed and FDIC that the alternative was to risk a systemic crisis in the financial sector. Later in 1984, at a congressional subcommittee hearing, Representative Stewart McKinney summed up the lesson of the rescue effort by saying: "Let us not use bandy words. We have a new kind of bank. It is called too big to fail, T.B.T.F., and it is a wonderful bank". Since then, TBTF has become a generally accepted, if unwritten, rule in the financial world.

The doctrine persisted during the savings and loans crisis of the late 1980s and early 1990s, as the government saved uninsured lenders to big banks whenever it saw risk to the broader system, without doing the same to small banks. In the summer of 1991 Fed Chairman Alan Greenspan, who was not even a great fan of deposit insurance, said that "there may be some banks, at some particular times, whose collapse and liquidation would be excessively disruptive" (Gelinas, 2009). In that same year, the Bank of New England failed even though the Fed had been allowing the bank unlimited access to the discount window while the Treasury had awarded it a billion dollars in tax and loan accounts to boost its liquidity. Ultimately the bank was rescued by the FDIC with a package consisting of guarantees for all deposits and the infusion of $750 million worth of new capital (Beckner, 1996).

Extension to NBFIs

With time, the TBTF principle was extended beyond commercial banks to other financial institutions. In 1998 a hedge fund, Long-Term Capital Management (LTCM), was saved from bankruptcy after it had got into trouble by indulging in risky derivatives trading. Although the government said that no public money was used in the bailout, Greenspan's public statements during and after the crisis made it clear that the Fed would have used public funds if banks had refused to help (Dowd, 1999).

The LTCM rescue is a milestone in the history of TBTF. Following the bailout of Continental Illinois in 1984, Federal Reserve officials were trying to convince large institutions that they cannot count on Federal Reserve support if they get themselves into difficulties. That message seemed to be slowly getting through to financial institutions, but the LTCM rescue wiped out all that progress in one stroke, resulting in a complete loss of credibility, which is essential for circumventing the

TBTF problem. The reason given for the intervention—the Fed's fears of the effects of LTCM's failure on world financial markets—was nothing less than an emphatic restatement of the TBTF doctrine. As Dowd (1999) put it, "too big to fail was back again, with a vengeance". As a result of the LTCM case, a widespread belief emerged, that if the government protected lenders to a hedge fund, then it certainly would not let an investment bank collapse.

Introducing the FDICIA

The most significant change undertaken to reduce the moral hazard problem created by TBTF protection was the 1991 Federal Deposit Insurance Corporation Improvement Act (FDICIA). The Act requires the FDIC to choose the "least-cost alternative" in resolving failing banks, with the exception of banks whose failure would cause "serious adverse effects on economic conditions and financial stability". (Angbazo and Saunders, 1997). The exception is to be determined jointly by the FDIC, the Federal Reserve and the Treasury Secretary in consultation with the President. The FDICCIA was designed to boost the likelihood that uninsured depositors and other creditors would incur losses if their bank fails (unless, of course, it was TBTF). The FDICIA improved the supervision and regulation of banks and formally limited the Federal Reserve's ability to make loans to faltering banks as a means of keeping them afloat.

In reality, however, the FDICIA did little to change existing policy towards TBTF financial institutions. Most of the "new" measures it introduced to combat the moral hazard problem created by TBTF protection already existed in some form or another. According to Feldman and Rolnick (1997), "the fix was incomplete, however, because regulators can provide full protection when they determine that a failing bank is too-big-to-fail". They also argue that "while the limitations [introduced by the FDICIA] appear to constrain bailouts, they are not prohibitive". Stern and Feldman (2004) take the view that systemic risk exception is a loophole that can be used in cases when no systemic risk is present, which means that there has been no significant change in the incentives of regulators when they are confronted with a decision whether or not to bail out a financial institution. Although the FDICIA may have helped on the margin, there remains room for substantial policy improvement.

2.4 TBTF rescue during the global financial crisis

Since the 1990s, the U.S. government has adopted a cherry-picking approach with respect to TBTF. While LTCM was saved, a prominent investment firm, Drexel Burnham Lambert, was allowed to declare bankruptcy in 1990. The cherry-picking approach was conspicuous during the global financial crisis. In September 2008 Henry Paulson was unapologetic about refusing to extend financial assistance to Lehman Brothers as the Bush administration signalled strongly that Wall Street should not expect help from Washington. Mr Paulson said that he never once considered it appropriate to put taxpayers' money at risk to resolve the problems at Lehman Brothers. Bank of America pulled out of its talks with Lehman after the government refused to take responsibility for losses on some of Lehman's most troubled real-estate assets, something it had agreed to do when JP Morgan bought Bear Stearns to save it from a bankruptcy filing in March 2008.

In 2009 some 150 U.S. banks were allowed to fail. These include Bank of Elmwood, Partners Bank, Georgian Bank, First State Bank, Bradford Bank, Community Bank of Nevada, Community Bank of Arizona, Bank of Wyoming, First Bank of Idaho, Colorado National Bank, National Bank of Commerce, and so on. None of these banks or others was TBTF, and so they were allowed to fail. But if Citigroup is TBTF why is it that 150 banks are not collectively TBTF? Or is it that small banks are not too politically connected to fail?

Another twist

TBTF was given yet another twist when in March 2008 the Federal Reserve acted to save the investment bank Bear Stearns, orchestrating the bank's sale to JP Morgan by providing Morgan with up to $30 billion in financing to cover Bear Stearns's portfolio of risky assets. The Bear Stearns deal means that the TBTF rule now applies to investment banks as well. The deal looked to many like a gift to JP Morgan. It is noteworthy that Jamie Dimon, JP Morgan's CEO and a prominent member of the Wall Street establishment, sits on the board of directors of the Federal Reserve Bank of New York, which (along with the Treasury Department) brokered the deal. In September 2008, we witnessed the sale of Merrill Lynch to Bank of America, the first bailout of AIG, and the takeover and immediate sale of Washington Mutual to JP Morgan—all of which were brokered by the U.S. government. In October 2008, nine large banks were recapitalized on the same day behind closed doors in Washington. This, in turn, was followed by additional bailouts for Citigroup, AIG, Bank of America, Citigroup (again), and AIG (again).

Alan Greenspan is quoted by McKee and Lanman (2009) as saying that he puts the blame for the resurgence of the TBTF doctrine on Paulson. In this respect Greenspan said: "at one point, no bank was considered too big to fail", but "that changed after the Treasury Department under then-Secretary Hank Paulson effectively nationalized Fannie Mae and Freddie Mac, and the Treasury and Fed bailed out Bear Stearns Co. and American International Group Inc.". Greenspan added: "It's going to be very difficult to repair their credibility on that because when push came to shove, they didn't stand up". Look who's talking! Why did not Greenspan think about his credibility when he enthusiastically advocated the rescue of LTCM a decade earlier?

Introducing TARP

In September 2008, Henry Paulson asked Congress for $700 billion to buy toxic assets from banks, with no strings attached and no judicial review of his purchase decisions. The underlying scheme has become known as the "Troubled Asset Relief Program" (TARP). TARP (or perhaps more appropriately, TRAP, as it turned out to be) allowed the U.S. Treasury to buy or insure "troubled" assets, defined as "residential or commercial mortgages and any securities, obligations, or other investments that are based on or related to such mortgages, that in each case was originated or issued on or before March 14, 2008". They also include "any other financial instrument that the [Treasury] Secretary, after consultation with the Chairman of the Board of Governors of the Federal Reserve System, determine the purchase of which is necessary to promote financial market stability" (Congressional Budget Office, 2009).

In a nutshell, TARP allowed the Treasury Secretary to buy illiquid, difficult-to-value assets (primarily CDOs) from financial institutions. In return, these institutions were required to issue equity warrants, equity or senior debt securities to the Treasury. Subsequently the TARP went through several changes that gave government officials more discretion in disbursing funds. The financial institutions that received funds in return for preferred stocks include Goldman Sachs, Morgan Stanley, JP Morgan, Bank of America, Citigroup, Wells Fargo and Bank of New York Mellon. Many observers suspected that the purpose of squandering TARP money was to overpay for toxic assets and thereby take the problem off the banks' hands. Indeed, that is the only way that buying toxic assets would have helped anything.

In effect the TARP money was used to recapitalize financial institutions, buying their shares on terms that were grossly favourable to those institutions. As the crisis deepened and financial institutions needed more help, the U.S. government became more and more creative in figuring out ways to provide financial institutions with subsidies that are too complex for the general public to understand. The first AIG bailout, which was conditioned on relatively good terms for taxpayers, was supplemented by three further bailouts whose terms were more AIG-friendly. The second Citigroup bailout and the Bank of America bailout included complex asset guarantees that provided those banks with insurance at below-market rates. The third Citigroup bailout, in late February 2009, converted government-owned preferred stock to common stock at a price significantly higher than the market price, which was effectively a subsidy.

By the end of 2009, big American banks were rushing to repay TARP funds before the end of the year. On 9 December Bank of America repaid the $45 billion of preferred stock owned by the Treasury. In total, the Treasury received $90 billion in December 2009, while banks were planning to raise some $50 billion in common stock. That rush was apparently motivated by the desire to go back to business as usual, to pay fat bonuses without having the government complaining about it. *The Economist* (2009b) quotes a hedge fund manager as saying that "the banks aren't afraid of the government any more". The problem is that there is no guarantee that these banks are out of the woods and that they would not resort to TBTF protection, thus demanding taxpayers' money, in the future. According to *The Economist* (2009b), the banks' "level 3" assets, which are illiquid and hard to value, stood at $346 billion, almost as much as their core capital.

Back with extra vengeance

The year 2008, in the midst of the global financial crisis, witnessed the return of the TBTF doctrine with extra vengeance. Officials made it clear and explicit that they were prepared to devote the resources necessary for preventing financial panic. According to Moss (2009) federal agencies in the U.S. dispersed some $2 trillion in responding to the crisis and have taken a potential commitment in excess of $10 trillion. That money covered even shadowy financial institutions. As a result, Moss argues, "there can be no doubt that federal policymakers view many of the nation's largest financial institutions as too big—or, more precisely, too systemic to fail". The Federal Reserve Bank of Minneapolis suggests, based on a series of studies, that the "government's response to the 2007–08 financial turmoil... expanded the safety net normally reserved for banks and exacerbated the existing too big to fail (TBTF) problem" (www.minneapolisfed.org/publications). In these studies it is argued that "a large TBTF problem is costly, having the capacity to sow the seeds of future financial crises".

2.5   Has the TBTF problem become worse?

The TBTF problem has certainly become worse, as the global financial crisis (or rather the bailouts resulting from the crisis) has created what Moss (2009) calls the "mother of all moral hazards". It is worse in the sense that regulators have lost credibility with respect to refusing a bailout and letting a failing institution fail. Unless appropriate regulatory measures are taken or something is done about credibility (or lack thereof), it will be business as usual for big financial institutions.

But even before the onset of the global financial crisis, the TBTF problem got progressively worse, particularly since wholesale deregulation started in the 1980s. Stern and Feldman (2004) suggested the following six reasons why the TBTF problem became worse even prior to the global financial crisis:

1. Banking consolidation has made big banks even bigger, more politically connected, and more likely to be bailed out if and when they fail.
2. Bank consolidation has created a greater number of big banks that can claim the TBTF status on the grounds that their failure poses significant systemic risk.
3. Technology has allowed small banks to play a more important role in the payments system to become too interconnected to fail (see Chapter 6).
4. Technology has improved the quality of information, and thus the development of capital markets. This has encouraged banks to depend increasingly on capital markets to fund their operations, thus becoming more vulnerable.
5. As a result of so-called "financial innovation", banking operations have become increasingly complex, making the unwinding of a failed institution rather difficult. This is the too-complex-to-fail problem.
6. Deregulation played a big role, as was pointed out earlier.

TBTF sceptics, such as Mishkin (2006), argue that while these points are valid, the FDICIA legislation has made things better, in which case they disagree with the proposition that the TBTF problem has become worse. But that was before the global financial crisis. Arguing that there is no TBTF problem, or that it is insignificant, in the aftermath of the global financial crisis is a triumph of wishful thinking over reason. Arguing that there is a problem but we have to live with it and keep on bailing out failed institutions is tantamount to defeatism, surrendering to the will of financiers.

3
Some Notorious TBTF Cases

3.1 Continental Illinois

In May 1984 the eighth largest bank in the U.S. at that time, Continental Illinois, found itself deep in trouble as a result of a faulty funding model (similar to the messy funding model that led to the collapse of the British bank, Northern Rock, in 2007). Beyond using funds from FDIC-insured small depositors and other stable long-term lenders such as bondholders, Continental relied more than most banks on short-term, uninsured lenders worldwide (particularly large short-term depositors and foreign money markets, which are typically more risk averse than the average retail depositor). This left the bank exposed to the risk of changes in attitude towards risk. On the assets side (the uses of funds), things were just as bad. Tight money, Mexico's default and plunging oil prices followed a period when the bank had aggressively pursued a commercial lending business, a Latin American syndicated loans business, and loan participations in the energy sector. The bank held a significant stake in the highly-speculative oil and gas loans of Oklahoma's Penn Square Bank. In a nutshell, Continental had two fundamental problems in its risk management system: (i) its appraisal of credit risk was faulty, and (ii) it had almost no core deposits to tide itself over if it got into trouble (Gup, 2004a).

When Penn Square failed in July 1982, Continental's distress became acute, culminating in press rumours of failure and a depositor run in early May 1984. To prevent immediate failure, the Federal Reserve announced categorically that it would meet any liquidity needs that Continental might have, while the FDIC gave depositors and general creditors a full guarantee (not subject to the $100,000 FDIC deposit-insurance limit) and provided direct assistance of $2 billion. Money centre banks assembled an additional $5.3 billion unsecured facility pending a resolution and resumption of more normal business. Those measures slowed, but did not stop, the outflow of deposits from Continental.

The fear of complications

Besides generic concerns of size, contagion of depositor panic and bank distress, regulators feared a significant disruption of national payment and settlement systems. Of special concern was the wide network of correspondent banks with high percentages of their capital invested in Continental Illinois. Essentially, the bank was deemed TBTF, and the "provide assistance" option was reluctantly taken. In a Senate hearing afterwards, the then Comptroller of the Currency, C.T. Conover, defended his position by admitting that the regulators would not let the eleven largest banks fail (Conover, 1984). Regulatory agencies (FDIC, Office of the Comptroller of the Currency, the Fed, etc.) feared that the failure of Continental may cause widespread financial complications and a major bank run that may easily spread by financial contagion. On 17 May 1984, the FDIC issued a press release saying (Todd and Thomson, 1990):

> In view of all the circumstances surrounding Continental Illinois Bank, the FDIC provides assurance that, in any arrangements that may be necessary to achieve a permanent solution, all depositors and general creditors of the bank will be fully protected and service to the bank's customers will not be interrupted.

However, there is no evidence suggesting that those fears were justified. William Isaac, a former FDIC Chairman, commented on the rescue of Continental by saying (Trigaux, 1989):

> I wonder if we might not be better off today if we had decided to let Continental fail, because many of the large banks that I was concerned might fail have failed anyway.... And they probably are costing the FDIC more money by being allowed to continue several more years than they would have had they failed in 1984.

On 26 July 1984, the then Chairman of the House Banking Committee, Fernand St Germain, made it clear that he was unhappy about the bailout of Continental, arguing that it was expensive and that the decision to go ahead with it was not considered carefully (Sprague, 1986). He said:

> The rescue of Continental dwarfs the combined guarantees and outlays of the Federal Government in the Lockheed, Chrysler and

New York City bailouts which originated in this Committee. More important is the fact that the Federal Government provided assistance to these entities only after the fullest debate, great gnashing of teeth, the imposition of tough conditions, and ultimately a majority vote of the House and the Senate and the signature of the President of the United States.

The dawn of the TBTF era

Although Continental was not the first bank to be bailed out by the U.S. government, this costly rescue operation marked the dawn of the TBTF era. What is also alarming about this bailout is that "Continental is an example of a big bank that forgot its history". Sprague (1986) tells a story from 1937 when Continental protested the payment of deposit insurance premium, sending the FDIC a cheque for $831.96 with a note in which the bank argued that "the deposit insurance law was invalid and unconstitutional".

3.2   Long-Term Capital Management

Long-Term Capital Management (LTCM) was founded in March 1994 by John Meriwether, a former Salomon Brothers trading "star", along with a small group of associates, most notably Robert Merton and Myron Scholes, two economists who received the economics Nobel Prize in 1997. The fund initially specialized in high-volume arbitrage trades in bond and bond-derivatives markets but gradually became more active in other markets and more willing to speculate. The project thus started as an arbitrage fund but gradually became more like a macro fund. LTCM, however, was as far away as possible from long-term capital management—that is, the management of capital with a long-term perspective. Initially LTCM was rather successful: by the end of 1997 it had achieved annual rates of return of around 40 per cent and had nearly tripled its investors' money. But that was the time when any leveraged fool could have done just as well.

The rise and fall of LTCM

That track record and the prestige of its associates (among them a "star trader" and two Nobel Prize winners) made LTCM very popular with rich individual and institutional investors. By that stage, it appeared that the fund's assets had grown to about $120 billion and its capital to about $7.3 billion. Although the fund was highly leveraged (an assets-to-equity ratio of over 16 to 1) the management of LTCM concluded that the capital base was too high to earn the rate of return on capital for which they were aiming. Consequently, $2.7 billion of capital was returned to shareholders, thus cutting the fund's capital to $4.8 billion and increasing its leverage ratio to around 25 to 1.

In effect, the management of LTCM had taken a major gamble: they made the fund much more risky, hoping to bolster return on equity. It is rather strange, therefore, that Myron Scholes (2000) claimed that "the increase in volatility (particularly in equity markets) and the flight to liquidity around the world resulted in an extraordinary reduction in the capital base of the firm that I was associated with, Long-Term Capital Management". In truth what happened to LTCM was simply a case of greed combined with overconfidence. Why not, when two finance (economics, as it is formally known) Nobel Prize winners are calling the shots? The LTCM management chose to overlook a very important fact of financial life: that leverage is good while things are going well, but it can be fatal when things turn sour. This principle was demonstrated vividly by the destruction of a large number of hedge funds during the global financial crisis.

Market conditions deteriorated sharply in the summer of 1998, leading to major losses for LTCM in July of that year. Disaster struck in August when the Russian government devalued the ruble and declared a moratorium on future debt repayments. Those events led to a major deterioration in the creditworthiness of many emerging-market bonds, which had an adverse effect on LTCM because the fund had bet massively on the narrowing of the price spreads between U.S. Treasury bonds and emerging-market bonds. To make matters worse, the fund sustained major losses on other speculative positions because their "highly sophisticated models" had told them that what actually happened subsequently could only happen once in a few billion years.

By the end of August 1998 LTCM's capital was down to $2.3 billion, and the fund had lost over half of the equity capital it had held at the start of the year. By that time, its asset base was about $107 billion, raising the leverage ratio to over 45 to 1, which is very high by any standard and certainly not the kind of leverage ratio you want to have in that volatile environment. As its losses mounted, the fund had increasing difficulty meeting margin calls and needed more collateral to ensure that it could meet its obligations to counterparties. The fund was running short of high-quality assets that could be used as collateral to maintain its positions, and it also had great difficulty liquidating those positions. Many of the positions were relatively illiquid, difficult to sell in normal times, and even more difficult to sell (particularly in a hurry) in nervous bear markets. A combination of high leverage and low liquidity can be nothing short of a recipe for disaster, as numerous financial institutions found out the hard way during the global financial crisis. Morris (2008) explains the failure of LTCM as follows:

> Hubris, along with the drive to improve yields, may have been the real cause of LTCM's failure. The patterns began to drift away from their core disciplines into arenas in which they had little experience, like currency trading and equity arbitrage (betting on takeovers), even as they steadily increased leverage ratios.

On 2 September 1998, the partners of LTCM sent a letter to investors acknowledging the fund's problems and seeking an injection of new capital to sustain it. That information soon leaked out and the fund's problems became common knowledge. LTCM's situation continued to deteriorate in September, forcing its management to look for assistance in an increasingly desperate effort to keep the fund in business as it was facing insolvency. Not surprisingly, no immediate help materialized, and by 19 September the fund's capital had reached a low level of $600 million. The fund had an asset base of $80 billion at that point, and its leverage ratio was skyrocketing, signalling an impending disaster.

The Fed steps in

Investors and regulators were observing LTCM's deterioration with mounting concern. Many financial institutions had large stakes in LTCM, and there was also widespread concern (justified or otherwise) about the potential impact of its failure on financial markets. The Fed felt obliged to intervene, and a delegation from the New York Federal Reserve and the U.S. Treasury visited the fund on 20 September to assess the situation. At that meeting, the fund partners persuaded the delegation that LTCM's situation was not only bad but potentially much worse than market participants imagined. They also portrayed the fund as TBTF, having once conveyed the message that it was so sophisticated and run by such intelligent people that it could not fail.

The Fed accepted the proposition that LTCM was TBTF, concluding that its failure was feared to have disastrous effects on financial markets. In a testimony to the House Committee on Banking and Financial Services (1998), Greenspan put it as follows:

> Financial market participants were already unsettled by recent global events. Had the failure of LTCM triggered the seizing up of markets,

substantial damage could have been inflicted on many market participants, including some not directly involved with the firm, and could have potentially impaired the economies of many nations, including our own... .

But those contemplated consequences were grossly exaggerated. LTCM was a hedge fund investing (recklessly) rich people's money, people who accepted the risk involved and had reaped the benefits when things were going well. Also at stake was the money borrowed from banks, but banks also accepted the risk involved. In any case, the amounts involved were not so great as to cause systemic failure or "substantial damage" (a few billion dollars is a drop in the ocean relative to the assets of the financial sector or GDP). If LTCM had been allowed to go down, investors and creditors would have endured sustainable losses and that would have been the end of the matter. Instead, regulators opted for a hazardous precedent: granting the TBTF status to a hedge fund.

The New York Federal Reserve invited a number of the creditor firms to discuss a rescue package, and it was soon agreed that this consortium would mount a rescue if no one else took over the fund in the meantime. However, when representatives of that group met on 23 September, they learned that another group had just made an offer that would expire at lunchtime that day. It was therefore decided to wait and see how LTCM responded to that offer before proceeding any further. A group consisting of Warren Buffett's firm, Berkshire Hathaway, along with Goldman Sachs and American International Group (yes, the same AIG), offered to buy out the shareholders for $250 million and put $3.75 billion into the fund as new capital. That offer would have saved the fund from insolvency, but existing shareholders would have lost everything except for the $250 million takeover payment. By the same token the fund's managers would have been fired (deservedly so).

That would have been a fair solution to the problem without any regulatory involvement. The precedent of granting the TBTF status to a hedge fund could have been avoided at the modest cost of the fund staff losing their highly-paid jobs (these are not the kind of people who would have sought unemployment benefits) and rich individual and institutional investors losing some of the gains they had made earlier. The alternative for the LTCM management would have been to lose their equity, their jobs, and their management fees and get nothing in return—in short, to lose everything. They would therefore have been insane to turn the Buffett group down, and we must suppose they would not have done so. There is thus a very strong argument that the

Fed could have abandoned the rescue as late as the morning of 23 September without letting LTCM fail (Dowd, 1999).

But that was not to be, as Dowd (1999) put it. The management of LTCM rejected the offer, although they were in no position to negotiate, demand or put conditions. One can only assume that they did so because they were confident of getting a better deal from the Federal Reserve's consortium. To please the LTCM management, the Fed reconvened discussions to hammer out a rescue package, which was agreed on by the end of the day. The package was promptly accepted by LTCM and made public immediately. Under the terms of the deal, 14 prominent banks and brokerage houses (including UBS, Goldman Sachs, and Merrill Lynch) agreed to buy 90 per cent of the fund's equity for $3.65 billion. Existing shareholders would retain a 10 per cent holding, valued at about $400 million. This offer was clearly better for the existing shareholders than was Buffett's offer. It was also better for the managers of LTCM, who would retain their jobs for the time being and earn management fees that they would have lost had the Buffett group taken over. Control of the fund was passed to a new steering committee made up of representatives from the consortium. The announcement of the rescue ended concerns about LTCM's immediate future.

Rewarding recklessness

The LTCM case is a textbook example of rewarding recklessness. Although stakeholders were happy that the failure of LTCM had been avoided, some observers expressed concern about the long-term implications of the rescue, particularly because it was engineered by the Fed and motivated by the TBTF doctrine. Indeed, there was considerable criticism of the management of LTCM for getting into difficulties and of the Federal Reserve for bailing out the fund. The Fed should have sat back and let the Warren Buffett group do the job. James Leach, Chairman of the House Committee on Banking and Financial Services, expressed the following opinion at the 6 May 1999 hearing (House Committee on Banking and Financial Services, 1999):

> I am very worried about a precedent that has gotten almost no review, and that is that this Fed-led, treasury-endorsed bailout of Long-Term Capital Management had the effect of putting the United States Government in collusion with a group of private parties against a private party alternative bid, and that is the only rationalization for government action, was that there was no private alternative on the table. But there was, and very credible one and

one that was every bit as secure as the one that was put together by the government.

What is more tragic about this event is that those who oppose regulation and cheer deregulation use it as a case study to demonstrate the hazard of regulatory intervention, in the sense that the private sector would have sorted out the mess on its own. But this argument is flawed and no less than a travesty because it overlooks the distinction between prevention and cure. The failure of LTCM came about because hedge funds are unregulated beasts. Proper regulation of liquidity and leverage would have prevented the saga.

So, the question that begs for an answer is the following: why did the Fed force a settlement? Many observers are sceptical about the official explanation that a disorderly failure would have been violently disruptive, but Morris (2008) suggests that the real motive was to avoid a scandal. How could anyone justify the fact that a small group of people managed to borrow hundreds of billions of dollars from banks, while banks and their regulators had no idea of how much that group had borrowed and what they did with it?

3.3   The Royal Bank of Scotland

The Royal Bank of Scotland (RBS) has not only become TBTF, but it has (through acquisitions) become the largest company in the world (Lanchester, 2009). The RBS fought off three takeovers/mergers in the 1970s and 1980s before growing stronger and launching takeovers of its own—that is, the prey becoming a predator. In 1999 the RBS became the second largest bank in Britain after the Hong Kong and Shanghai Banking Corporation (HSBC) which made Fred Goodwin, the bank's CEO, some sort of a hero in the banking world. The "success" of RBS was recognized to the extent that a case study entitled *The Royal Bank of Scotland: Masters of Integration* was taught at Harvard Business School. The bank continued to live up to its reputation and grew by embracing not only banking interests but also a wide range of insurance products. Subsequently, the RBS acquired a 10 per cent share in the Bank of China, the world's fifth largest bank and launched a takeover bid for the Dutch bank ABN Amro. A consortium that also included the Belgo-Dutch bank Fortis and the Spanish Banco Santander won the bid against Barclays, by paying €71 billion for the deal although ABN had sold off its American subsidiary, LaSalle, which was one reason for the RBS to be interested in the deal in the first place.

A bad deal and concealment of the truth

The ABN Amro deal turned out to be a fatal mistake, not only because it was extremely expensive but, perhaps more importantly, because ABN Amro had a significant exposure to the kind of toxic assets that RBS had accumulated massive amounts of. By April 2008, RBS was resorting to the markets to raise more capital to cover losses from the deal. Within months of the deal, the ABN Amro takeover destroyed RBS. According to Lanchester (2009), "along with the AOL-Time Warner merger and the Daimler-Chrysler merger, the ABN Amro takeover is one of the biggest flops in corporate history". *The Economist* (2009c) describes the purchase of ABN Amro as "disastrous".

According to Kay (2009a), the RBS was crippled by activities that more than 169,000 employees (out of a total of 170,000) did not know about and were not engaged in. A careful examination of the 2007 financial statements may reveal why RBS went down. The balance sheet shows that derivatives amounted to £337 billion as opposed to £116 billion in 2006. However, the annual report makes it sound as if derivatives were used for the purpose of hedging risk. The report says: "Companies in the Group transact derivatives as principal either as a trading activity or to manage balance sheet foreign exchange, interest rate and credit risk" (Lanchester, 2009). Furthermore, the annual report is rather vague about the notorious subprime mortgage derivatives, which caused the global financial crisis. It says the following about subprime products:

> The Group has a leading position in structuring, distributing and trading asset-backed securities (ABS). These activities include buying mortgage-backed securities, including securities backed by US subprime mortgages, and repackaging them into collateralised debt obligations (CDOs) for subsequent sale to investors. The Group retains exposure to some of the super senior tranches of these CDOs which are all carried at fair value.

During a board meeting in the summer of 2006, Sir Fred Goodwin was asked by fellow directors whether the bank had any plans to move into the subprime market. He told the board that the bank would not move into subprime products and that, as a result, "RBS is better placed than our competitors". In the foreword to RBS's 2006 annual report, published in April 2007, Sir Fred wrote: "sound control of risk is fundamental to the Group's business... central to this is our long-standing aversion to subprime lending, wherever we do business". In reality, however, RBS turned out to have quite a significant exposure to subprime products, and to be steadily acquiring more. On the 2007 balance sheet, this exposure appears under "debt securities". This item includes £68.302 billion of mortgage-backed securities, up from £32.19 billion the previous year.

In her book, *Fool's Gold*, Gillian Tett (2009) has RBS "aggressively" growing its exposure to collateralized debt obligations during this period. In 2007, its American subsidiary, Greenwich Capital, bought a chunk of subprime mortgages from New Century Financial, a major player in the market that was facing bankruptcy. RBS lent another subprime player, Fremont General, $1 billion. Yet another American subsidiary of RBS, the Citizens Bank, was buying up U.S. subprime products, "allegedly without seeking approval from the RBS board". It was not until the summer of 2007, as Northern Rock was facing meltdown, that Goodwin told the board that RBS had, in fact, built up a substantial subprime exposure. A spokesman for RBS declared (Lanchester, 2009):

> The reality is that, like many others, RBS was heavily exposed to problems in subprime markets via its own operations and those inherited from ABN Amro. This is despite the fact that we did not engage directly in sub-prime issuing. The Board was in possession of full information and the details provided to the market in all financial reporting reflected the Group's honestly held opinion at the time.

The rescue

During the weekend of 11–12 October 2008, RBS received an emergency injection of government (taxpayers') cash to the tune of £20 billion. On 26 February 2009, RBS gave a preliminary announcement of its annual results: it had lost £24 billion, the largest loss in British corporate history, and required yet more help from the taxpayers to remain solvent. An extra £25.5 billion was paid, taking the government's share of the bank to around 95 per cent. In addition, RBS put £302 billion of its assets into the government's asset protection scheme, a sort of insurance plan under which the government, in return for a fee, promised to underwrite future losses from toxic assets (these assets used to be worth £325 billion but their value has already been written down). As a result of this rescue operation and others, the British government has put itself in a position that no one knows how it will get out of. So much public debt has been created, putting enormous pressure on the national currency and, more importantly, threatening the solvency of the nation as a whole.

Fred the Shred

No wonder that Sir Fred Goodwin has become "Fred the Shred" or the "world's worst banker" (Lanchester, 2009). *The Economist* (2009c) went as far as describing him as a "bad banker and dishonourable man". But then whoever took over from "Fred the Shred" wanted business as usual for RBS. In December 2009, the board announced the intention to pay out £1 billion in bonuses, arguing that it was not fair to apply different standards to RBS from those applied to other banks, overlooking the fact that the bank is owned predominantly by taxpayers. On 25 February 2010, the RBS announced that it had paid £1.3 billion in bonuses (more than what had been announced previously) for the "excellent job" of losing only £3.6 billion in 2009 (some 100 employees received around £1 million each). Despite the strong rhetoric from the British government (Brown and Darling), they seemed incapable of acting decisively by demanding the resignation of the RBS board. Brown actually was talking about unifying bonuses across the world, something that we are unlikely to see in our life times. The RBS action is probably the main reason why the British government decided in December 2009 to impose a tax on bankers' bonuses.

Even Goodwin himself insisted that he was entitled to his full pension of over £700,000 a year due at once (at the young age of 50). If the British government had not rescued the RBS, his pension would have been paid out to the pension-protection fund at the much lower rate of £28,000 a year, due at the age of 65. *The Economist* (2009c) describes Goodwin as "the failed chief executive of a bank that was judged too big to fail" who had become an "accidental millionaire". As a result of mounting public outrage, Goodwin decided to accept less than the full pension, which he announced while in his luxury hideaway in Southern France (Tryhorn and Inman, 2009). It remains to say that when Goodwin got his golden handshake, the RBS paid the tax on his end-of-service benefits.

3.4 Northern Rock

Northern Rock Building Society was formed in 1965 as a result of the merger of Northern Counties Permanent Building Society (established in 1850) and Rock Building Society (established in 1865). During the 30 years that followed, Northern Rock expanded by acquiring 53 smaller building societies, most notably the North of England Building Society in 1994. The Rock was subsequently listed on the stock exchange, making the FTSE 100 Index in 2000.

Northern Rock did not collapse because of excessive exposure to subprime risk. Rather it had an extreme funding model and a significantly wide funding gap (the difference between loans and deposits). To fund its loans, the Rock depended on capital markets, and that seemed fine when things were going well. But when the subprime crisis struck, the resulting credit squeeze made it difficult for the bank to raise money to fund its business.

On 14 September 2007, the bank sought and received a liquidity support facility from the Bank of England. This led to customers queuing outside branches to withdraw their savings (a run on the bank). On 22 February 2008 the bank was taken into state ownership. The nationalization came in the aftermath of two unsuccessful bids to take over the bank, neither being able to commit fully to repayment of taxpayers' money. In October 2009 the European Commission approved a plan to restructure Northern Rock by separating it into a good bank and a bad bank. The good bank would have the bulk of retail deposits and low risk mortgage loans, and it would be sold off. Other mortgage assets would be held by the bad bank (company) that would remain nationalized.

There is a conspiracy theory about the rescue of Northern Rock. While the rescue operation conducted by the Bank of England was justified on the grounds that the alternative could have been a systemic failure, Spring (2008) argues that the British government committed billions of taxpayers' pounds to rescue what he calls "Northern Wreck" because "the workforce, borrowers and individual investors [of the Rock] are concentrated in the [labour] party's Northeast England heartland".

3.5   American International Group

Founded some 90 years ago in Shanghai, AIG moved its headquarters to New York City as the world headed towards war in 1939. After Maurice Greenberg took over in 1967, AIG consolidated its global empire. By the time Greenberg was forced out in an accounting scandal 38 years later, AIG had become one of the world's biggest public companies, providing insurance to U.S. municipalities, pension funds and other public and private bodies through guaranteed investment contracts and other products.. In 2006, the company's sales amounted to $113 billion, while it had 116,000 employees in 130 countries. Indicative of the size of AIG is that it has written more than 81 million life insurance policies, with a face value of $1.9 trillion.

Going into uncharted territory

Problems at AIG did not come from its traditional insurance business but primarily from its business of insuring mortgage-backed securities and other risky debt against default. Its losses centred on the financial products unit (FPU), which until March 2008 was led by its high-rolling head Joseph Cassano. The FPU was some sort of a hedge fund attached to a large and stable insurance company.

AIG had gone into uncharted territory, which is yet another example of diseconomies of scope. Backed by an AAA rating, the company made huge profits by selling credit default swaps (CDSs) to Wall Street's top firms and the biggest companies in Europe and Asia. The CDSs covered $441 billion worth of fixed-income securities to guard against potential bankruptcies and hence default. The FPU made $2.5 billion in pre-tax profits in 2005, largely by selling underpriced insurance on complex, poorly understood (mortgage-backed) securities. Often described as "picking up nickels in front of a steamroller", this strategy is profitable in ordinary years, and catastrophic in bad times. And when bad times came, it turned out to be catastrophic (Lewis, 2009b).

Serious problems started to emerge in September 2008 when Moody's revised AIG's credit rating downwards, forcing the company to seek more cash for collateral against its insurance contracts. The state of the market at that time made it difficult for AIG to sell some of its assets. Without adequate cash, it could default on its obligations to the buyers of its insurance policies. Almost $20 billion was wiped off AIG's balance sheet on 15 September 2008.

Claiming the TBTF status

It is at this stage that AIG claimed its status as a TBTF company on the grounds that "the extent and interconnectedness of AIG's business is far-reaching and encompasses customers across the globe ranging from governmental agencies, corporations and consumers to counterparties" (Saporito, 2009). The failure of AIG, it was argued, could create a chain reaction of enormous proportion. Among other effects, it could lead to mass redemptions of insurance policies, which would theoretically destabilize the industry, the withdrawal of $12 billion to $15 billion in U.S. consumer lending in a credit-short universe. The company even warned of the damage that would be inflicted on Boeing and General Electric, since AIG's aircraft-leasing unit bought more jets than anyone else.

The U.S. government bought the argument. "Uncomfortable as this was, we believe we had no choice if we are to pursue our responsibility for protecting financial stability", Fed Vice Chairman Donald Kohn testified to the Senate Banking Committee (Barnes, 2009). He further said:

> Our judgment has been and continues to be that, in this time of severe market and economic stress, the failure of AIG would impose

unnecessary and burdensome losses on many individuals, households and businesses, disrupt financial markets, and greatly increase fear and uncertainty about the viability of our financial institutions... Thus, such a failure would deepen and extend market disruptions and asset price declines, further constrict the flow of credit to households and businesses in the United States and in many of our trading partners, and materially worsen the recession our economy is enduring.

Treasury Secretary Timothy Geithner (who took office on 26 January 2009) said that government officials "agreed that the collapse of AIG could cause large and unpredictable global losses with systemic consequences, destabilizing already weakened financial markets and further undermining confidence in the economy, and constricting the flow of credit" (Barnes, 2009). The Federal Reserve believed that the collapse of AIG could also "lead to substantially higher borrowing costs, reduced household wealth and materially weaker economic performance" (NECN.com, 2008). In short, the U.S. Treasury Department believed that if AIG went down, the potential losses to the U.S. and global economy would be "extremely high", suggesting that if there was no improvement, more money would have to be "invested". In September 2008, the U.S. government agreed to provide an $85 billion emergency loan to rescue AIG, in return for a 79.9 per cent equity stake. In October 2008, after taking billions in bailouts, AIG sent some of its executives on an $86,000 British hunting trip. When the news of the event broke, AIG apologized. Then it cancelled yet another retreat that it had scheduled for later in the month.

That was the first bailout, but AIG's troubles persisted. In total, the company has cost the taxpayers some $170 billion. As a result, it turned out that AIG had become the banking industry's ATM, essentially passing along $52 billion of TARP money to an array of U.S. and foreign financial institutions (from Goldman Sachs to Switzerland's UBS). Those institutions were counterparties to the credit default swaps that AIG sold at least through 2005. In the midst of the pay-the-counterparties frenzy, AIG paid out $165 million in bonuses to executives at the FPU, the same people who compelled the government to bail out the company in the first place. That incidence triggered public outrage, and justifiably so. In March 2010 it was announced that AIG would sell its Asian business to Prudential, a British insurance company, for some $30 billion. The damage inflicted on AIG by the wizards of the FPU could not be repaired by bailout money alone.

Despite their public comments that a failure of AIG could sink global financial markets, U.S. government officials considered (in late January and early February 2009) allowing AIG to file for bankruptcy, according to documents obtained by FOX Business (Barnes, 2009). The documents consist of e-mails about AIG between officials at the Treasury Department and the Federal Reserve, as well as with two attorneys from Davis Polk & Wardwell LLP. Details of the bankruptcy discussions were not clear from the e-mails, which FOX Business obtained under a Freedom of Information Act request. The very fact that allowing AIG to fail was actually considered a reminder that those officials must have felt that the human race was capable of surviving the failure of an insurance company. At least they must have felt that the envisaged consequences of the failure of AIG were exaggerated.

3.6 Citigroup

Citigroup (or Citi) was born on 7 April 1998 as the offspring of one of the world's largest mergers in history involving the banking giant Citicorp and the financial conglomerate Travelers Group. The history of the company encompasses several firms that over time amalgamated into Citicorp (a multinational banking corporation that operated in more than 100 countries) and Travelers Group (whose businesses covered credit services, consumer finance, brokerage, and insurance). As such, the company's history dates back to the founding of the City Bank of New York (later Citibank) in 1812, Bank Handlowy in 1870, Smith Barney in 1873, Banamex in 1884, and Salomon Brothers in 1910. The merger produced the world's largest financial services network, spanning 140 countries with approximately 16,000 offices worldwide. At one time, the company had approximately 300,000 employees around the world, and held over 200 million customer accounts in more than 140 countries.

Although presented as a merger, the deal was actually more like a stock swap, with Travelers Group purchasing the entirety of Citicorp shares for $70 billion while issuing 2.5 new Citigroup shares for each Citicorp share. Through this mechanism, the existing shareholders of each company owned about half of the new company. While the new company maintained Citicorp's "Citi" brand in its name, it adopted Travelers' distinctive "red umbrella" as the new corporate logo, which was used until 2007. The chairmen of both parent companies, Sandy Weill and John Reed, were announced as co-chairmen and co-CEOs of the new company, Citigroup. The vast difference in management styles between the two men immediately presented question marks over the wisdom of such a setup.

Since the remaining provisions of the Glass-Steagall Act forbade banks to merge with insurance companies, Citigroup was allowed between two and five years to divest any prohibited assets. However, Weill stated at the time of the merger that "over that time the legislation will change" and that "we have had enough discussions to believe this will not be a problem". Indeed, the passing of the Gramm-Leach-Bailey Act in November 1999 vindicated Reed and Weill, opening the door to financial services conglomerates offering a mix of commercial banking, investment banking, insurance underwriting and brokerage. Thus, the roots of Citi's downfall were sown in 1999 as the efforts of Sandy Weill to repeal the Glass-Steagall Act produced results. Weill has been deservedly placed on the *Time* (2009) list of "25 People to Blame for the Financial Crisis".

The rise and fall of Citi

For some time, the megabank model adopted by Citi worked well, as handsome profit was generated from a variety of operations, including credit cards, mortgages, merger advice, and trading. Meanwhile, according to Dash and Creswell (2008):

> Citigroup was ensnared in murky financial dealings with the defunct energy company Enron..., it was criticized by law enforcement officers for the role one of its prominent research analysts played during the telecom bubble, ..., and it found itself in the middle of regulatory violations in Britain and Japan.

Heavy exposure to mortgage-backed securities (MBSs) and collateralized debt obligations (CDOs), compounded by poor risk management, put Citigroup in trouble as the subprime crisis worsened in 2008. The company had used "elaborate" mathematical risk models to examine mortgages in particular geographical areas, overlooking the possibility of a national housing downturn and the prospect that millions of mortgage holders would default on their obligations. Like LTCM, Citi was a victim of its own models and the people who trusted those models.

On the board of directors of Citigroup, Robert Rubin (a former Treasury Secretary) and Charles Prince (the CEO) were said to have been influential in pushing Citi towards toxic assets. This is the same Prince who in July 2007 told *Financial Times* that "as long as the music is playing you've got to get up and dance", referring to Citi's involvement in the leveraged buyout market. Dash and Creswell (2008) quote a former Citigroup executive as saying: "Chuck [Prince] didn't know a CDO from a grocery list, so he looked for someone for advice and support", and that person turned out to be Rubin, who believed that "you have to take more risk if you want to earn more". According to Dash and Creswell (2008), the bank's risk managers failed to investigate adequately the claim made by Thomas Maheras, who oversaw trading, that "no big losses were looming", although Citi had accumulated some $45 billion in mortgage-backed securities.

As the crisis began to unfold, Citigroup announced on 11 April 2007 that it would eliminate 17,000 jobs, or about 5 per cent of its work force, in a broad restructuring designed to cut costs and bolster its long under-performing stock. Even after Bear Stearns ran into serious trouble in the summer of 2007, Citigroup decided that the possibility of trouble with its toxic assets was so tiny (less than 1/100 of 1 per cent) that they excluded them from their risk analysis. With the crisis worsening, Citigroup announced on 7 January 2008 that it was considering cutting another 5 per cent to 10 per cent of its work force.

Insolvency followed by rescue

By November 2008, Citigroup was insolvent, despite its receipt of $25 billion in TARP money. On 17 November, the company announced plans for about 52,000 new job cuts, on top of 23,000 jobs already lost in 2008 in a huge downsizing resulting from four quarters of consecutive losses and reports that it was unlikely to be in profit again before 2010. Many senior executives were fired but Wall Street responded by dropping its stock market value to $6 billion, down from $300 billion two years prior (Landon, 2008). As a result, Citigroup and federal regulators nego-tiated a plan to stabilize the company and put an end to the deterioration in its market value.

The arrangement called for the government to back about $306 billion in loans and securities and directly invest about $20 billion in the company. Lewis and Einhorn (2009) describe the $306 billion guarantee as "an undisguised gift without any real crisis motivating it". The plan was approved late in the evening on 23 November, 2008. A joint state-ment by the Treasury Department, the Federal Reserve and the FDIC announced: "With these transactions, the U.S. government is taking the actions necessary to strengthen the financial system and protect U.S. tax-payers and the U.S. economy". That was a hell of protection of taxpayers.

According to New York Attorney General Andrew Cuomo, and as reported by the *Wall Street Journal*, after having received its $45 billion

TARP bailout in late 2008, Citigroup paid hundreds of millions of dollars in bonuses to more than 1038 of its employees. That included 738 employees each receiving $1 million, 176 employees each receiving $2 million, 124 each receiving $3 million, and 143 each receiving bonuses of $4 million to more than $10 million (Grocer, 2009).

Perhaps a word on relations with the government would be useful here. Citigroup is the 16th largest political campaign contributor in the U.S. According to Matthew Vadum (2008), a senior editor at the conservative Capital Research Center, Citigroup is also a heavy contributor to left-of-center political causes. This makes Citi too politically connected to fail.

3.7　Lehman, Merrill and Bear

Lehman Brothers, Merrill Lynch and Bear Stearns had similar stories of evolution and, more or less, the same reasons for failure, but they had different fates. The U.S. government allowed Lehman to go down but arranged nice deals (marriages under the gun, some would say) for Merrill and Bear. *The Economist* (2009d) compares the failure of Lehman Brothers with that of Bear Stearns by describing the former as "[probably] the most spectacular event in the humbling of Wall Street", while describing the latter as the event that "first exposed the fragility of America's seemingly mighty investment banks".

The rise and fall of Lehman

Lehman Brothers was founded in 1850 by two cotton brokers in Montgomery, Alabama. The firm moved to New York City after the Civil War and grew into one of Wall Street's investment giants. Lehman's collapse began as the subprime crisis unfolded in the summer of 2007 when its stock began to fall steadily from a peak of $82. The firm was a major player in the subprime market under the "leadership" of Dick Fuld, its CEO. Lehman fought a running battle with short sellers who were accused of spreading rumours to drive down the stock price. Short sellers responded by accusing Lehman of not coming clean on the true size of losses.

When the U.S. government, represented by Henry Paulson, refused to extend financial assistance and potential buyers, Barclays and Bank of America, rejected an acquisition deal, Lehman filed for bankruptcy on 15 September. With the disappearance of Lehman, its CEO (Dick Fuld) vanished from the scene. Fuld has been deservedly placed on the *Time* (2009) list of the "25 People to Blame for the Financial Crisis". "For all this wealth destruction", *Time* explains, "Fuld raked in nearly

$500 million in compensation during his tenure as CEO, which ended when Lehman did".

The rise and fall of Merrill

Merrill Lynch, which was the largest brokerage firm in the world, was founded in 1914 to become one of the pillars of Wall Street, acquiring the reputation that it was the "stockbroker for Main Street". In recent years Merrill grew to encompass two companies: a thriving wealth management company with $1.4 trillion of assets managed by 16,000 brokers and a fixed income operation focusing on high-risk high-return securities backed by subprime home mortgages.

Under the direction of Stan O'Neal, Merrill Lynch became the biggest underwriter of CDOs, and that brought about its demise. In late October 2007, the company posted a write-down of $8.4 billion to recognize the loss of value of these securities. Shortly afterwards, Stan O'Neal, who was the driving force for Merrill's entanglement in the subprime market, was removed as chief executive with a golden handshake. In November John Thain was named as O'Neal's successor, and he promptly started to negotiate with the Bank of America. In July 2008 Merrill sold $31 billion worth of securities for a few cents on the dollar.

In December 2007, Bank of America shareholders signed off on the acquisition, but the subprime losses forced BOA to seek assistance from the government, obtaining an emergency infusion of $20 billion. As criticism of the deal mounted, the CEO of Bank of America, Ken Lewis, told a Congressional Committee in April 2009 that he was considering pulling out of the Merrill deal but regulators had pressured him to complete it. On 14 September 2008, Merrill announced that it had agreed to be purchased by BOA rather than run the risk of going under. Only $3.6 billion was paid in bonuses to Merrill staff before the acquisition, which brought outrage from shareholders and taxpayers.

The rise and fall of Bear

Once upon a time in the not-too-distant past, Bear Stearns was recognized as the "Most Admired" securities firm in *Fortune*'s "America's Most Admired Companies" annual survey, and second overall in the securities firms section. The survey is a prestigious ranking of employee talent, quality of risk management and business innovation. On that occasion, James Cayne, Chairman and CEO said: "This accomplishment substantiates my belief that our commitment to clients, the strength of our culture, and the quality of our people truly sets Bear Stearns apart from our peers" (All Business, 2005). Bear Stearns was also one of the largest underwriters of mortgage bonds that signalled the beginning of the global financial crisis. As losses mounted in 2006 and 2007, the company actually increased its exposure to mortgage-backed securities that were central to the subprime crisis.

The collapse in June 2007 of two of its hedge funds, which had invested heavily in mortgage-backed securities, heralded the collapse of Bear Stearns. In December 2007 Bear announced the first loss in its eight-decade history of about $854 million for the fourth quarter. The firm also announced that it had written down $1.9 billion of its holdings of mortgage-backed securities. The failure of Bear Stearns was caused by a massive run on its liquidity, as clients and trading partners feared that Bear would not be able to meet its obligations. *The Economist* (2009d) quotes an executive as saying "it was 24 hours from solvent to dead".

In *House of Cards*, William Cohan (2009) attributes the failure of Bear Stearns to a violation of one simple principle of finance: risk reduction via diversification. Cohan argues that Bear put too many of its eggs in one basket and that "by failing to diversify, Jimmy Cayne, Bear's longtime boss, became a Sophoclean tragic hero, ruined by his own terrible choices". The one basket was mortgage-backed securities, which (according to Cohan) "Cayne never fully understood". Furthermore, Cayne "oversaw the ballooning of Bear's balance sheet to as much as 50 times its equity". *Time* (2009) justified putting Cayne on the list of "25 People to Blame for the Financial Crisis" as follows:

> Plenty of CEOs screwed up on Wall Street. But none seemed more asleep at the switch than Bear Stearn's Cayne. He left the office by helicopter for 3$\frac{1}{2}$ day golf weekends. He was regularly out of town at bridge tournaments. Back at the office, Cayne's charges bet the firm on risky home loans.

In March 2008, the Federal Reserve approved a credit line to help JP Morgan acquire Bear. A class action lawsuit was filed on behalf of shareholders, challenging the terms of JP Morgan's acquisition of Bear Stearns. On the same day, a new agreement was reached that raised JP Morgan's offer to $10 a share, up from the initial offer of $2, which Bear's shareholders accepted. The revised deal was aimed to quiet upset investors and any subsequent legal action brought against JP Morgan as a result of the deal. It was also intended to prevent employees, many of whose past compensation consisted of Bear Stearns stock, from leaving for other firms. The fact remains, however, that JP Morgan bought Bear for less than the value of its asset building (*Time*, 2009). The Bear Stearns bailout was seen as an extreme-case scenario, and continues to raise significant questions about the Fed's intervention.

Leverage and concentration killed Bear. There is also a conspiracy theory explanation for the collapse suggested by Cook (2008). He quotes John Olagues, a leading authority on stock options, saying that "Bear Stearn's collapse was artificially created to allow JP Morgan to be paid $55 billion of taxpayer money to cover its own insolvency and acquire its rival Bear Stearns". Olagues adds: "this was allegedly achieved through a combination of coordinated campaign of market rumor coupled with manipulation of Bear Stearns using a form of derivatives called a 'put' option".

4
Far Too Big and Politically Connected

4.1 No longer humble intermediaries

Financial institutions are no longer, as they are supposed to be, humble intermediaries that channel funds from lenders to borrowers and from savers to investors. This is what students are taught in *Financial Markets and Institutions 101*, where they are told at the very beginning that financial institutions perform the task of intermediating between deficit units and surplus units. Financial institutions have become the means for a small group of people (bankers, financiers, traders, brokers, financial engineers, etc) to earn fat bonuses and amass huge individual fortunes by taking excessive risk with other people's money while counting on government bailouts when things go wrong. What they have been doing is a clear manifestation of "heads I win big, tails you lose it all".

Big winners

One of those who won big while others lost it all has been described as a "villain whose reign of terror over 400 employees brought the company [AIG], the U.S. economy and the global financial system to their knees" (Lewis, 2009b). This is Joseph Cassano, the former head of AIG's Financial Products Unit who, according to Lewis (2009b), is "the man who crashed the world". Cassano managed to amass a personal wealth of some $280 million from salaries and bonuses. And even after he had been fired by AIG, he was still earning a humble consultancy fee of (only) one million dollars per month from the same company that had fired him. By the way, in 2009 that same company posted the biggest ever quarterly loss in U.S. corporate history and subsequently received $170 billion in taxpayers' money to pay for an adventure in an uncharted territory (derivatives). Why? Because it was too big to fail, or so it managed to convince the U.S. government. Another failed institution, Merrill Lynch, collapsed because its CEO, Stan O'Neal, thought it was a good idea to go heavily into the subprime market. He even fired one of his colleagues for voicing concern about over-indulging in subprime products. For that "achievement", O'Neal was paid $51 million in 2006 and $160 million when he was fired at a time when Merril Lynch was begging for government bailout and share-holders were watching the value of their shares evaporate. Yes, it has been absolute bonanza for some.

Oligopolistic markets

The markets for financial services have become oligopolistic, consisting of institutions that are big, powerful and politically connected. This is why financial institutions have, more or less, a monopoly over the TBTF status. The *status quo* has become that bankers and financiers call the shots, demanding more and more deregulation and govern-ment bailouts whenever they get in trouble, even though trouble results invariably from greed and incompetence, as manifested by the global financial crisis. The irony is that, through taxpayers' money and government-assisted mergers and acquisitions, financial institutions have become even bigger and more powerful.

The trend towards oligopoly in general is a negative development, even for those who believe in the power (and beauty) of the market and object to government intervention to regulate market structure. In a genuinely free market (at least in theory), there are potentially unlimited numbers of small/medium-sized firms competing for approx-imately equal footing in a level playing field. There are no barriers to entry into the market and no single firm (or a small group of firms) can control the price or the quantity of the underlying product. Typically, such a market is supervised (not directed or controlled) by the govern-ment. With the advent of big businesses, truly free competitive markets have gone the way of the dinosaurs. The trend has become for firms to buy each other to grow bigger and obtain more market power, prevent-ing new firms from entering the market, controlling prices, and exert-ing pressure on the government for concessions and less regulation.

4.2 Internalization and "King of the Mountain"

The growth of financial institutions may be explained in terms of the same reasons as why other firms seek to grow bigger. This is an issue that is dealt with in microeconomics under the heading "theory of the firm". An important reason for a firm to grow big is to avoid the transaction costs resulting from using markets. Transaction costs that can be avoided (or reduced) by centralizing them in one firm include the difficulty of price discovery and the costs of brokering deals and raising capital from outsiders. This proposition is sometimes referred to as the "internalization hypothesis", which is an extension of the original idea put forward by Coase (1937), stipulating that certain marketing costs can be saved by forming a firm. Coase considered four main types of costs: (i) the cost of discovering the correct price, (ii) the cost of arranging the contractual obligations of the parties in an exchange transaction, (iii) the risk of scheduling of goods and inputs, and (iv) the taxes paid on exchange transactions.

The advantages of internalization are the avoidance of time lags, bargaining, and buyer uncertainty. Indeed, the main motive for internalization is the presence of externalities in goods and factors markets. If markets in intermediate products are imperfect, firms have an incentive to bypass them by creating internal markets, such that the activities linked by the markets are brought under common ownership and control (Buckley and Casson, 1976). Internalization, therefore, can be used to explain why firms are created in the first place and why they grow bigger.

Another motivation for growth that is relevant to financial institutions in particular is that of managerial interests. Managers pursue growth to enhance their salaries and personal prestige (a "king of the mountain" kind of attitude). This is what Berger *et al* (1999) call "empire building", arguing that "executive compensation tends to increase with firm size, so managers may hope to achieve personal financial gains". Carney (2009) lists real-life examples by referring sarcastically to the "vision" of some heavy-weight American bankers (the bosses at Citigroup, JP Morgan and Bank of America). He writes:

> We know the story of Sandy Weill's imperial ambitions, Jamie Dimon's heroic vision of global banking, Ken Lewis's attempt to prove the Land of the Lost Cause could beat the Yankees at banking.

As we saw in each of the cases examined in Chapter 3, particular individuals stood out as the driving force behind the quest for growth. Typically, these individuals do well for themselves but not necessarily for the shareholders, which is a typical agency problem.

4.3 The quest for market power

An important reason for the growth of firms is the desire to be big enough to have significant market power, a term that refers to the ability of a firm to manipulate the market by dictating the price without losing all of its customers to competitors. In other words, a firm with market power faces a downward-sloping demand curve, implying that the firm can retain customers even if it raises its price while competitors maintain theirs. Indeed if demand is sufficiently inelastic—that is, a price hike produces a small drop in sales—such a move will even boost sales revenue. A firm with no market power faces a horizontal demand curve, in the sense that any small increase in the price causes a total loss of customers to competing firms. In extreme cases, market power is monopoly power but in less extreme cases, market power results from a big market share when a small number of big firms dominate the market (oligopoly) or differentiated products (actual or perceived through advertisement). The presence of a large number of firms and differentiated products characterizes the situation known as "monopolistic" or "imperfect" competition.

Monopoly power

Although the structure of the market for financial services is not monopolistic, it may be worthwhile considering monopoly power as the extreme form of market power, at least to put things into perspective. A monopoly exists when a (big) firm has almost total control over a particular product so that it is in a position to determine the terms on which customers obtain the product (price and quantity). Monopolies are thus characterized by a lack of competition for the product they provide. Monopoly power exists when a firm has the ability to control a price within its product market or its geographic market, and when this firm has the ability to exclude a competitor from doing business within these markets. A monopolist, therefore, is in a position to sell a smaller quantity of goods at a higher price than would firms under perfect competition where there are numerous buyers and identical products. As a result, monopolies tend to become less efficient and less innovative over time because they do not have to do much to sell their products. In the jargon of microeconomics, monopolies produce "deadweight loss", which reduces social welfare. This is why countries typically have legislation against monopolies, the so-called antitrust or anti-monopoly laws. When a monopoly is not broken through the open market, the government may step in to regulate it, turn it into a publicly-owned monopoly, or forcibly break it up. Unfortunately, it seems that financial institutions are exempt from government action of this kind. Much fuss has been made on both sides of the Atlantic about the alleged monopolistic practices and market abuse of Microsoft, but no financial institution has received similar treatment. The global financial crisis has intensified calls for the use of anti-monopoly laws to break up financial institutions.

Firms may establish a monopoly position in the market through mergers and acquisitions, which could be horizontal (between two firms in the same industry at the same stage of production) or vertical (in the same industry but at different stages of the production process). Of approximately 350,000 mergers and acquisitions in all industries valued at \$26.4 trillion in 1985–2005, 124,000 transactions valued at \$10.1 trillion involved financial institutions (Schmid and Walter, 2006). Of these transactions, about 20 per cent were cross-market transactions, involving at least two areas of finance (commercial banking, investment banking, insurance, asset management and financial infrastructure services), whereas 7 per cent were cross-border transactions involving more than one country. The motivation for growing through mergers and acquisitions is the belief that value can be maximized by boosting market power, by improving efficiency, and by reinforcing access to the safety net (claiming the TBTF status). However, the empirical evidence does not support this proposition. Metais (2009) suggests that "the vast majority of acquisitions do not create value and may even destroy it", explaining this observation in terms of: (i) the "marital" problem of the two different, often competitive companies; and (ii) economies of scale and synergies that do not materialize. Why, then, do they do it? Because of (i) the attitude of "eat or be eaten", (ii) the perceived importance of size in a globalized market, (iii) the ego and economic interests of leaders, and (iv) "copy-cat" business behaviour. Dash (2009) adds to this list the notion of "grow or die". There is certainly support for these propositions in reality. At one time the Royal Bank of Scotland was the target for acquisition by another bank, then it became (under the "leadership" of Fred Goodwin) the "king of mergers and acquisitions". Goodwin made personal gains by making the RBS the largest bank in the world, but he ended up destroying it as he embarked on one of the worst mergers in corporate history with ABN Amro.

Monopoly power also comes from the ownership of patents and copyright protection or the exclusive ownership of assets. AIG, for example, had more or less a monopoly over the notorious credit default swaps that brought about the company's demise (strange that in its heyday, AIG was not subject to the kind of action that Microsoft was subject to on several occasions). Otherwise, a firm can become a monopoly via internal growth as it attempts to exploit the economies of scale and scope.

From monopoly to oligopoly

In today's banking and finance, markets are basically oligopolistic, where a few big firms dominate. In the U.S., where there are thousands of banks, the few largest banks are dominant and the distribution of assets is extremely skewed. In Europe, the predominant model is that of big, universal banks. Therefore, it is oligopoly all around. The problem, however, is that oligopoly has all of the disadvantages and repercussions of monopoly. Because oligopolists often develop agreements among themselves and avoid price wars (which would be damaging to all), they end up being like a collective monopolist. If they engage in a struggle for market share through expensive advertising campaigns, and otherwise, the situation may be more precisely described as "oligopolistic competition". But let us stick to oligopoly for the purpose of the following discussion. On this issue, J.K. Galbraith (1952) wrote:

> A vast difference separates oligopoly from the competition of the competitive model.... The power exercised by a few large firms is different only in degree and precision of its exercise from a single-firm monopoly... not only does oligopoly lead away from the world of competition... but it leads toward the world of monopoly. In the... oligopoly, the practical barriers to entry and the convention against price competition have eliminated the self-generating capacity of competition.

He also wrote:

> With oligopoly, there is no longer any certainty of technical advance... prices no longer reflect the ebb and flow of consumer demand... and it leads to profitable and comfortable stagnation.

The fact remains that, in the presence of big business and without government intervention, an unregulated market leads inexorably to oligopoly. This process is known as consolidation or concentration.

Consolidation versus competition

A large body of literature finds empirical support for the notion that banking consolidation leads to anti-competitive outcomes. In a review of the issue, Berger *et al* (1999) suggest that banks in more concentrated markets charge higher rates on small business loans and pay lower rates on retail deposits. Furthermore, they (banks) respond more slowly to central bank changes in interest rates, making it more difficult to get out of a recession. The study warns that banking consolidation could boost systematic risk, the risk that cannot be eliminated or reduced via diversification. This is simply because consolidation reduces the scope for diversification. Results of theoretical and empirical research show that high concentration in banking tends to reduce competitiveness (Gilbert, 1984) and that the market power of banks raises the cost of capital (Smith, 1998). It has also been found that a monopolistic banking system has a negative impact on income and the business cycle (Smith, 1998). Under monopoly, banks ration credit more heavily than competitive banks, which results in negative consequences for capital accumulation and growth (Guzman, 2000). Empirical work conducted by Chong (1991) and by Hughes and Mester (1998) indicates that bank consolidation makes bank portfolios more risky.

There is also ample empirical evidence on the "concentration-fragility view", that a more concentrated banking system is more fragile than otherwise. Boyd and de Nicolo (2005) found a positive relation between concentration and fragility and thus the probability of systemic distress. Likewise, Caminal and Matutes (2002) show that less competition can lead to higher probability of failure if loans are subject to "multiplicative uncertainty". The TBTF doctrine is conducive to the fragility of concentrated banking systems. Typically, regulators are more concerned about bank failure when there are a few banks only. Therefore, banks in concentrated systems receive TBTF subsidies, which intensifies risk taking incentives and therefore system fragility (Mishkin, 1999).

Johnson (2009) goes as far as attributing the global financial crisis to lack of competition in the financial sector. He writes:

> ... this crisis was in many ways spawned and largely perpetuated by the decision of U.S. citizens and politicians to allow banks to merge into un-competitive juggernauts and to then trust them to take tremendous risks with our nation's wealth. A more sensible approach would focus not just on rescuing pre-existing financial institutions but, instead, on creating a structure for more contained and competitive ones.

Why consolidation has accelerated

Consolidation in the U.S. banking industry has been rampant. In 1985 there were more than 14,000 banks, but since then the market structure has changed dramatically, as banks began to consolidate for several reasons, such as the deregulation of interstate banking. At present there are only about half the number of banks that existed in 1985, as shown in the Figure 4.1. Consolidation has brought with it big financial institutions that can claim the TBTF status. Between 1998 and 2008, the share of global financial assets accounted for by the world's five largest banks (as measured by *The Banker* magazine) doubled from 8 to 16 per cent (Ford and Larsen, 2009).

Berger *et al* (1999) attribute the acceleration of consolidation to "changes in economic environments that alter the constraints faced by financial services firms". Specifically, they identify five factors that have reinforced the trend for consolidation: (i) technological progress that has produced economies of scale, (ii) improvements in financial conditions such as low interest rates and high stock prices, (iii) accumulation of excess capacity or financial distress, (iv) international consolidation of markets, and (v) deregulation. In practice, deregulation played a vital role in encouraging consolidation. For example, Jayaratne and Strahan (1998) suggest that mergers and acquisitions activity flourished in states after they joined interstate banking agreements. Other deregulatory measures, particularly the abolition of the Glass-Steagall Act, played a similar role.

Figure 4.1   Number of Banks in the U.S.

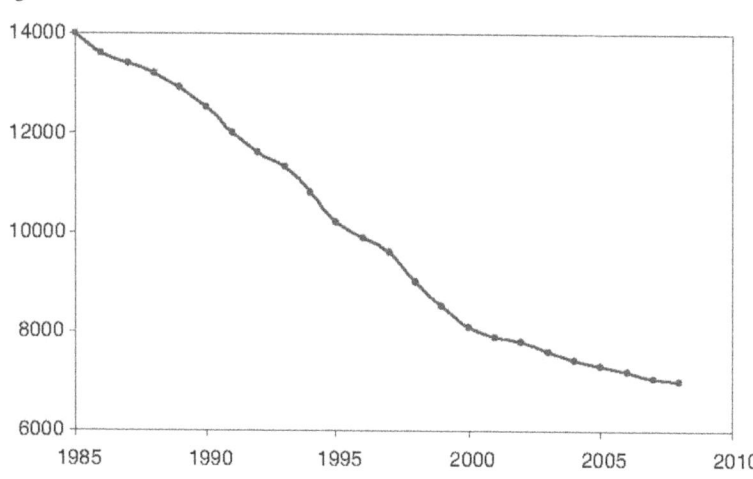

Data Source: Federal Reserve

Concentration post-financial crisis

The global financial crisis has intensified bank concentration in the U.S., boosting the oligopolistic power of the super-banks. In a *Washington Post* article entitled "Banks Too Big to Fail Have Grown Even Bigger", Cho (2009) quotes Mark Zandi, chief economist of Moody's Economy.com, as saying that "there has been a significant consolidation among the big banks, and it's kind of hollowing out the banking system". He adds: "You'll be left with very large institutions and small ones that fill in the cracks", and "the oligopoly has tightened". Following the change of status of Goldman Sachs and Morgan Stanley from investment banks to bank holding companies to enable them to acquire failed institutions such as Merrill Lynch and Bear Stearns, the commercial banks' share of the $24 trillion assets of the financial system (170 per cent of GDP) rose from 37 per cent in June 2008 to 46 per cent in October 2008. The situation now is that six banks account for two thirds of the assets of the banking system, as shown in Figure 4.2. The six super-banks are: Bank of America, Citigroup, JP Morgan, Goldman Sachs, Morgan Stanley and Wells Fargo. The acquisition of Merrill Lynch by the Bank of America (with the help of taxpayers' money) created a financial giant rivalling Citigroup, the biggest U.S. bank in terms of assets. Bank of America had earlier bought Countrywide Financial, the troubled mortgage lender, and the two deals put BOA at the pinnacle of American finance as the largest brokerage house and consumer banking franchise.

Figure 4.2   The Distribution of Assets in the U.S. Banking System (October 2008)

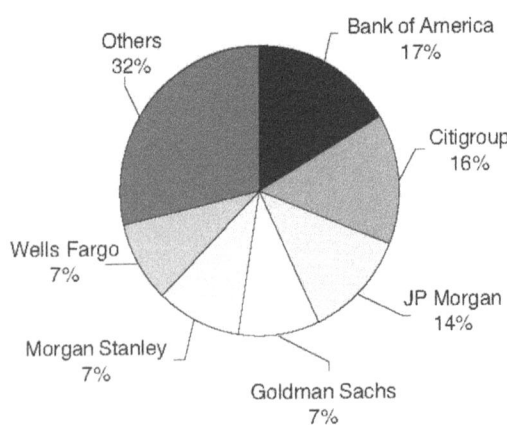

Data Source: Federal Reserve

Figure 4.3   Concentration of Assets in U.S. Banking (50 Largest Banks)

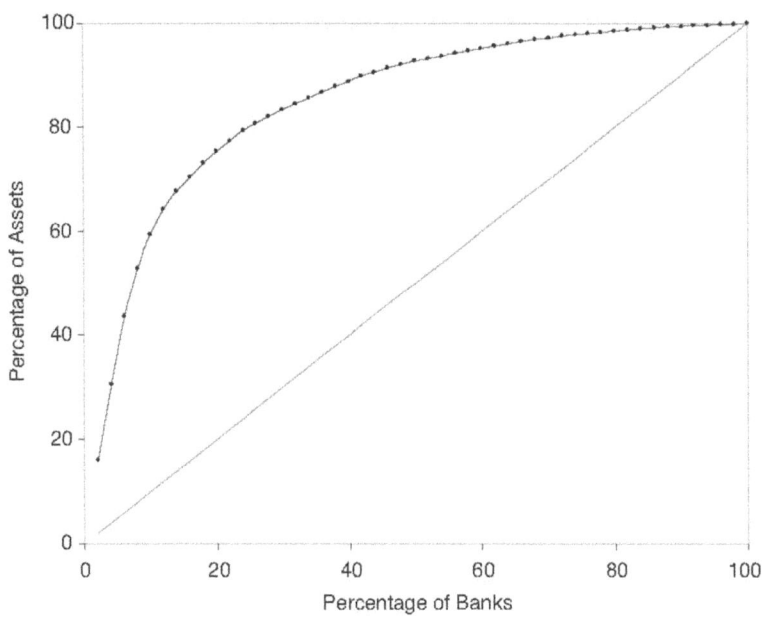

Data Source: FDIC

Figure 4.3 shows the "Lorenz curve" of the distribution of the total assets of the 50 largest U.S. banks at the end of September 2009. The cumulative value of the percentage of assets held by x per cent of the largest 50 banks is plotted against the value of x. The diagonal line provides a benchmark for measuring the concentration of assets. The largest four banks hold about 53 per cent of the assets. The concentration is conspicuous, confirming that the market is indeed oligopolistic.

In mid-October 2009, it was announced that, due to less competition, Goldman Sachs made huge profit in the third quarter and that it intended to distribute bonuses worth billions of dollars. Likewise, JP Morgan recorded profit of $3.6 billion in the third quarter. The explicit reason given by the BBC Business News on 15 October was less competition, particularly the disappearance of Lehman Brothers.

4.4   Exploiting the economies of scale and scope

One advantage of big firm size (at least from the firm's perspective) is the exploitation of economies of scale and scope. Economies of scale are cost advantages that result from business expansion as the average cost per unit of output falls. These economies arise from several sources, including purchasing (bulk buying of materials through long-term contracts), managerial (managers become more specialized), financial (obtaining lower cost of capital), and marketing (spreading the cost of advertising over a greater number of units of output). Each of these factors reduces the long-run average cost of production. Furthermore, as the firm expands, the initial investment of capital is diffused (spread) over an increasing number of units of output, which makes the marginal cost of producing one extra unit of output less than the average cost per unit.

Economies of scope are conceptually similar to economies of scale. But while economies of scale refer to efficiencies associated with supply-side changes (changes in the scale of production of a single product), economies of scope refer to efficiencies associated with demand-side changes, such as changes in the scope of marketing and distribution of different types of products. In other words, economies of scope refer to the reduction in average cost resulting from the production of a wider variety of products.

The difference between economies of scale and economies of scope is therefore straightforward. While economies of scale are obtained by producing more of the same product, economies of scope result from the production of relatively small quantities of a wide variety of products. Hence, the difference between the two concepts lies in the phrases "single product" and "variety of products". Because economies of scope typically involve marketing and distribution efficiencies, they are more dependent on demand than economies of scale. Economies of scope provide motivation for bundling products and creating a whole line of products under one brand. But like economies of scale, economies of scope can help firms grab more market power and boost competitive advantage. This is because economies of scope help to reduce average cost, putting the firm in a position where it can force less-cost-efficient competitors out of business while discouraging would-be rivals from entering the market. Furthermore, it is likely that firms seek economies of scale and scope jointly by growing bigger and becoming more diversified (hence conglomerates emerge).

Economies of scope: Sources and importance

There are several sources of economies of scope. In advertising, for example, as the number of products promoted is increased and broader media used, more people can be reached with each dollar spent on advertising. Selling several products can often be more efficient than selling one product. The cost of the travel time of the sales force is distributed over a greater revenue base, leading to an improvement in cost efficiency. Synergies may arise by offering a complete range of products, because that would give the consumer a more desirable product offering than a single product would. Economies of scope can also arise from distribution efficiencies. It can be more efficient to ship a range of products to any given location than to ship a single type of product to that location. Further economies of scope occur when cost savings arise from by-products in the production process. An example would be the benefits of heating from energy production having a positive effect on agricultural yields. Finally, a firm that sells many products, sells the same product in many countries, or sells many products in many countries, benefits from reduced risk levels as a result of the economies of scope. If one of its product lines falls out of fashion or if one country experiences economic slowdown, the firm will, most likely, remain in business. This is the portfolio management principle of risk reduction via diversification.

Not all economists agree on the importance of economies of scope. Some argue that the concept only applies to certain industries, and then only rarely. Furthermore, efficiency may not last: at some point, additional advertising expenditure on new products will start to be less effective (an example of diseconomies of scope). Also, the creation of new products is not without problems and may adversely affect efficiency. For example, there is a need for additional managerial expertise, while higher raw material costs, a reduction in competitive focus and the need for additional facilities may lead to higher average costs. What, then, has happened to specialization and the division of labour on which Adam Smith wrote more than two centuries ago? And what has happened to the law of comparative advantage, which tells us that a firm or a country must specialize in the production of goods and services in which it has a comparative advantage relative to other firms or countries?

Economies of scope in banking

In banking the abolition of the separation between commercial and investment banking (enshrined in the Glass-Steagall Act of 1933) as well as other measures of deregulation, enabled banks to seek more economies of scope. Instead of having loans and deposits as their products, banks now offer a wide variety of products. A bank may offer the same customer a deposit, mortgage, credit card, insurance, fund management, financial planning and other services.

Not only has the abolition of the Glass-Steagall Act produced an oligopolistic finance industry dominated by TBTF institutions, it has also created severe conflict of interest and abusive market power. A financial institution that can do commercial as well as investment banking may make the granting of a loan to a customer conditional upon the requirement that the customer uses part of the loan to buy securities in a new issue managed by the same institution. The customer may oblige even though it is felt that these securities are of inferior quality, or that they are not appropriate in terms of risk-return trade-off. By all means, this kind of practice represents abuse of market power and requires consumer protection.

Arguments for and against diversification

There is no agreement in the literature on the benefits of diversification. Schmid and Walter (2006) make the following arguments for diversification, with particular reference to financial institutions:

- Cost and revenue economies of scope. Examples include the sharing of joint costs (on the cost side) and cross selling of multiple financial services to clients (on the revenue side).
- Better co-ordination across highly specialized activity lines and monitoring of capital expenditure makes internal capital market efficiency exceed external capital market efficiency.
- More profitable use of private information, given that financial institutions are more opaque than non-financial firms.
- The ability to allocate human capital optimally across functions, given that diversification produces an environment in which internal labour market efficiency exceeds external labour market efficiency.
- More efficient use of proprietary client-related information in revenue generation, pricing and risk assessment. One example pertaining to risk assessment is that big and diversified financial institutions are allowed under Basel II to use the advanced measurement approach to calculate regulatory capital.
- Reduced bankruptcy risk due to less than perfectly correlated revenue streams across functions.
- Incremental financing capacity in financial conglomerates, allowing investment in highly profitable projects that might otherwise be forgone.
- Increased market power.
- Lower tax burden as a result of intra-firm transactions (transfer pricing).
- Too big to fail guarantees.

Some of these arguments are based on ideas that are too abstract and may have no presence in reality. The points on internal and external labour and capital market efficiency in particular sound more like rhetoric. Some other points pertain to advantages derived from malpractices, which may be due to regulatory gaps. These malpractices should be discouraged rather than be claimed as advantages. For example, the Basel II Accord allows big and diversified banks to calculate regulatory capital on the basis of their internal models. But this kind of advantage is obtained from a deliberate but flawed regulatory design that should not have been suggested in the first place. The Basel II Accord has been criticized severely for allowing such malpractice and for giving preferential treatment to big and diversified institutions (see Chapter 9). Increased market power is something that we strongly argue against in this book, calling for regulation to curtail it. And reducing the tax burden through fraudulent transfer pricing is illegal (Moosa, 2002).

On the other hand, several arguments can be suggested against diversification in financial institutions (Schmid and Walter, 2006):

- Cross subsidization across business lines, and hence inefficient allocation of resources and reduced performance incentives in profitable business lines.
- Excess free cash and unused borrowing capacity lead to overinvestment in low-return projects.
- Conflict between central and divisional management in the presence of internal information asymmetries.
- Inter-divisional conflicts with respect to compensation systems and attribution of revenues, costs and risk.
- Excessive premiums paid in the process of activity diversification.
- Inability of investors to obtain clean exposure to specific areas of financial services activity and hence to construct efficient portfolios based on their asset allocation objectives.
- Conflict of interest among clients and activity areas of financial conglomerates that create reputational risk.

The arguments against diversification seem to make more sense than the arguments for. The empirical evidence on this issue reveals the following:

- As the product range widens, unit costs rise—that is, diseconomies of scope emerge—in the world's 200 largest banks (Saunders and Walter, 1994).
- Extremely weak evidence for the presence of economies of scope in some 300 banks with assets ranging between $100 million and $500 million (Mitchell and Onvural, 1996).

- Mergers between bank holding companies and securities or real estate firms boost risk (Boyd *et al*, 1993).
- Diversification from lending into non-interest activities damages risk-adjusted performance. Any scope-related gains are more than offset by the higher volatility of these activities (Stiroh and Rumble, 2006).
- All diversification of bank-based financial services firms is value-destroying (Laeven and Levine, 2007).
- A large body of international evidence indicates the presence of a conglomerate discount, the loss of value resulting from mergers compared to specialized stand-alone firms (Berger and Ofek, 1995; Lang and Stulz, 1994; Lins and Servaes, 1999; Chen and Ho, 2000; Beiner and Schmid, 2005; Schmid and Walter, 2006).

4.5   A reality check

While growing big to exploit economies of scale and scope may be bad for the economy at large because it creates oligopolistic markets, the picture for firms pursuing this goal may not be entirely rosy either. Such an endeavour may prove to be problematical and counterproductive. Sears Roebuck and Company tried to diversify into financial services but quickly realized the error of that course of action and got back to its core business (retailing) and sold off its Allstate insurance unit, Coldwell Banker real estate operations, and its Discover Card financial services unit. In April 2010 the Google stock price declined, despite the announcement of spectacular operating results, in reaction to news that the company wanted to diversify away from its core business into hardware. And while the failure of Citigroup was not entirely due to diversification (rather, it was mainly due to management incompetence), the last thing that should be done is to put an incompetent management in charge of a wide range of products.

Two anecdotes on Swiss banking

There are also two anecdotes on what used to be the mighty Swiss banking industry. The first one starts on 3 June 2002, when it was announced that two Swiss banks, Lombard Odier and Darier Hentsch, had merged. These two banks were traditionally involved in private banking, managing the wealth of rich individuals. The merger followed in the wake of the demise of Swiss private banking, which lost its true appeal (its famed secrecy) because of an international drive against money laundering and tax evasion. This came at a time when the two banks were having other troubles and were showing signs of weakness and loss making. For example, Darier Hentsch suffered a blow in October 2001 when a senior partner, Benedict Hentsch, stepped down because of his involvement (as vice-chairman) in the collapse of Swissair. Lombard Odier, on the other hand, put itself in trouble by venturing into alien territory, trying to ride the equity boom that came to an end in 2000. The merger came as an attempt by the two banks to reinvent themselves and to find some economies of scale and scope. However, some observers believe that by going for scale, the two banks destroyed their traditional attraction, attentive service to (wealthy) clients. In the process they abandoned the lucrative business of private banking, which has traditionally produced returns as high as 30 per cent. This anecdote also demonstrates how mergers can destroy value.

The second anecdote is about Credit Suisse, Switzerland's second largest financial institution. In the spring of 1997, Lukas Muhlemann, the chairman and chief executive, was quoted by *The Economist* (1997) as having made fun of the idea of combining banking and insurance by saying "why buy a cow when all you want is a glass of milk?". A few months later the man himself decided to buy the cow, in the form of Winterthur Insurance. In 2001 things started to go wrong as Credit Suisse sold the insurance arm that served multinational firms, Winterthur International, at a rather low price. Then the fall in stock markets hit Winterthur's life insurance business, ending up booking a SF4 billion fall in shareholders' equity. In the first quarter of 2002, Winterthur booked a post-tax loss of SF150 million on its life-insurance business. All this punished the Credit Suisse share price, which declined by over 40 per cent between January 2000 and June 2002. Diversification in this case did not reduce, but rather augmented, business risk.

4.6   The big motive: Mission TBTF

While financial institutions, like other firms, grow big to reduce transaction costs, to enjoy market power and to exploit economies of scale and scope, there is a particular motive for them to do so. Obtaining the TBTF status is perhaps the reason why financial institutions want to be big because they are in a privileged position when it comes to receiving the TBTF status.

"Life is beautiful when you are too big to fail", as Dennis Berman (2007) puts it. Two Federal Reserve economists made an attempt to estimate how much a financial institution would be prepared to pay for the privilege of being TBTF. In general, the benefits of TBTF may be represented in a number of ways, including: (i) gaining favour with uninsured creditors and market participants, (ii) operating with lower regulatory costs, and (iii) increasing the institution's chances of receiving regulatory forbearance (Brewer and Jagtiani, 2007). The TBTF status is not only useful when a TBTF institution gets itself into trouble, but also when things are going well. The status provides easy access to politicians and law makers and puts TBTF institutions in a strong position to negotiate (or demand) more and more deregulation. For example, Citi's former CEO, Sandy Weill, played a big role in the faulty decision to repeal the Glass-Steagall Act in 1999, which allowed TBTF institutions to grow even bigger.

Take the following anecdotal evidence on the TBTF motive for growth. Four of the largest mergers in U.S. history occurred in 1998 in the banking sector when Citicorp merged with Travelers, BankAmerica merged with NationsBank, Banc One merged with First Chicago and Norwest merged with Wells Fargo. I am not sure about the timing of these mergers relative to the rescue of LTCM, but that rescue must have given big banks the impression that "if they are prepared to rescue a relatively small hedge fund, they will rescue a big bank". The justification for saving LTCM in 1998, which was public knowledge, might have provided motivation for growing big to maximize the probability of being rescued, should things go wrong.

The empirical evidence

Brewer and Jagtiani (2007) examined banking merger data over a period of many years and found that banks were willing to pay a premium on a deal that would take them over $100 billion in assets, deemed by them to be the threshold for TBTF. Specifically, they found that nine banks that did such deals paid $14–16.5 billion to get what Berman (2007) calls the "gold-plated TBTF status". They point out that if there is a significant value to achieving TBTF status, financial institutions should be willing to pay more for acquisitions that enable them to reach such a size. If there are a limited number of suitable acquisitions that would allow an institution to become TBTF, and if this institution has to outbid other institutions with similar motivation, the extra acquisition premium could provide an indication of the value of TBTF.

Some economists have suggested that banks seek growth to boost the probability that the FDIC will cover 100 per cent of deposits, which is consistent with the notion of too big to fail or what they call "too important to fail" (Hunter and Wall, 1989; Boyd and Graham, 1991). This is the so-called "deposit insurance put option enhancing hypothesis", which suggests that banks may pursue growth even if it is socially suboptimal (Benston *et al*, 1995). Likewise, Mishkin (2006) argues that "the presence of too-big-to-fail encourages banks to grow in size to take advantage of the too-big-to-fail subsidy, so banks will be larger than is socially optimal and there will be too many bank mergers". Mishkin describes this outcome as misallocation of resources and cost-inefficient behaviour on the part of banks.

Support for the "mission TBTF" hypothesis is also provided by Harada and Takatoshi (2008), Hosono *et al* (2007) and by Norman (2008). Harada and Takatoshi (2008) examined bank mergers in Japan in the 1990s and concluded that "a primary objective of a merger was to take advantage of the perceived too-big-to-fail policy, rather than to pursue a radical reform". Likewise, Hosono *et al* (2007) examined the Japanese banking industry over the period 1990–2004 and found that "the government's too-big-to-fail policy played an important role in the mergers and acquisitions". Norman (2008) investigated the situation in the U.S., arguing that the TBTF status confers a funding advantage not available to non-TBTF banks (small competitors). As a result, "this imbalance creates an incentive for banks to merge in order to create a bank considered TBTF, or for existing TBTF banks to purchase smaller banks". In either case, he asserts, "the purpose is to capture the gains from the too big to fail status".

4.7   Growing big: A recap and evidence

While we have examined economies of scale and scope separately, they invariably go together. Financial institutions grow big typically by diversifying (through mergers and acquisitions) to form financial conglomerates. Hughes *et al* (2001) demonstrate that better diversification is associated with larger economies of scale, while Beck *et al* (2006) point out that "larger banks tend to be better diversified than smaller banks". It is in this sense that we evaluate the arguments for and against big financial institutions in this section.

Arguments for and against big financial institutions

There are, it seems, stronger arguments against than for big financial institutions. The main argument for big financial institutions is the efficiency derived from economies of scale and scope. However, it is often the case that economies of scale and scope turn out to be diseconomies of scale and scope. Another argument is that diversification may result in less risk for the institution, as diversification reduces reliance on the demand for any single service or product. But branching out in new territories may prove fatal, and it is the antithesis of specialization and the law of comparative advantage. Some would suggest that big and diversified financial institutions provide convenience to individuals and firms with various financial needs that they can satisfy with one conglomerate. And the units of a financial conglomerate may generate some new business just because they offer convenience to clients who already rely on its other services. These advantages seem to be rather trivial and pale into insignificance when we judge them against the disadvantages of big financial institutions.

Yet another argument for big financial institutions is the need to be big in the age of globalization. Big size, the argument goes, is important for financial institutions to operate around the world and cope with massive cash flows. There is simple anecdotal evidence (call it casual empiricism) against this proposition. Some financial institutions have grown by a factor of 5 over a period of ten years. This kind of hyper-growth cannot be benign, as it is disproportional to the growth of the world economy. Why did the "optimal" size of the Royal Bank of Scotland rise from £89 billion to £2.4 trillion in ten years? Why did the "optimal" size of Citigroup rise from $740 billion to $1.9 trillion between 1998 and 2008? Why did two Icelandic banks grow by a factor of 20 in seven years, to the extent that one of them became nine times the size of the entire economy of Iceland? Why did big financial institutions become even bigger in the midst of the global financial crisis when the world economy was experiencing the worst recession since the Great Depression? Why would a financial institution grow faster than the economy it is supposed to serve?

The problems associated with big size have been recognized for a long time. Dash (2009) refers to the "curse of business", a term that was coined nearly a century ago by Louis Brandeis who warned that "banks, railroads and steel companies had grown so huge that they were lording over the nation's economic and political life". "Size, we are told, is not a crime", Brandeis wrote, but "size may, at least, become noxious by reason of the means through which it is attained or the uses to which it is put". Brandeis even expressed concern that the big firms of his days could imperil democracy through concentrated economic power. Before Brandeis, Adam Smith argued in his classic, *The Wealth of Nations*, that "large joint stock companies were wasteful and inefficient and could survive only if given special government assistance, as evidenced by the examples of the South Sea Company and the East India Company" (Leathers and Raines, 2004).

Simon Johnson (2009) argues forcefully against big financial institutions. He sums up his case as follows:

> For years, we have accepted a theory of financial concentration—not only across all lines of previously differentiated sectors (insurance, commercial banking, investment banking, retail brokerage, etc.) but in terms of sheer size. The theory was that capital depth would permit the various entities, dubbed financial supermarkets, to compete and provide full service to customers while cross-marketing various products. That model has failed. The failure shows in gargantuan losses, bloated overhead, enormous inefficiencies, dramatic and outsized risk taken to generate returns large enough to justify the scale of the organizations, ethical abuses in cross-marketing in violation of fiduciary obligations, and now the need for major taxpayer-financed capital support for virtually every major financial institution.

I suppose that Johnson sums it up rather eloquently. Let us now see what the formal empirical evidence tells us about the curse of big size.

Empirical evidence against size

There is ample empirical evidence against size. Hughes *et al* (2001) point out that "most academic studies of bank production fail to find evidence of these scale economies". Berger *et al* (2002) have shown that large banks are less willing to lend to small businesses, unwilling to lend to businesses with informal book-keeping, and exacerbate credit constraints, stifling business development. Hence they conclude that small banks are in a better position to collect and act upon soft information than large banks. Boyd and Gertler (1994) found that "large banks were mainly responsible for the unusually poor performance of the industry in the 1980s". This finding is attributed to two factors: deregulation and TBTF protection. The rescue of Continental Illinois in 1984 created the perception that large banks would enjoy TBTF protection.

Research results show that "a robust negative correlation exists between size and performance". This finding is attributed to "an increased perception of a TBTF subsidy", following the announcement of the Comptroller of the Currency in September 1984 (in a testimony to the U.S. Congress) that 11 bank holding companies were too big to fail (O'Hara and Shaw, 1990). A 2002 report of the Federal Reserve examined banking mergers around the world and concluded that scale provided advantages only up to about $50 billion. Beyond this limit, disadvantages start to appear as a result of the difficulty of running big institutions (Ford and Larsen, 2009). The report also revealed that some very large banks may achieve high return only because of the TBTF status. de Nicolo (2000) found a significantly positive relation between bank size and the probability of failure for banks in the U.S., Japan and several European countries.

Berger *et al* (1993) surveyed the literature on the efficiency of financial institutions, concluding that the average cost function in the banking industry has "a relatively flat U-shape, with medium-sized forms being slightly more scale efficient than either very large or very small firms". The survey conducted by Humphrey (1990) arrived at the same conclusion. Studies that used only banks with under $1 billion in assets, those that used banks of all sizes, and one study that included all banks of over $100 million in assets found average costs to be minimized between $75 million and $300 million in assets (Berger *et al*, 1987; Ferrier and Lovell, 1990; Berger and Humphrey, 1991; Bauer *et al*, 1993). Studies that used only banks with over $1 billion in assets found the minimum average cost point to be between $2 billion and $10 billion in assets (Hunter and Timme, 1986, 1991; Noulas *et al*, 1990; Hunter *et al*, 1990). McAlister and McManus (1993) found substantial scale inefficiencies for small banks, that full scale efficiency reached by about $50 million in assets, and approximately constant average costs thereafter (up to $10 billion in assets). Similar to banking, the literature on thrifts and governmental financial institutions shows that the average cost curve is U-shaped with scale economies for institutions below $100 million in assets and constant costs or diseconomies for large institutions (Murray and White, 1983; Kim, 1986; Goldstein *et al*, 1987; Mester, 1987, 1989, 1991; Le Compte and Smith, 1990).

The efficiency implications of bank mergers have been investigated in a number of empirical studies. The studies are based on a comparison of pre-merger and post-merger financial ratios, such as operating costs as a ratio of total assets, and the return on equity or assets (Rhoades, 1986, 1990; Linder and Crane, 1992; Cornett and Tehranian, 1992; Spindt and Tarhan, 1992; Srinivasan, 1992; Srinivasan and Wall, 1992). Most of these studies found no benefits from mergers.

The hazard of being big

It has been recognized that without government policies to protect the wider community, big businesses (of any kind) would ultimately end up with an excess of abusive power that they utilize to make more and more money. It is not only that big means oligopoly and market power. Big financial institutions are too big to manage, and when they are sufficiently diversified in terms of product, conflict of interest will arise (hence the Glass-Steagall Act). The most serious consequence of big size, however, is that big financial institutions claim the TBTF status and thus expect taxpayers' money when they get themselves in trouble.

4.8   The growing political influence of financial institutions

Financial institutions and their bosses have become so influential and politically connected that they have been capable of pushing governments for more and more deregulation while demanding (and obtaining) taxpayers' money when things go wrong, even if things go wrong as a result of greed and incompetence. Johnson (2009) calls this phenomenon a "quiet coup". In his speech to the G20 finance ministers in November 2009, the former British Prime Minister, Gordon Brown, argued forcefully for a "better economic and social contract between financial institutions and the public, based on trust and a just distribution of risks and rewards". Brown posed the question as to whether or not the economic and moral relationship between financial institutions and taxpayers is symmetrical and fair, the answer being an unequivocal "no". He also called for bringing financial institutions into "closer alignment with the values held by the mainstream majority". It was another British Prime Minister, Winston Churchill, who in the 1940s articulated the best description of the contemporary relationship between the financial sector and society. He said "never in the history of conflict has there been so much owed by so many to so few". Churchill was then referring to the RAF pilots as the few, but this statement is equally valid for the situation involving the few financiers and the many taxpayers. The only difference is that the current conflict is between the few and the many as their interests are extremely misaligned.

Johnson argues that financiers played a central role in creating the global financial crisis, indulging in gambles that caused the collapse with the implicit backing of the government. More alarming, he argues, is that "they [financiers] are now using their influence to prevent precisely the sorts of reforms that are needed, and fast, to pull the economy out of its nosedive". He also writes:

> Policy changes that might have forestalled the crisis but would
> have limited the financial sector's profits—such as Brooksley Born's

now-famous attempts to regulate credit-default swaps at the Commodity Futures Trading Commission, in 1998—were ignored or swept aside.

Not even the global financial crisis has changed anything as financiers are still defiant, expecting bailouts and bonuses despite the damage they inflicted on middle-class Planet Earth. They refuse to admit responsibility for the crisis, blaming it on macroeconomic factors (such as low interest rates) and global imbalances (like everything else, blame it on China or even Rio, to borrow the title of a Michael Cane movie). Big banks, it seems, have only gained political strength since the crisis began, exploiting fear of systemic failure to strike favourable deals with the government. Bank of America obtained its second bailout package (in January 2009) after warning the U.S. government that it might not be able to go through with the acquisition of Merrill Lynch, a prospect that the Treasury did not want to consider. We must not forget that financial institutions make so much money, and spread enough of it around, that they gain significant political power. This is one reason why it will be so difficult to reform financial regulation.

4.9   Victims or villains?

Denial, by financiers and their advocates, of responsibility for the advent of the financial crisis and claims of victimization, vilification and demonizing are quite common these days. In April 2009, for example, a financial sector enthusiast and advocate, Pejman Yousefzadeh, was quoted by Salmon (2009) as saying:

> The brain drain that the American financial services industry may face thanks to increasing regulation, the pursuit of class warfare rhetoric and the policies by the Obama administration and its allies, and the tendency to blame the current economic downturn on entities like hedge funds, which had nothing to do with the financial crisis, will only serve to hurt American financial services industry down the road.

How painfully ludicrous and outrageous! Mr Yousefzadeh (who is upset according to Salmon) is not only calling for a carpet exoneration of the culprits who have destroyed the world economy but also that we should allow financiers to do more damage next time and give them bigger bonuses to stop the "brain drain". This kind of rhetoric can only be ideologically-driven, coming from someone who describes himself as a libertarian-conservative Republican. When President Obama was awarded the Nobel Prize for peace, Yousefzadeh used his website to denounce the award, calling it a "truly absurd decision, with no basis, no material support, and no justification whatsoever save the decision to bandwagon in favor of a political figure whose personal popularity may well be transient, and who has achieved nothing tangible whatsoever to deserve the Peace Prize". Not even Dick Cheaney could have said it better.

Responding to the libertarian-conservative Republican

Felix Salmon responds, in a deservedly sarcastic manner, to Mr Yousefzadeh's rhetoric by declaring that he (Salmon) wants to hurt the American financial industry down the road if "hurt" means bringing down the size of the financial sector and its share of corporate profit. He describes a measure like this as a "Pigovian policy response: you tax and regulate the stuff you want less of". Yousefzadeh should at least acknowledge the fact Obama and his "allies" (not sure who they are) have been spending bailout money on big financial institutions to the extent of taking the U.S. budget deficit to $1.4 trillion (10 per cent of GDP), a shortfall that was not seen even during World War II. Salmon, however, does not comment on the "brain drain" and the claim that hedge funds had nothing to do with the global financial crisis. Therefore, I will respond to these outrageous allegations.

The brain drain

To start with, I thought for a while that Yousefzadeh was talking about NASA, because that is what I associate brain power with. So, what brain drain are we talking about here? *The Economist* (2008c) makes the interesting observation that banks "seem to be poor at nurturing talented managers" (recall the drama of appointing successors to the departing CEOs at Merrill Lynch and Citigroup). While managerial skills are important, basic banking and finance (which is all we need to support economic activity) does not require big brains. It requires hard work, honesty, transparency and good customer service (this is not to say that "honest but dumb" will suffice).

Yousefzadeh must be talking about the drain of the brains that invented CDOs, CDSs and the other toxic products. If that is the case, then a brain drain is good for everyone. If he means the brains of financiers like Joseph Cassano, Stan O'Neal and "the worst banker in the world", Fred the Shred (of the RBS), then a brain drain is good for the shareholders of these firms and the economy at large. Or is he talking about the big brains of Milken and Madoff who defrauded people of billions of dollars? The real brain drain (and this is serious) may involve some brilliant mathematicians, physicists and real engineers who were lured to the finance industry by big financial rewards. A brain drain involving people leaving financial institutions is also good because mathematicians, physicists and engineers can do a better job doing science and real engineering than inventing and pricing hazardous financial products. It could be that the brain drain pertains to the academics who were lured to the finance industry from academia and who would now go back to academia. Again, this is good for everyone (the role of academics in the present mess and the rising star of the financial sector will be discussed in Chapter 5). So a brain drain from financial institutions is a positive development for everyone, and it should not be hampered.

If anything, the real brain drain has been inflicted by financial institutions on all sectors of the economy. Financial institutions are, therefore, not the victims but rather the perpetrators of the brain drain. The finance industry has been attracting top-notch mathematicians, physicists and engineers from other sectors of the economy where they have a comparative advantage and where they can produce something useful and advance our knowledge of the world around us. It is never in the interest of the society and economy to convert a mechanical engineer, who could work on the improvement of the fuel efficiency of the internal combustion engine, to a financial engineer working on making derivatives more complex and opaque.

The role of hedge funds

The second allegation, that hedge funds had nothing to do with the global financial crisis, is simply preposterous. Hedge funds are unregulated, secretive and highly leveraged financial institutions that take excessive risk, hence constituting a recipe for disaster. Given that most observers agree that the crisis was caused by a combination of excessive leverage and risk taking, hedge funds cannot be exonerated because that is what they do for living. The first sign of stress for Bear Stearns was that two of its hedge funds got into trouble as a result of heavy involvement in the mortgage-backed securities market. In June 2007, Bear Stearns demanded cash from the hedge funds, but these were not in a position to oblige. Bear Stearns seized the assets of the hedge funds but failed to liquidate them, leading to enormous financial difficulties.

It also seems that Yousefzadeh has a short memory, which can be convenient. In 1998 a hedge fund, LTCM, managed by big brains (the outcome of the brain drain inflicted by the financial sector on academia), lost $4.5 billion and claimed the TBTF status. Yes, one could say that hedge funds are victims of the CDOs and CDSs that financial engineers invented, but they only have themselves to blame for greed-motivated excessive leverage and reckless risk taking. In the process they lost money borrowed from banks, and a big chunk of that money came from small depositors.

Morris (2008) suggests that hedge funds were the force that propelled the CDO market, as they were heavy buyers of toxic assets. This is how he explains it:

> Well, they must be investors willing to take on tremendous risk to earn superior returns. And they must have considerable freedom to invest as they choose. Ideally, they wouldn't have to disclose the details of their positions to nervous shareholders or trustees. They would need access to huge amounts of investable funds and must be free to leverage up their positions to enhance returns. Yes, as the reader has already guessed, it's the hedge funds. And the entire industry is dancing to their tune.

It would take a big suspension of disbelief just to entertain the idea that hedge funds had nothing to do with the global financial crisis. This is reality, not Dreamland or Wonderland.

In defence of big pay

Another finance industry enthusiast is Thomas Donohue, the President of the U.S. Chamber of Commerce who defended Wall Street compensation packages in a news conference held on 12 January 2010 (https://self-evident.org/?paged=2). Donohue described bonus recipients (financiers) as "mad scientists", and "very unique people". And they believe it: "we are special, so we are worth it", which explains why financiers have some sort of an inflated sense of entitlement. They are indeed special and unique because in no other profession do people get paid obscene amounts of money for doing work that is useless at best and destructive at worst. The problem is that even if, for the sake of argument, we assume that those people do something useful for humanity, some big bonus recipients who lost their highly-paid jobs do not know the difference between a bond and a shopping list.

Comparing these bonus recipients to scientists is an absolute insult to science. A very brilliant, small minority of scientists receive the Nobel Prize for coming up with an invention or a discovery that makes our lives more pleasant. In reward for some 40 years of hard work leading to the discovery or invention, a Nobel-Prize scientist will then receive a once-in-a-lifetime "bonus" that is less than one twentieth of the annual bonus of a financial guru who ends up blowing up his company and the economy of Iceland. A disenchanted former computer programmer at Citigroup in Dallas once wrote "I can't help but believe that their [Citi's] financial and upper management gurus are incompetent, narrow-minded and as self absorbed as the folks who were running the show in their information technology department" (Drum, 2009).

Villains, not victims

As far as I am concerned, financiers are villains, not victims. President Obama acknowledged this fact in an interview with Steve Kroft in December 2009 when he said explicitly that the global financial crisis was "caused in part by completely irresponsible actions on Wall Street". He also said: "Bankers have not shown a lot of shame about their behavior and outsized compensation despite the bank bailouts and economic downturn". No wonder, then, that Mr Yousefzadeh believes that Mr Obama is not worthy of the Nobel Prize.

5
The Jewel in the Crown

5.1   Some facts and figures

Since the beginning of the 1980s, the financial sectors of most (actually, all) advanced countries have grown at a much faster pace than other sectors of the economy to grab an ever increasing share of GDP and total corporate profit. Indeed, the financial sector has become a world of its own, an entity that exists for its own sake, not for the purpose of supporting real economic activity (the production of goods and services that we need or want). It has become an end—not the means to achieve the end of lubricating economic activity by providing credit, liquidity and means of payment. The financial sector as a whole has become much larger than can be justified on the basis of its basic function of supporting real economic activity, perhaps too big for the good of the economy—or "too big for its boots", as *The Economist* (2009f) puts it. And it has become the jewel in the crown of the economy. This is why some scholars use the term "financialization of the economy" (Metais, 2009).

The financial sector's share of GDP

Thomas Philippon (2008) studied the growth of the U.S. financial sector over the period 1860–2007 and concluded that the growth seemed to reflect fundamental economic needs up to 2001, but that it was not clear why the sector kept growing so quickly after 2002. His analysis and consequent conclusion are based on the proposition that financial institutions provide services to households and companies and that the financial sector's share of aggregate income reveals the value that the rest of the economy attaches to these services.

Figure 5.1 traces the share of the U.S. financial sector in GDP for selected years with a superimposed trend. It was around 1.5 per cent of GDP in the mid-19th century. The first significant increase in the

Figure 5.1   The U.S. Financial Sector's Share of GDP in Selected Years

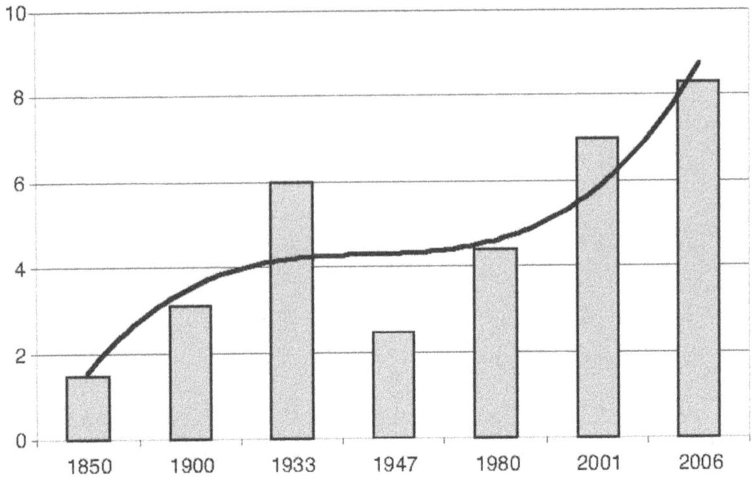

Data Source: Philippon (2008)

financial sector's share of GDP, which occurred between 1880 and 1900, is attributed by Philippon to the financing of railways and early heavy industries. As a result, the financial sector's share rose to more than 3 per cent in 1900. The second big increase took place between 1918 and 1933 as a result of the financing of the electricity, car and pharmaceutical industries. This increase took the share of the financial sector in GDP to just under 6 per cent in 1933. After a continuous decline in the 1930s and 1940s, the share of finance was down to only 2.5 per cent in 1947, but that was the low point. The third big increase, which occurred between 1980 and 2001, is attributed by Philippon to the financing of the IT revolution. By the end of 2001 the share of the financial sector in GDP was just over 7 per cent. The trend continued following the collapse of IT stocks, taking the financial sector's of GDP to 8.3 per cent in 2006.

Based on a simple model, which attributes changes in the size of the financial sector to corporate demand for financial services, Philippon found that the financial sector was about one percentage point of GDP too big. In April 2008, Justin Lahart of the *Wall Street Journal* interviewed Philippon and summed up the discussion in the following way (Philippon, 2008):

Mr. Philippon argues that the surge of financial activity that began in 2002 created an employment bubble that is now bursting. His model suggests total employment in finance and insurance has to fall to 6.3 million to get back to historical norms, and that means losing an additional 700,000 jobs in the sector.

Philippon disputes this interpretation of his results, arguing that his model is not about the number of jobs but about the GDP share, which means that it would be more accurate to say that the annual wage bill of the financial sector needs to shrink by approximately $100 billion. However, he admits that his model cannot explain the continuation of the growth of the financial sector from 2002 onwards, suggesting that he was not sure that "the services provided by insane trading volumes and real estate derivatives were worth the price tag".

The main defect in Philippon's work is the proposition that the size of the financial sector reflects the value that the rest of the economy attaches to financial services. As the subsequent discussion will reveal, the expansion of the financial sector was sustained even when the wider community started to realize that some products of the so-called "financial engineering" were useless and did not serve any meaningful purpose. This is why Philippon is bewildered by the continued growth of the financial sector after 2001. He actually underestimates the size of the financial sector, and his explanation of its growth in the period since 1980 overlooks an important explanatory factor: financial deregulation.

The financial sector's share of corporate profit

The U.S. financial sector commands a large portion of corporate profit and likewise for the wage bill. *The Economist* (2009e) estimates that between 1996 and 2007 the profits of finance companies in the S&P 500 dramatically jumped from $65 billion to $232 billion or from 19.5 per cent to 27 per cent of the total. Johnson (2009)puts forward the following interesting facts and figures:

> From 1973 to 1985, the financial sector never earned more than 16 percent of domestic corporate profits. In 1986, that figure reached 19 percent. In the 1990s, it oscillated between 21 percent and 30 percent, higher than it had ever been in the postwar period. This decade, it reached 41 percent. Pay rose just as dramatically. From 1948 to 1982, average compensation in the financial sector ranged between 99 percent and 108 percent of the average for all domestic

private industries. From 1983, it shot upward, reaching 181 percent in 2007.

These are staggering figures, which Salmon (2009) comments on by writing:

> Financial services companies are meant to be intermediaries, middlemen. And any time that the middleman is taking 41 percent of the total profits in what's meant to be a highly competitive industry, there's something very wrong.

Morris (2008) quotes Martin Wolf of the *Financial Times* as saying that "over the very long term global financial services profits are about twice as high as those in the rest of the industry", which "runs counter to a fundamental proposition of free-market economics, that profits across enterprises should even out over time". Morris attributes what he calls "the permanent advantage of financial services" to the fact that "they don't really compete in free markets". This is how he explains what he calls the "inordinate privileges of financial services":

> They [financial institutions] earn high profits because they take big risks, as evidenced by their very high degree of leverage compared to other industries. In truly free markets, however, periods of high risks and high profits are offset by periods of large losses. But in financial services, although the high profits accrue to managers and shareholders, their losses are usually partly socialized.

Sustained growth post-2001

Consider the growth of the financial sector in the post-war period over two sub-periods: 1947–80 and post-1980. Between 1947 and 1980, the share of the financial sector in GDP rose from 2.5 to 4.4 per cent. Rapid growth of the sector started in 1980 and has been sustained since, which is not a coincidence because 1980 was the year marking the advent of wholesale financial deregulation. The growth of the financial sector was sustained by deregulation and favouritism by the government, and this is why the end of the IT revolution caused no change in the trend.

It seems that deregulation has played a more important role in the growth of the financial sector than economic growth. The nexus between the financial sector and the whole economy is fragile. Economic growth in the 1960s was rather rapid, but seemed to require little financial intermediation. Finance grew quickly in the 1980s while the economy stagnated, and the pattern changed again in the 1990s. So it is certainly not true that a large financial sector is required to sustain economic growth. And even if casual observation reveals that finance is positively correlated with growth, this is simply correlation, not causation. All we really know is that richer countries have more financial flows relative to GDP, not that more finance boosts GDP in any shape or form.

Is the financial sector too big?

The global financial crisis has intensified the belief that the financial sector is too big and that it should be reduced in size. Philippon (2007), for example, argues that "the current financial crisis tells us that we might not need to spend more than 8% of our economic resources to buy these financial services". His estimate is that "the financial sector should be around 7% of GDP if the U.S. remains an innovative, relatively finance-intensive economy". He makes a justifiably sarcastic remark about the destiny of financial engineers, suggesting that "they could always go back to being engineers".

Many would argue that even at 7 per cent of GDP the financial sector is still too big. In an interview with *Prospect* (2009), Lord Turner of the Financial Services Authority (FSA, the former U.K. financial regulator) points out that the U.K. financial sector has grown too big, that some of its activities are worthless from a social perspective, and that it is destabilizing the U.K. economy. He suggests that excessive pay in a swollen financial sector can be stopped by reducing the size of the sector or by applying special taxes. Iceland has learned this lesson the hard way when its banking system collapsed, having outgrown its tiny economy. In Switzerland, the country that is typically associated with prestigious banking, officials have declared that the Swiss government could not afford to take on all the liabilities of the UBS and Credit Suisse, its largest banks. It was back in the 1980s that Sprague (1986) said explicitly that "individual banks should not grow faster than the economies they serve, and the regulators should no longer allow them to do so".

It is not only the amounts involved that cause concern, it is also the quality of financial services and products that we allocate a tremendous amount of resources to for the benefit of the financial sector and its bosses. Just as Turner believes that some financial activities are useless from a social perspective, Johnson (2009) wonders whether modern finance is more like electricity or junk food. "It is more like junk food", Johnson believes. He points out that "there is growing evidence that the vast majority of what happens in and around modern financial markets is much more like junk food—little nutritional value, bad for your health, and a hard habit to kick".

5.2 Financial markets and financial engineering

For those who do not accept the proposition that the financial sector has become too big, consider the following staggering figures pertaining to the size of financial markets in relation to the U.S. GDP, which is about $14 trillion, and the world GDP of just over $60 trillion. The size of the world stock markets was estimated at about $36.6 trillion at the beginning of October 2008 (and that was when markets went down by no less than 30 per cent from earlier peaks). The daily trading volume in the foreign exchange market is $3.2 trillion, of which only a tiny fraction is used to finance international trade. The nominal value of the total world derivatives market has been estimated at about $791 trillion, 13 times the size of the entire world economy. The notional value of the notorious credit default swaps was around $62 trillion in 2007 (Figure 5.2). In 1990 there were just 610 hedge funds, but by 2006 that number had risen to 4500 (Figure 5.3). The market value of hedge funds rose from $75 billion in 2000 to $390 billion in 2007 (Figure 5.4). It was only because of the

Figure 5.2 The Notional Value of Outstanding Credit Default Swaps ($ trillion)

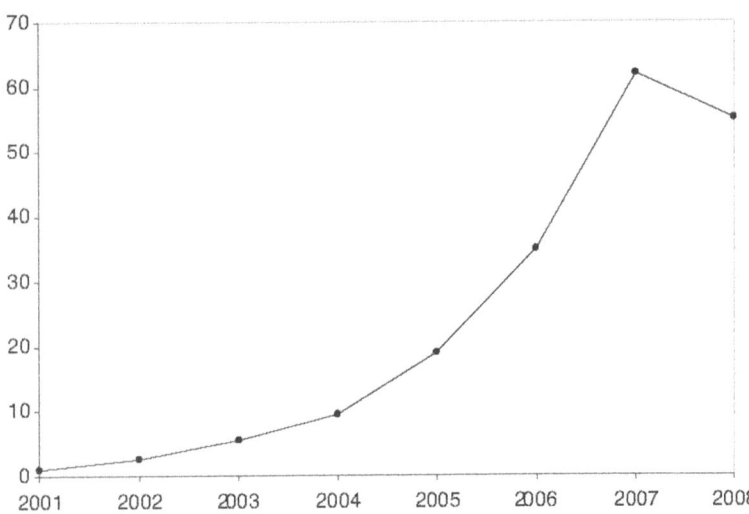

Data Source: International Swaps and Derivatives Association

global financial crisis that the number and value of hedge funds dropped in 2008. This is why Ferguson (2008) correctly argues that "Planet Finance was beginning to dwarf Planet Earth".

Figure 5.3 The Number of Hedge Funds

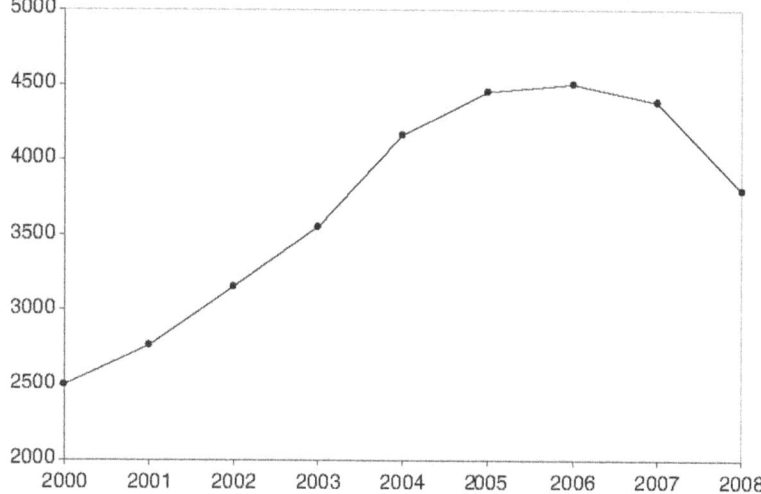

Data Source: Lipper TASS Database

Figure 5.4 The Value of Hedge Funds

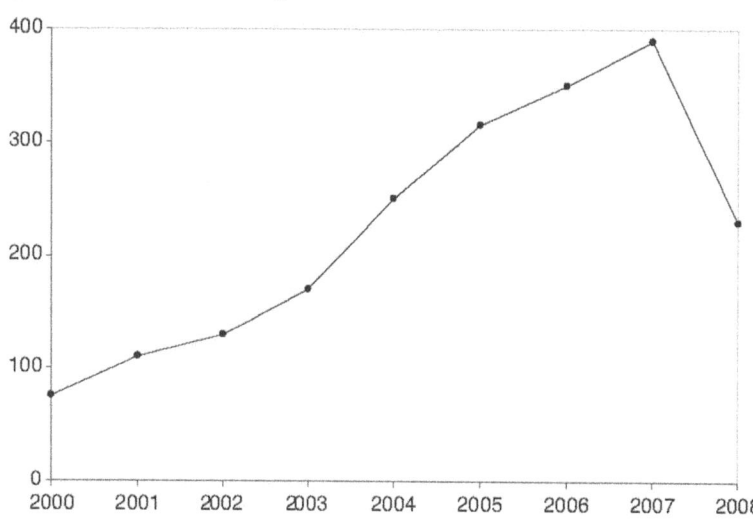

Data Source: Lipper TASS Database

Financial "engineering"

It is so-called "financial innovation" and "financial engineering" that have led to the explosive growth of financial markets. Instead of producing tools for risk management, financial engineers have been producing tools for more risk exposure, tools that can hardly be understood by anyone. In his review of Gillian Tett's book, *Fool's Gold*, Dominic Lawson (2009) tells a story about an e-mail sent by one of the inventors of complex credit derivatives, which were a prime cause of the global financial crisis, to one of his colleagues. The e-mail said: "What kind of monster has been created here? It's like you've raised a cute kid who then grew up and committed a horrible crime". Lawson also argues that these derivatives were invented by JP Morgan, and this is why Morgan was much more cautious about exposure to the subprime mortgage-based instruments that brought up the demise of Merrill Lynch, Lehman Brothers and Bear Stearns.

As financial assets became more complex and harder to price, investors who were oblivious of the impending disaster were reassured by the rating agencies and regulators (who rely on these agencies) that some complex models provided by the issuers of securities predicted nothing to worry about (Norris, 2008). Commenting on this state of affairs, George Soros (2008) wrote:

> The super boom got out of hand when the new products became so complicated that the authorities could no longer calculate the risks and started relying on the risk management methods of the banks themselves. Similarly, the rating agencies relied on the information provided by the originators of synthetic products. It was a shocking abdication of responsibility.

In his review of Kevin Phillips' book, *Reckless Finance, Failed Politics, and the Global Crisis of American Capitalism*, Robert Solow, an economist who won the Nobel Prize in 1986, writes (Solow, 2008):

> Modern financial engineering creates unlimited opportunities for bets that are only remotely related to productive activity, if at all. A can bet B that C will be unable to meet its obligation to pay D. (A may then try to manipulate the odds by spreading rumors about C's financial condition).

No one should care if A and B want to have bets, irrespective of whether these bets involve horse racing, poker, dice throwing, coin tossing or credit default swaps. The problem is that these bets may produce negative externalities if (which is typically the case) they seek leverage—that is, borrowing to finance the bets. By borrowing from banks and other financial institutions, larger amounts can be placed on bets than one's own private capital would permit. Leverage is tantalizing when things are going well because it boosts return on equity, but for the society as a whole the involvement of the banking system in these bets means more risk for everyone, gamblers and otherwise. If things go wrong, the whole system can be hit so hard by defaults that the financial system becomes so paralysed that it is unable to perform its basic function of financing real economic activity. The total volume of bets (and bets on bets made possible by some ingenious derivatives) can vastly exceed the amount of underlying real activity, but this is fine for some people. Since the fees of those who manage and direct the bets (and the interest income generated by providing leverage to finance the bets) depend on the gross volume of debt, this state of affairs is bonanza for financiers who generate enormous incomes for themselves.

After all, it is the combination of financial engineering and leverage that caused the global financial crisis and the consequent world recession. In the prelude to the crisis, major commercial and investment banks (and the hedge funds that ran alongside them) were the big beneficiaries of the twin housing and equity market bubbles in the U.S. and other countries. Their profits were fed by an ever-increasing volume of parasitic transactions founded on a relatively small base of actual physical assets. Each time a loan was sold, packaged, securitized, and resold, banks took their transaction fees, and the hedge funds buying those securities reaped increasingly large fees as their holdings grew.

Basic products of financial engineering may be useful, but financial engineers have taken things too far, just to boost the size of business for their bosses. While relatively simple derivatives provide scope for risk transfer, increasingly complex and opaque derivatives are used to raise leverage and circumvent investment restrictions, bank capital rules and tax legislation. Take, for example, the notorious credit default swaps, which were mainly used to bet against default on mortgage-backed securities. Lewis and Einhorn (2009) describe CDSs as "insurance that most people do not know". These derivatives, they argue, are "more like buying fire insurance on your neighbor's home... from a company that does not have any real ability to pay you if someone sets fire to the whole neighborhood". That company, as we know, is called AIG.

Engineers and "engineers"

We depend on engineers in crucial matters such as the maintenance of, among other things, the planes that we use to fly, the power grid, gas pipes, roads, bridges and tunnels. It is engineers who design and execute the production of cars, consumer durables, computers, ships, buildings and every piece of physical capital that we use or see every day. We, therefore, owe our easy life in big part to engineers. I am talking about mechanical, electrical, chemical, structural, civil, control, marine and aeronautical engineers.

But financial engineers, oh no! These are the inventors of the collateralized debt obligations and credit default swaps, the derivatives that blew up the world financial system and bankrupted Iceland, a tiny isolated country that is as far as it could be from the epicentre of financial engineering. These are the "engineers" who designed structured products, which derived their values from a weird combination of promised cash flows, to the extent that the financial engineers themselves, the people who sold them and (naturally) the people who bought these products had no clue about the risk embodied in them. By talking about investors who bought structured products, I do not only mean naïve investors. Stan O'Neal, the former CEO of Merrill Lynch, destroyed his firm and pushed it to extinction by taking it heavily into CDOs, firing anyone who dared to express dissent. Fred Goodwin, the former boss of the Royal Bank of Scotland who is now hiding in Southern France, sealed the fate of his bank by doing exactly the same thing, which he did not admit at the beginning.

Exotic financial products

As I said earlier, the basic products/derivatives are useful. These include forward contracts, futures, basic call and put options and basic kinds of interest rate and currency swaps. These tools, and combinations thereof, are more than adequate for the purpose of hedging and speculation. Futures were invented to circumvent some problems associated with forward contracts (such as the lack of liquidity) whereas the versatility of options provides the means to hedge against any state of the world as well as contingent exposures. Basic swaps are adequate for reducing the cost of borrowing and hedging foreign exchange risk exposure. Why on Earth do we need options on futures, futures on options, options on options, futures on options on futures, options on futures on options, and so on and so forth? Why do we need the so-called exotic options? And is there any value for production and our wellbeing in the so-called knockout options (also known as down-and-out options, barrier options, extinguishable options and activate/deactivate options), path dependent options and chooser options? These derivatives serve no meaningful purpose, apart from allowing gamblers to bet on rather complex outcomes.

Derivatives can bankrupt countries and destroy the lives of their citizens. Greece, for example, got itself in deep financial trouble because the Greek government was at one time persuaded by some unscrupulous bankers to use some derivatives to accumulate enormous and unsustainable debt while avoiding external scrutiny. In early 2010, worries over Greece rattled world markets as its debt exceeded by far the limits imposed by the European Union. According to the *New York Times*, "instruments [some exotic swaps] developed by Goldman Sachs, JP Morgan and a wide range of other banks enabled politicians to make additional borrowing in Greece, Italy and possibly elsewhere" (Story *et al*, 2010). In this sense, banks (with the help of financial innovation) enabled Greece to borrow beyond its means. In 2001, the Greek government paid Goldman $300 million in fees for arranging such deals. The *New York Times* states that "such derivatives, which are not openly documented or disclosed, add to the uncertainty over how deep the troubles go in Greece". In effect, Greece held a "garage sale", mortgaging airports and highways (as well as revenue from taxes on national lottery) in return for immediate cash.

An idea has occurred to me while pondering the messy situation in Greece. People are warned against smoking, using such slogans as "smoking kills" and "smoking causes cancer and heart disease". Why is it, therefore, that countries are not warned (say by the IMF, BIS, or even the UN) against derivatives? They indeed kill. There is normally outrage if a particular multinational causes environmental damage somewhere. What financial institutions have done to Greece, and other countries, should be met with the same level of outrage.

Weapons of mass destruction

Basic investment does not need all of the cosmetic sophistication provided by financial engineering. Warren Buffett, probably the best investor in the world, uses a simple strategy that does not need these tools: buying undervalued assets and reaping capital gains. This brilliant investor calls derivatives "weapons of mass destruction", which is absolutely on the spot. George Soros, probably the most successful currency speculator, made his fortune by taking currency positions based on fundamental considerations. A friend of mine, who has had a successful career as an investment banker and portfolio manager, told me once that he could not understand why an investor needs derivatives to be successful. He said that he would only buy an asset if he thought that its price would go up (sounds like the Buffett strategy). He does not believe in short selling or the use of instruments that allow him to speculate on a market downturn. This is a successful investor who has done well for himself without the need for the arsenal produced by "gifted" financial engineers.

Teather (2008) argues that if, as Warren Buffett believes, derivatives are "weapons of mass destruction", then Blythe Masters is "one of the destroyers of the World". Masters, according to *The Guardian*, is a member of an elite group dubbed the "JP Morgan Mafia" that invented the complex credit derivatives that lie at the heart of the global financial crisis. After the fact, Masters was unapologetic about the destruction of the world. In an exchange of e-mails with *The Guardian*, Masters blamed it on the misuse of derivatives, not on the very essence of the derivatives. With respect to credit default swaps, she blithely said: "I do believe that CDSs have been miscast, as much as workmen tend to blame their tools" (Teather, 2008).

Likewise, Robert Merton, who contributed to the failure of LTCM and blamed it (with Myron Scholes) on "external forces", argues along the same lines. In a panel discussion at Harvard, Merton argued that "the management and boards of directors of financial institutions were out of their depth, unable to understand the new products created by the new financial economics" (McDonald, 2009). No one can deny that Professor Merton is brilliant in solving partial differential equations and that he has a super understanding of stochastic calculus, measure theory, copulas, etc. However, to expect ordinary people to be as smart as he is way off the mark. While managers and directors are blamed for risking other people's money by trading the inventions of "new financial economics", it is the responsibility of the inventors of these products to label them "handle with extreme care". I can only wonder why it is that Buffett and Soros, who presumably have no understanding of these products, have done extremely well whereas those who supposedly understand the products destroyed the firms they worked for and along with them the rest of the world. It is about time the advocates of "new financial economics" came down to Planet Earth.

The *status quo* as far as derivatives are concerned is totally unsatisfactory. Seidman (2009) writes:

> In the rush to create financial 'products', banks lost sight of their core mission. In truth, their role is to safeguard the financial resources of their customers and to help allocate capital to productive uses in

society. In the future, bankers should worry less about their own 'innovation' and more about supporting the real innovations of the entrepreneurs and others who create tangible value. Wall Street is supposed to be in the financial services business—that is, the business of serving others.

Indeed, going back to basics is all we need. Banks and other financial institutions should send engineers back to where they belong: factories and labs.

5.3   The government's love affair with the financial sector

The finance industry, particularly in the U.S., has lifted itself to super stardom by creating an image, boosted by groupthink, that a flourishing financial sector necessarily means a flourishing economy. Politicians, including law makers and those in government, have not only embraced this image of the finance industry but have also reinforced it. The U.S. government contributed to the rising star of finance through changes in monetary policy. In October 1979 the Fed switched policy from interest rate targeting to money supply targeting, making interest rates highly volatile and bond trading rather lucrative, boosting such institutions as Goldman Sachs.

The support of politicians and regulators

The Economist (2009e) suggests that "the [finance] industry's profitability allows it to gain political influence, either through the funding of candidates or via the desire of the government to protect taxpaying businesses". Johnson (2009) points out that although the finance industry has become one of the top contributors to political campaigns, at the peak of its influence it did not have to buy favours the way, for example, the tobacco companies or military contractors might have to. Johnson argues that the finance industry "benefited from the fact that Washington insiders already believed that large financial institutions and free-flowing capital markets were crucial to America's position in the world." Policymakers, who are supposed to regulate and supervise financial institutions, have nothing but praise for these institutions. Alan Greenspan's views in favour of unregulated financial markets are well known, while Ben Bernanke (2006) said the following:

The management of market risk and credit risk has become increasingly sophisticated. ... Banking organizations of all sizes have made substantial strides over the past two decades in their ability to measure and manage risks.

As we know now, and at a very high cost, the proposition that financial institutions have the ability and/or willingness to manage risk properly is ludicrous. Chairman Greenspan and President Bush insisted, even when the ship was sinking, that the economy was "fundamentally sound" and that the tremendous growth in complex securities and credit default swaps was evidence of a "healthy economy" where risk was distributed safely. But in the aftermath of the crisis, Greenspan was apologetic about the way he had viewed the world. In October 2008, he admitted that he was shocked because he had realized that his view of the world and his ideology were not right (Fox, 2009).

The revolving door

One explanation for the love affair between the U.S. government and the finance industry is the movement of personnel from finance to government and vice versa, the so-called "revolving door" between the government and the financial sector. This is what Jagdish Bhagwati (2009) calls "the Wall Street-Treasury Complex". Robert Rubin, once the co-chairman of Goldman Sachs, served in Washington as Treasury Secretary under Clinton, and later became chairman of Citigroup's executive committee. When he was Treasury Secretary, Mr Rubin was instrumental in the loosening of banking regulation, which made the creation of Citigroup possible by allowing banks to expand far beyond their traditional role and permitting them to profit from a variety of financial activities. He also impeded the tighter oversight of exotic financial products. Rubin is one of many influential figures who have been through the "revolving door".

Henry Paulson, CEO of Goldman Sachs during the long boom, became Treasury Secretary under George Bush, and in this capacity he initiated the bailout of AIG (to protect the interests of Goldman). John Snow, Paulson's predecessor, left to become chairman of Cerberus Capital Management, a large private-equity firm that also has Dan Quayle as one of its executives. After leaving the Federal Reserve, Alan Greenspan became a consultant to Pimco, perhaps the biggest player in international bond markets. These movements strengthen ties between the government and the financial sector. Goldman Sachs in particular has seen these movements frequently, and it has become a tradition for Goldman's staff to go into public service after they leave the firm, perhaps to return to better positions when they leave the government.

The Dutch disease

In the U.K. a lot of people believe in the idea of "who needs manu-facturing industry when we have the City". This is the idea that as long as the financial sector is doing well, it generates wealth that com-pensates for the wealth lost by dismantling manufacturing industry. Yet it turned out that the U.K. was more badly bruised by the global financial crisis than continental European countries for the very reason that the City was (and still is) too big for the U.K. economy. The City, it seems, has become a curse, creating another version of the so-called "Dutch disease". Likewise, Iceland's economy has been shattered by the crisis because its financial sector was disproportionately big for its tiny economy.

The proposition that the financial sector on its own can support a modern economy is nonsense, but it is the kind of nonsense that many people believe. I recall talking to one of my colleagues at a party in 1994 where I expressed dismay at the disappearance of the steel indus-try from the northern British city of Sheffield, once the world supplier of steel. He replied by saying: "Who cares? The U.K. now has a service-based economy". I responded by saying: "Well, there are two ways to eliminate a current account deficit: exporting computers and exporting prostitutes. Are they the same?"

In December 2009 a row erupted over planned bonus payments by British banks, including those bailed out by the government (most notably RBS). The government threatened to impose a special windfall tax on bonuses, a measure that was not ruled out by the opposition Conservative Party. Bankers, as always, argued that this would hurt the banking system and affect growth adversely, claiming that the banking system is the main artery of growth! They also predicted that some British-based banks would move out to other places such as Geneva. It was rather refreshing to watch a British government spokesman announcing on BBC news that "the government cannot be held to ransom". He even declared: "If they want to go, they can go. The financial sector is too big anyway". He went as far as suggesting that bankers were behaving like Arthur Scargill, the leader of the British Union of Miners during the Thatcher years. At last, some official real-ization that the British financial sector (at 10 per cent of GDP) is far too big for a healthy economy.

5.4   The role of deregulation

In both the U.S. and the U.K. the rise of the finance industry to its status of the jewel in the crown of the economy started when Ronald

Reagan and Margaret Thatcher came to power and pursued extreme measures of financial deregulation. In the good old days, financial institutions had well-defined functions: commercial banks took deposits and gave loans; investment banks dealt with corporate finance (mergers and acquisitions, IPOs, etc); securities firms traded securities on behalf of their clients; and mutual funds managed diversified portfolios for shareholders. Each of these functions was supervised by a designated regulator. Competition between different functions was limited and financial institutions were slim and healthy.

Deregulation coupled with free market ideology played an important role in raising the status of the financial sector. We described specific acts and rulings of deregulation in Chapter 2, but the following is a general description of the deregulatory measures that reinforced the financial sector and boosted its image:

- Insistence on free movement of capital across borders.
- The repeal of the Glass-Steagall Act, thus allowing commercial and investment banks to merge.
- A congressional ban on the regulation of credit default swaps.
- Measures allowing investment banks to be extremely leveraged.
- The Basel II Accord that allows banks to determine their own risk and regulatory capital (see Chapter 9).
- Failure to update regulation to keep up with the tremendous pace of financial innovation.

The demise of conventional banking

One consequence of deregulation is the demise of the conventional "three-six-three" model of banking, whereby bankers borrow money at 3 per cent, lend it at 6 per cent and are on the golf course by 3 pm (*The Economist*, 2009g). These figures are not necessarily exact or representative of the banking business, but they serve to indicate that bankers traditionally sought reasonable spreads without taking excessive risk or exposing themselves to complex derivatives.

Commercial banks have been attracted to the investment banking business where margins are higher. They started using their capital to back up their advisory operations, which is the kind of conflict of interest for which the Glass-Steagall Act was designed. As a result, investment banks abandoned the traditional partnership structure and raised money on the stock market or alternatively they were bought by commercial banks. One reason why commercial banks manage to outgun investment banks is their low cost of capital resulting from deposit insurance and the TBTF status that was at one time reserved for commercial banks.

5.5 The role of academia

I spent the first ten years of my career as an investment banker before I took the heroic decision in 1991 to become an academic at the cost of taking of an 80 per cent salary cut. The move has been insightful, at least for the purpose of writing this section. In the world of banking and finance the word "academic" can be as bad as an insult. Practitioners believe that academics can say what they like because they do not use real money and because they do not have their jobs in the line of fire. Academics, on the other hand, think that they are always ahead of practitioners because they are the smart people who do things rigorously. It is astonishing, therefore, that there has been a marriage of convenience between practical finance and academic finance. Posner (2009) provides an explanation by arguing that "the entwinement of finance professors with the financial industry has a dark side" because "if they criticize the industry and suggest tighter regulation, they may become black sheep and lose lucrative consultantship".

Academia has certainly played a (dirty) role in creating the rosy image of the finance industry, as well as contributing to its growth and the destruction of 2008–09. As mathematical finance was gaining acceptance by practitioners, finance academics increasingly took positions as consultants or partners in financial institutions. Two Nobel Prize winners, Myron Scholes and Robert Merton, took board seats at the hedge fund Long-Term Capital Management in 1994 and contributed to its crash in 1998. Finance academics gave their seal of approval to finance practices and provided justification for *laissez faire* finance that has caused the carnage we have witnessed. In a survey of financial economics, *The Economist* (2009h) makes the interesting remark that "financial economists helped to start the bankers' party, and some joined with gusto". And Morris (2008) points out that "options and futures markets exploded with the advent of the Black-Scholes formula", which is an invention—or a discovery—of two financial economists.

The role of financial economists

Financial economists have come up with the efficient market hypothesis (EMH), which is the extrapolation of the macroeconomic hypothesis of rational expectations. It was Eugene Fama, a financial economist at the University of Chicago, who brought the EMH to prominence.

The hypothesis stipulates that financial prices reflect all available information relevant to the values of the underlying assets, which means that the price of an asset converges on its value fairly quickly. EMH enthusiasts, such as Michael Jensen (1978), went as far as claiming that "there is no other proposition in economics which has more solid empirical evidence supporting it than the efficient market hypothesis". When in 1985 Andrei Shleifer presented a paper in the annual meeting of the American Finance Association, in which he presented compelling evidence against the EMH, Myron Scholes described what Shleifer said as "rabbi economics" (Fox, 2009). Scholes was referring to his rabbi who would "tell a story about something that happened to his family, then go on to generalize the story to some big moral about the whole world". He was accusing Shleifer of the same. This is the Myron Scholes who was awarded the Nobel Prize in the following decade, and in that same decade he contributed to the failure of a hedge fund that triggered the first TBTF rescue of a non-bank financial institution. Critics of the EMH were always rebuffed with lethal force.

However, "theories based on market efficiency, though internally consistent and mathematically elegant, nevertheless are not a reflection of what happens in the market place" (Dehnad, 2009). According to the EMH, Warren Buffett and George Soros should not exist because they belong to that species of traders who can outperform the market consistently. Buffett's view of the EMH, as expressed by Dehnad (2009), is interesting: the EMH "advocates no due diligence when investing—just buy the market—so it is good for his [Buffett's] business". The EMH also implies that investment companies should not exist: why form a company and bear administrative costs, utility bills and other overheads if you cannot beat the market? If the EMH were valid, then the best course of action would be to close down the company and put net receipts (shareholders' equity) in an index fund that tracks the market or in index futures.

To its benefit, the finance industry interpreted the EMH, with the help and encouragement of academia, to imply that the market is capable of pricing financial assets correctly and that deviations from fundamental values could not persist. The development of financial engineering was propelled by the EMH, in the sense that any complex security can be priced correctly through the market mechanism of arbitrage. As a result, financial sector gurus convinced politicians, regulators and investors that what they were doing was in the interest of the economy as they found alternative investment outlets and means of risk management. Furthermore, belief in the EMH made the authorities reluctant to restrain either the dotcom or the housing and credit bubble (*The Economist*, 2009g).

The global financial crisis has dealt a severe blow, not only to the EMH but to the whole discipline of financial economics. According to Harper and Thomas (2009), who were referring to what happened during the global financial crisis, "the disappearance of buyers... from major financial markets, especially over-the-counter markets for derivatives, reinforces disaffection with Efficient Market Theory". But don't you dare say something like this to any one of the majority of academic financial economists. They still marvel at the EMH and their contribution to human welfare. For example, Myron Scholes (again) argues that recent events cannot be blamed on models and theories but rather on the practitioners who pushed these models and theories in practice (*The Economist*, 2009i). He seems to forget an important observation that is put sarcastically by Ferguson (2008) who refers to Planet Finance as "an abstract, even absurd world... where mathematical models ignored both history and human nature, and value had no meaning". I can only wonder if Professor Scholes pushed models and theories too far when he was with LTCM in 1998. More recently, another fund he was involved in, Platinum Grove, took a big hit although Professor Scholes, has been since the LTCM fiasco, preaching about the hazard of ignoring some real life factors while utilizing economic models.

It is refreshing, however, that a growing number of economists and observers feel that the EMH is a fallacy that has been exposed by the global financial crisis. Quiggin (2009) points out that "the failure of the efficient markets hypothesis will have ramifications throughout economics and finance, and will require a thorough rethinking of the analysis of financial regulation". Fox (2009) declares the triumph of the efficient market's critics "by showing why traditional market forces can sometimes be just as pervasive as the rational ones".

The EMH is not the only theory that served the financial sector. Financial economists, or the majority of them, managed—through some defunct theory as opposed to conjectural evidence from history—to convince policymakers that self-regulation could control systemic risk, thus providing justification for the deregulatory measures that started in 1980. Shojai and Fieger (2010) suggest that "the more one delves into the intricacies of academic finance the more one realizes how little the understanding is among a majority of academics... and how difficult it really is to implement the theories that are devised in so-called scientific finance institutions and major business schools in the West". Shojai and Fieger call it a "sad fact" that "academic finance has failed in its effort to even provide valuation models that can price simple assets". They further argue that "expecting these models to perform any better for highly complex instruments is nothing more than wishful thinking".

The mavericks of behavioural finance

I must say, however, that those mavericks who have embraced behavioural finance as an alternative paradigm are more humble, less arrogant and more accurate in their predictions and explanations. Robert Shiller, for example, gave an early warning that the U.S. housing market was dangerously overvalued. Unlike the EMH brigade, the behavioural finance mavericks do not believe that investors are rational decision makers and that prices reflect the true and intrinsic value of each trade. Rather, they believe that market participants are human beings who have emotions, fears, greed and hopes. As a result, some decisions and patterns of behaviour may appear to be inconsistent and irrational. This perspective is shared by a successful trader who should not exist according to the EMH, George Soros, who argues that "the mathematical tools and techniques that are used to study the markets and investors' behavior miss one important point that human beings can influence the course of events" (Dehnad, 2009). An important policy implication of behavioural finance is that one argument for regulation is the protection of people from themselves, since they do not necessarily act in their own best interest (McDonald, 2009).

The contribution of macroeconomists

Apart from coming up with the rational expectations hypothesis, which has long been defunct, it is the ideas and models of academic macroeconomists that have been guiding macroeconomic policy. Recall that it was the Federal Reserve policy shift to money supply targeting in 1979 that made interest rates highly volatile and bond trading a lucrative, but risky, business. And it was Alan Greenspan's easy monetary policy that fuelled the housing boom (and bust).

Criticism of the discipline has been coming from within. Paul Krugman, a Nobel Prize winning macroeconomist, describes contemporary macroeconomics as "spectacularly useless at best and positively harmful at worst" (*The Economist*, 2009i). It is the principles of modern macroeconomics that led central bankers to worry about goods price inflation while ignoring financial asset price inflation (Greenspan always insisted on focusing on consumer price inflation while ignoring asset price inflation). Morris (2008) argues that while "academics can adduce technical reasons why central banks should not concern themselves with asset prices", "common sense demands some intervention when prices of a major asset class are soaring beyond reason".

A typical macroeconomic model of the economy overlooks the financial sector, hence it makes sense to "leave the financial sector alone became what happens there is inconsequential". In a typical macroeconomic model, financial institutions do not exist, insolvencies do not occur and leverage does not matter. In Don Patinkin's (1956) neo-classical framework, the financial sector was limited to the demand for and supply of money and bonds, and financial institutions played no significant role in the economy. Likewise, Karl Brunner and Allan Meltzer (1963) and James Tobin (1969) envisaged a minor role for financial institutions in determining macroeconomic equilibrium. With reference to more recent work, Spaventa (2009) emphasizes this point by writing:

> DSGE-type models neglect financial assets and intermediaries and cannot accommodate heterogeneous agents, asymmetric information, agency problems, coordination failures and so on—it has been said that there is nothing in those models that can be of interest to central bankers. There may be concurrent explanations for the lack of concern for financial variables in modern macro modeling; the acceptance of the efficient market hypothesis and of neutrality theorems; the illusion that the volatility of financial markets had come to an end with the Great Moderation.

How unrealistic and how convenient for financial institutions! The message is clear: the activities of financial institutions are inconsequential, so leave them alone.

Economists (not only macroeconomists) have come up with a number of theories and propositions that have been made defunct by the global financial crisis. Apart from the efficient market hypothesis, Quiggin (2009) identifies five others: the Great Moderation, central bank independence, trickle down, the case for privatization and individual retirement accounts. These theories and propositions have been guiding economic policy for a long time. Thank goodness, not everything written by economists is taken seriously. As a part of a survey conducted by Mason *et al* (1992), a disenchanted economist commented on what is published in economics/finance journals by saying:

> I find most of the contents [of journals] to be of possible interest only to the authors. Data-free mathematical masturbation is not my

preferred source of enlightenment. I suspect that the average reader-per-article is less than one, even among academics.

Referring to economics, or rather neoclassical economics, Horn (2009) argues that "we are witnessing the dismantling of an approach that, at least in its shallow mainstream version, has to make a series of absurd assumptions in order to reach any conclusion—with both the assumptions and the conclusions being astonishingly out of touch with reality. She goes as far as saying, and justifiably so, that "the Nobel Prize in Economics does not really deserve its name", and that "the prize is, of course, no guarantee of quality". To remedy the situation, Horn calls for widening the scope of economics. She writes:

> Economics must also again be understood as an encompassing social science, deeply ploughing the rich common ground with philosophy, sociology, politics and history. The use of formal mathematical methods should certainly be part of this approach—but not their long practiced senseless misuse, with many mainstream scholars indulging in an obsession with mathematical virtuosity for its own sake, forgetting to ask the relevant questions.

However, old habits are hard to kick, and mainstream economists still marvel at the old ideas. For example, Taylor (2009) believes that policy is now in a "massive cleanup mode", and recommends "returning to the set of principles for setting interest rates that worked well during the Great Moderation".

The gimmicks of financial econometrics

It is because of the gimmicks of financial econometrics that many people who can crunch numbers (being econometricians), but do not know the difference between a grocery shop and a bank and between a bond and a cheque, are employed as professors of finance in universities around the world. The work done by this group of academics is irrelevant at best, and dangerous at worst. It is these people who have been telling the finance profession that they (econometricians) can come up with models for forecasting financial prices and their volatility. They have also been suggesting the tantalizing prospect of coming up with trading rules that can be used as a license to print money. One must remember that, as far as making big money is concerned, those who know do not tell and those who tell do not know.

Some elaborate models have been developed, including ARMA, ARIMA, ARFIMA, TAR and SETAR models. We also have neural networks, wavelet analysis and multi-chain Markov switching models (sounds like electrical engineering). And we have "dymimic" models (yes, that is dymimic, not dynamic). The Nobel Prize was awarded to Robert Engle for inventing ARCH models (and the same prize was awarded to Fleming for the discovery, or invention, of penicillin). ARCH models can supposedly explain and predict financial volatility, but things did not stop there. There have been more sequels to ARCH than to Jaws, Rocky, Rambo and Die Hard put together. These sequels include GARCH, EGARCH, XARCH and XYARCH where X and Y can be replaced by any letter of the alphabet. Then came Threshold GARCH and ANST-GARCH, which stands for Asymmetric Nonlinear Smooth Transition-Generalized Autoregressive Conditional Heteroscedasticity. One can only say "wow!". This is what will take us to Mars and enable us to find a cure for cancer, not to mention inflation and unemployment. The finance industry bought this stuff and used it as a sales tool because it looks and sounds cool. But I am yet to meet someone (an econometrician or otherwise) who tells me that he or she has managed to make profit on the basis of forecasts generated from any of these models. After all, this is the ultimate test of forecasting accuracy.

Foley (2009) suggests that econometric models suffer from "fatal flaws". He writes:

> The best models they have are of two types, both with fatal flaws. Type one is econometric: empirical statistical models that are fitted to past data. These successfully forecast a few quarters ahead as long as things stay more or less the same, but fail in the face of great change. Type two goes by the name "dynamic stochastic general equilibrium". These models assume a perfect world, and by their very nature rule out crises of the type we are experiencing now.

As a result, Foley argues, "policy makers base their decisions on anecdotal analogies to previous crises". As he puts it, "the leaders of the world are flying the economy by the seat of their pants".

The contribution of statisticians and mathematicians

Statisticians and mathematicians have come up with some risk models that do nothing apart from instilling complacency. It is nice to have a model that a financial institution can use to measure its maximum loss with a confidence level of 99.9 per cent, a degree of precision unheard of in the physical sciences that are based on controlled lab experiments. Regulators bought this idea to the extent that Basel II, the international accord on capital adequacy, allows banks to determine their regulatory capital on the basis of their own models (with a confidence level of 99.9 per cent). When the financial crisis struck, it became abundantly clear that most financial institutions were inadequately capitalized. We must not forget that financial institutions do not like to hold too much capital, as this reduces return on shareholders equity.

It is statisticians who provide the means for financial institutions to minimize regulatory capital while appearing compliant with regulation. It is also statisticians who have come up with the so-called "Gaussian Copula", a technique that was used (with disastrous results for AIG and its counterparties) to measure the joint probabilities of default. In his review of Gillian Tett's *Fool's Gold*, Dominic Lawson (2009) argues that the formulas devised by the best and brightest as tools for dispersing risk (and even avoiding it altogether) ended up so badly misused that they helped precipitate the "first depression of the globalized economy". Lawson made it explicit that the people who blew up the world did not realize that they were playing with fire because their models told them that "everything was going to be all right". Lawson also believes that the moral of Tett's tale is that "money is too important to be left to the mathematicians" (actually, statisticians in this case). I must, however, disagree with Lawson on the "misuse" of the models devised by the "best and brightest". It was not the "misuse" of the models that contributed to the disaster, it was the models themselves as they failed the ultimate test of reality.

Shojai and Fieger (2010) are not impressed by the models developed by academics to deal with risk in financial institutions, arguing that "all of the models fail when put under intense scientific examination". They make the interesting remark that "the main worry is that it is not always academics who fail to realize this fact, practitioners also believe that these models work even without having a holistic view of the risks within their organizations". They add:

> Few can deny that there were serious failures in risk management... perpetrated in all probability by the belief that the models developed work and that they can withstand environments such as the recent financial crisis.

Mathematicians or mathematical economists provided the abstract models demonstrating that the worst thing for the economy is for the government to hamper its workings via intervention through regulation and supervision. After all, it was the mathematical models of Thomas Sargent and Robert Lucas that took the brilliant idea of John Muth that rational people cannot make systematic expectation errors and converted it, with the help of an incredible set of assumptions, to the proposition that the government should not intervene or regulate the economy or any of its sectors. That is the same Lucas who once said that he was "skeptical that the subprime mortgage crisis would contaminate the whole market", and the same Lucas who, in September 2007, cast a big shadow of doubt on the possibility that the economy would slip into a recession (Posner, 2009). It is the same Lucas who still believes that the EMH was a great discovery.

This brand of academics seem to overlook the fact that excessive government intervention in economic activity is unwarranted under normal conditions, but when a big shock strikes then government intervention is necessary (you do not need to see a doctor when you cut yourself shaving, but you definitely need the intervention of a doctor if you are involved in a major car accident). Morris (2008) correctly argues that "only the most invincible dogmatists could survey the history of financial booms and busts and come away with the notion that markets are always right". They also seem to ignore the fact that mathematical methods have been developed to study natural science where people's attitudes do not affect the outcome of natural events (if you jump from a high place, you will be killed or injured by the force of gravity, irrespective of how you feel about gravity). According to Shojai and Feiger (2010):

> Economists have drifted into realms of sterile, quasi-mathematical and a priori theorizing instead of coming to grips with the empirical realities of their subjects. In this sense, they have stood conventional scientific methodology, which develops theories to explain facts and tests them by their ability to predict, on its head.

Mathematical models have also been used to prove that privatization is always, and under any set of circumstances, good for the economy. I recall a seminar presentation in which the presenter described a rather elegant mathematical model to demonstrate that privatization is always good. When it was time for Q&A, I asked the presenter the following question: "when you embarked on the construction of the model, were you motivated by the desire to unravel the 'truth' or did you start from the stance that you wanted to prove that privatization works under any circumstances?". Needless to say, I did not get a satisfactory answer but my reckoning at the time was that he constructed the model in such a way as prove that privatization is always good for our welfare. For a long time, saying that privatization was always good opened the door for academics to obtain research grants and consultancy jobs from the government.

The glory of academic finance

Within universities, finance has been in a world of its own. Finance professors are more highly paid than professors of other disciplines, and this is normally justified on the grounds that it is necessary to avert the brain drain to the financial sector. Higher salaries for finance professors and the availability of plentiful resources in finance departments (because they attract large student numbers and research grants) explain why there has been a brain drain within universities, as brilliant brains leave the less lucrative areas of mathematics, science and engineering to join finance departments. With a move like this, some "beautiful minds" (to borrow the title of the Russell Crowe movie in which he played John Nash) stop working on the development of semi-conductors and fiber optics to come up instead with yet another sequel to ARCH.

Finance departments typically have staff consisting of economists, accountants, statisticians, econometricians, mathematicians, physicists and even chemists (I know of at least one such case). This group of heterogeneous people typically share one opinion and a feeling of elitism. "Finance is not economics", they say, not because this is a valid statement, but to keep away from economics departments where resources are less plentiful and salaries are lower.

I have always argued that finance is financial economics because it deals with the study of financial markets, financial firms and the pricing of financial assets, which makes finance a branch of economics, as the definition of finance in the *Palgrave Dictionary of Finance* says. Once I even dared to give a presentation in a finance department entitled "what is finance?", in which I argued that finance is financial economics and that it is different from labour economics, for example, only in as far as financial markets differ significantly from the labour market. I did ask the audience the following question: "if you guys are not economists, what do you call yourselves: financiers, financists, financial accountants, or what?". They listened with dissent, but the discussion revealed one thing: "we do not want to be part of the economics department".

The failure of academic finance

Economic (financial) theory and the mathematical and econometric models used for representation, estimation, hypothesis testing and forecasting are the constituent components of academic finance, which according to Blommestein (2009) has failed, and this failure is one of the symbols of the financial crisis. Blommestein attributes the failure of academic finance to account for real world phenomena to: (i) treating economics not as a "true" social science, but as a branch of applied mathematics inspired by the methodology of classical physics; and (ii) using economic models as if the empirical content of economic theory is not very low. He further writes:

> Failure to understand and appreciate the inherent weaknesses of these conventions had fatal consequences for the use and interpretation of key academic finance concepts and models by market practitioners and policymakers. Theoretical constructs such as the efficient markets hypothesis, rational expectations, and market completeness were too often treated as intellectual dogmas instead of (parts of) falsifiable hypotheses.

Blommestein accuses academics of failing to communicate the limitations of their models and to warn against (potential) misuses of their research, and of introducing (often implicitly) ideological or biased features in research programmes. In addition, he argues, "there is wide-spread failure to incorporate the key implications of economics as a social science". To remedy the situation and go forward, Bloomestein suggests five principles: (i) economists need to take the implications of the nature of economics as a social science more seriously; (ii) academic economists should make efforts to reduce as much as possible the political or ideological features in their theories; (iii) more emphasis should be placed on explaining the working of institutions; (iv) allowing a role for moral (ethical) standards; and (v) the profession needs to acknowledge the econometric modelling implications of the "semantical insufficiency of economic and financial theory". In a nutshell, the profession needs an overhaul and a big dose of reality check. Coming down to Earth will be nice.

A positive note

I will close this chapter on a somewhat more positive note. I am not saying that all academics working in economics, finance and related fields that are relevant to the finance industry are guilty as charged in the case of the financial sector versus the rest of the society. I have already said that those financial economists believing in behavioural finance, such as Robert Shiller, warned of things to come. Referring to economists, Garnaut (2009) acknowledged that "parts of our profession were guilty of believing a model of risk that was chosen for its elegance above its relevance to the behaviour of real economies". He also acknowledged that "economists are accused of propagating the idea that unregulated markets can deliver a maximum of economic welfare" and that "we [economists] are accused of being hired agents of vested interest"—in other words, "hired guns". However, he correctly reminds us that economists like Pigou, Musgrave and Stiglitz came up with "insights into what markets cannot do alone". In the same context (of positive contributions) he mentions Keynes, Stigler, Buchanan, Mill, Carlyle, Krugman and Corden. I would add to his list Minsky, Galbraith and many others. Horn (2009) argues that "the verdict of narrowness and non-scientific shallowness cannot be directed against those economists who have made their career outside the mainstream... in institutional economics..... or in public choice, in law and economics, game theory and behavioural finance".

Unfortunately, however, economists like Stiglitz and Krugman, and those working outside the orthodoxy, are still a small minority fighting against the ideology of mainstream majority that is shared by the political establishment. Spaventa (2009) makes the remark that "though some scholars have initiated thoughtful soul searching exercises, the prevailing mood seems to be that of business as usual, as if nothing happened". However, if people like George Bush and Alan Greenspan can change their views about the beauty of markets, then there is hope for humanity. Let us hope that academic free marketeers will follow the foot steps of the new Bush and Greenspan, only in as far as free markets are concerned.

6
Worthy of Bailout: To be or Not to be?

6.1 Cherry picking?

Sprague (1986) argues that "bailout is a bad word", that "to many it carries connotations of preference and privilege and violation of the free market principles", and that "it sounds almost un-American". "Preference" and "privilege" are the key words in Sprague's statements, hence the title of this section "cherry picking". He examines four episodes of bailout, but right from the beginning he asks the questions: "why and how were four institutions selected to be saved", "why only these four?", and "why did you save Continental and not my bank?". He answers the question "why the four?", by saying that "we were afraid not to". But why were "we" afraid only in those four cases?

The recent record

Let us examine the recent record to see why the bailout practice has indeed been cherry picking. In 2008 Lehman Brothers was allowed to fail (by filing for bankruptcy) but Merrill Lynch and Bear Stearns were saved from bankruptcy by government-assisted and partly-financed mergers with Bank of America and JP Morgan, respectively. Citigroup and AIG (and Goldman Sachs indirectly) were saved by massive direct injection of cash from the U.S. Treasury. Yet in 2009 alone more than 150 other U.S. banks were allowed to fail. The TBTF status was given to Continental Illinois in the 1980s, but not to Drexel Burnham Lambert in the 1990s. Consider also the case of the hedge fund LTCM, which was saved by the intervention of the New York Fed that engineered (with a lot of arm twisting, some would say) a very attractive deal for the failed management, but another fund (Amaranth) that was twice as big was allowed to go down. In the U.K. a prestigious 300 year old bank, Barings Bank, was allowed to fail in 1995 but Northern Rock, a bank with an extreme and reckless funding model, was saved by taxpayers' money in 2007. On the surface at least, it seems that big size is a necessary but not a sufficient condition for obtaining the TBTF status.

The Economist (2009j) suggests a political explanation for why Bear was bailed out while Lehman was allowed to sink. When the Treasury and Federal Reserve bailed out Bear in March 2008, they were criticized for creating moral hazard, as other firms (including Lehman) started to believe that they would be spared as well. According to Kenneth Rogoff, a Harvard economist, political pressure at some point would have required a big firm to go bust. Rogoff said: "if you look at a financial crisis, the standard playbook is to let the fourth or fifth largest bank go under and you save everybody else". What I do not agree with here is the idea of picking the fourth or the fifth largest bank just because it happens to be so. The decision to let Lehman go under was indeed political, but not because Lehman was the fourth or fifth. It is because of what happened behind closed doors. Had Goldman failed, it would have been saved irrespective of whether it was fourth or fifth. As argued earlier, the bailout of AIG was largely motivated by the Goldman connection.

To be or not to be WOBO

The TBTF status is certainly a privilege that is worth billions of dollars, both in good times and bad times. An argument that was put forward in Chapter 4 is that a prime motive for financial institutions to grow is the desire to obtain the TBTF status. Also, recall the evidence presented by Brewer and Jagtiani (2007), indicating that financial institutions pay a premium for mergers and acquisitions that make them TBTF. The question that arises here is how the government decides which institution to bail out and which one to let go under. In other words, what are the factors that make an institution worthy of bailout (WOBO)?

The general qualitative definition of TBTF is a financial institution that has many customers or plays a large role in the financial sector (for instance, by processing a big portion of payments or security transactions). It is TBTF because its failure may threaten the solvency of other institutions that are financially connected to it and to each other. The underlying argument goes as follows: by creating a domino effect, the failure of a TBTF institution threatens to cripple the national economy. For instance, if a major institution, A, fails and other institutions rely upon A and its creditors to fulfil their obligations, then these institutions, and potentially others that they are financially connected to, may collapse as well. If the spillover effects generated via this process are large enough, the failure of a big financial institution triggers an economy-wide recession. The same reasoning has been used to justify the need to bail out Greece, as the proponents argued that if Greece defaulted, creditor banks would fail and demand bailout money from their governments. Therefore, it would be bailout one way or another.

How do we know before the fact which institution is TBTF, in the sense that its failure will bring about the failure of the financial system and perhaps the advent of a recession? A related question that arises immediately is whether or not any difference would have been made by not rescuing Merrill Lynch, Citigroup, Bear Stearns and AIG. Even with the rescue of these institutions, the credit market died and recession struck. Would things have been different had the U.S. government saved Lehman Brothers while allowing Bear Stearns to apply for bankruptcy? I doubt that. And why is it that the failure of one TBTF financial institution can be disastrous for the economy and the financial system but not the simultaneous failure of a hundred financial institutions that jointly have the same size?

6.2 Size as a determinant of systemic importance

The general qualitative definition of TBTF stated in the previous section has the words "many", "large" and "big", all of which are indicative of size. Seeling (2004) argues that "bigness implies size and the term 'too big to fail' implies either absolute or relative size". However, an argument that has been put forward is that the concept of too big to fail should be replaced with that of systemically important financial institutions (SIFI). Seeling argues that "in practice the term [too big to fail] may not necessarily be size related" and that "it may relate to the systemic importance of a firm or its role in the economy". This argument implies that size is not the only factor that matters and that other factors should be taken into account to determine systemic importance, including opacity and the degree of involvement with counterparties. It is argued, for example, that "while the systemic importance of an organization tends to be closely related to size, this is not always the case". There are, for example, "banks that are not particularly large but are still often perceived as too big to fail because they perform an essential activity in the smooth functioning of financial markets and the payment system" (Ennis and Malek, 2005). Genberg (2009) defines a systemically important financial institution as follows:

> A financial institution may be deemed systemically important if it can potentially pose significant risk to financial stability, where risks

to financial stability can be defined as the risks of severe disruptions to the smooth functioning of the financial system. It is generally agreed that size is the single most important characteristic of a systemically important institution.

Non-size criteria

In addition to size, Genberg suggests two other characteristics of a systemically important financial institution: (i) the institution tends to affect others by affecting confidence in the system as a whole (particularly depository institutions), and (ii) the institution's profitability tends to be positively correlated with financial market volatility (such as hedge funds and highly leveraged financial institutions). Genberg explains why hedge funds should be regarded as SIFIs as follows. As volatility provides greater profitable opportunities for hedge funds and highly leveraged financial institutions, these institutions have a strong incentive to manipulate markets where they enjoy monopolistic power, producing undesirable swings in financial markets that can threaten financial stability. If this is the case, and it is so, then there is every reason to regulate these institutions and undermine their ability to manipulate the market, which is fuelled by leverage. On the contrary, hedge funds have been largely unregulated.

Thomson (2009) has suggested criteria other than size that can be used to define systemically important institutions as an alternative to the concept of TBTF, which pertains to size only. These criteria include the four C's: contagion, correlation, concentration and (the underlying) conditions. So, instead of too big to fail, we could be talking about too systemically important to fail (TSITF), which could be too contagious to fail (TCTF1), too correlated to fail (TCTF2), too concentrated to fail (TCTF3) and too important under specific conditions to fail (TIUSCTF). According to these criteria, a financial institution may not have super size but it is TSITF. Thus an institution that is worthy of bailout (WOBO) is TSITF rather than strictly TBTF.

Undermining size?

A firm is considered systemically important if its failure would have economically significant spillover effects, which (if left unchecked) could destabilize the financial system and have a negative impact on the real economy. This is a conceptual definition that, according to Thomson (2009), "is unsatisfactory because it provides little guidance in practice". He therefore suggests that we need a workable (that is, operational) definition of "systemically important", arguing that "delineating the factors that might make a financial institution systemically important is the first step toward managing the risk arising from it".

Thomson believes that using a size threshold (whether it be asset-based, activity-based, or both) is flawed because, he argues, what matters is not size but rather the composition of assets. For example, a bank that holds a portfolio made up largely of government and agency securities is likely to have less serious systemic implications than a comparable bank with a portfolio of commercial and industrial loans, presumably because the former has a lower probability of failure—and even if it does fail, it will suffer smaller losses. But this argument has several loopholes. To start with, there is no indication that small banks tend to hold proportionately more loans relative to government securities than large banks. All banks reduce the ratio of consumer and business loans and boost their holdings of investment-grade securities when the economy is on the downturn (because of a higher incidence and probability of default), and *vice versa*. *The Economist* (2009k) argues that "they [banks] expose themselves to similar risks by making the same sorts of loans" and that "each bank's appetite for lending rises and falls in sync".

Let us not forget that banks face an asymmetric loss function because they use other people's money, and given that bankers have an insatiable urge to earn fat bonuses, they love high-risk, high-return business loans that also generate substantial fee income. They particularly like the risky loans used to finance leveraged buyouts and other highly-leveraged transactions. Lee (2007), for example, correctly argues that "banks do not like putting their assets into fixed-income securities, because the yield isn't that great", implying that the only reason for holding investment-grade securities is the need for liquidity. Lee considers three banks that vary in size: Wells Fargo, Sun Trust, and M&T Bank, demonstrating that the three banks hold respectively 16, 18 and 17 per cent of their earning assets (loans and securities) as securities. Irrespective of size, loans represent the majority of a bank's assets because they are the bank's "bread and butter".

Thomson does not deny the importance of size but argues that it is not the only factor that matters. Accordingly, he tries to use numbers to determine a size threshold for an institution to be SIFI. A financial institution would be considered systemically important if it accounts for at least 10 per cent of the activities or assets of a principal financial sector or financial market or 5 per cent of total financial market activities or assets. He goes on and on by stating thresholds for off-balance sheet activities, and stating similar criteria for non-bank financial institutions (NBFIs). For example, he argues that a non-bank financial institution (other than a traditional insurance company), such as an investment bank, might be considered systemically important if: (i) its total asset holdings would rank it as one of the 10 largest banks in the country; (ii) its total assets would rank it in the top 20 largest banks and its adjusted total assets (accounting for off-balance sheet activities) would rank it in the top 10 largest banks; and (iii) it accounts for more than 20 per cent of securities underwritten (averaged over the previous five years). The problem here is that these figures are arbitrary, probably chosen because they are round numbers. It is not clear why an institution that just makes the list could inflict havoc on the financial system if it fails but the failure of another institution that just misses out will be totally benign.

Elsinger *et al* (2006) have investigated the determinants of systemic importance for European banks. By measuring systemic importance in terms of incremental value at risk and the conditional expected short-fall (another VAR-related concept), they considered as determinants of systemic importance size (measured as the book value of total assets) as well as return on average assets, the value of equity over total assets and the interbank ratio. The results reveal the importance of size and the interbank ratio (presumably a measure of interconnectedness).

6.3   Contagion as a determinant of systemic importance

Thomson argues that the "two classic cases of contagion as a source of systemic importance are Herstatt Bank and Continental Illinois, both in 1984" (actually, the Hersttat event happened in 1974). It is not clear why the closure of a relatively small institution, Bankhaus Herstatt, "had the potential to disrupt the international payments system and imposed nontrivial losses on its counterparties". Roth (1994) argues that the unexpected failure of Herstatt "left many foreign banks exposed and temporarily paralysed the foreign exchange market". These statements are rather strange, given that the bank lost $400 million in foreign exchange trading, which is a small amount relative to the size of the foreign exchange market, even in 1974. The losses would have been shared by the many banks and other counterparties. To say that the loss of a $400 million paralysed the foreign exchange market is some sort of an overstatement. I do not recall anything catastrophic happening in the aftermath. However, it is more plausible to argue that the Herstatt incident raised the alarm that something like this could happen to a bigger bank. This is why the Basel Committee on Banking Supervision (BCBS) was established in 1975 to instate capital adequacy standards.

Contagion versus size

The stated rationale for the "generous" bailout of Continental Illinois in 1984 was the threat that losses would be transmitted to some 2300 community banks that had correspondent-banking relationships with Continental. But that is only because Continental was a big bank. No one would have paid attention to one or more of the 2300 community banks, just like no one paid attention to the more than 150 U.S. banks that failed in 2009. Actually, contagion arises because of interconnectedness in the system but the quantum of adverse consequences depends on size. Thomson (2009) argues that "the justification for the Federal Reserve Bank of New York's assisted acquisition of Bear Stearns by JPMorgan appears to have been concerns about contagion" resulting from "the potential of loss transmission through the credit-default-swaps market". This immediately raises a question: was Lehman Brothers less involved in the credit default swaps market? I do not believe so, as the trio of Lehman, Bear and Merrill were more or less equally in love with toxic assets, and they were equally interconnected. Therefore, the decision to let Lehman Brothers go down while saving Bear Stearns and Merrill Lynch was not motivated by contagion but rather by another factor. Lehman Brothers was twice as big as Bear in terms of assets, so size alone cannot explain why Merrill and Bear were WOBO but Lehman was not.

Take another example, that of the CIT Group, the 101-year-old finance company that attempted to claim eligibility for bailout in the summer of 2009, on the grounds that "being forced into Chapter 11 protection would spell disaster for its customers", a "wide swath of the nation's small and midsize businesses who rely on it". A decision was then taken to put CIT through a different kind of bankruptcy, one that would let it re-emerge from court protection by the end of the year under the ownership of its creditors, who widely supported the re-organization plan. In this episode, regulators concluded over the summer that even though CIT was vital to many small businesses that needed financing, the company's problems did not pose the type of systemic risk that led to the aggressive rescues of Citigroup and Bank of America. To claim the WOBO status on the basis of interconnectedness did not work for the CIT Group.

Measuring contagion

Todd and Thomson (1990) use interbank exposure as an indicator of potential contagion or systemic risk. They present arguments and anecdotal evidence that support three hypotheses: (i) high levels of interbank exposure reduce the safety and soundness of the banking system because it boosts the probability that the failure of a single bank or a few banks would impact on a larger number of banks; (ii) interbank exposure affects the ability of the FDIC to use market discipline as a constraint on risk-taking by banks; and (iii) a rising level of interbank exposure is indicative of reduced stability of the financial system. While there is merit in all of these hypotheses, contagion cannot be a substitute for size. Furthermore, it is plausible to suggest that interbank exposure increases with size. What is not clear, however, is why Todd and Thomson (1990, p. 141) argue that "interbank exposure... need not... constitute contagion or systemic risk that has significant public policy implications for the safety and soundness of the banking system".

Thomson (2009) tries to quantify the effect of contagion that makes a SIFI, arguing that a financial institution would be considered systemically important if its failure could result in: (i) substantial capital impairment of institutions accounting for a combined 30 per cent of the assets of the financial system; (ii) the locking up or material impairment of essential payments systems (domestic or international); and (iii) the collapse or freezing up of one or more important financial markets. He defines a substantial impairment of a payments system or market as "one that is large or long enough to affect real economic activity". Although a figure of 30 per cent sounds arbitrary, there is some indication in the quantitative measures of contagion that size does matter as the effect of contagion is defined in terms of size (the combined size of institutions accounting for 30 per cent of the assets of the financial system). This sounds inconsistent with Thomson's objection to size, "whether it is asset or activity based".

If contagion implies interconnectedness then it is plausible to suggest that the failure of a widely interconnected institution is less problematical than the failure of an institution that only deals with a limited number of other institutions. This is because in the first case total losses are shared by a large number of institutions, each of which incurs what would be a manageable loss.

6.3   Correlation as a determinant of systemic importance

Correlation, as a source of systemic importance, is what Thomson calls the "too many to fail" problem. The underlying idea is that if risk exposures are correlated, then a group of banks may become systemically important. Financial institutions have incentives to take on risks that are highly correlated with other institutions because regulators are less likely to close an institution if many other institutions would become insolvent at the same time. This may explain why, in the run-up to the global financial crisis, financial institutions over-exposed themselves to subprime mortgages, mortgage-backed securities, and related mortgage-derivative securities. This argument, however, is inconsistent with the earlier argument used by Thomson to undermine the importance of size, when he claimed that what matters is not the size but the composition of assets, implying that individual banks hold vastly different asset portfolios (particularly with respect to the amounts of investment-grade bonds *vis-à-vis* commercial loans). I pointed out earlier that this was not a valid argument because banks tend to hold similar portfolios. Here, Thomson uses the "all in a sinking boat argument" to justify correlation as a determinant of systemic importance. Thus Thomson contradicts himself while suggesting that correlation is a more important criterion than size. What matters here is the combined size because it has implications for the size of loans.

Too many to fail

The too-many-to-fail problem requires that a group or subset of institutions be classified as being jointly systemically important. It is completely impractical, although Thomson tries to assign parameters to correlated risk exposures (including the determination of what level of correlation across portfolios poses a systemic threat), asserting the importance for this purpose of risk models, stress testing and scenario analysis. Fortunately, Thomson argues, "some large financial institutions are doing this type of risk modeling and scenario analysis for looking at their own risk profile" and that "their work provides a good foundation for others to work from". But the global financial crisis has exposed the weakness of these techniques, not in the least because of the fact that rare events occur more frequently than what is predicted by value at risk models (the Black Swan problem of Taleb, 2008). The VAR models used by financial institutions are inadequate because the global financial crisis has demonstrated vividly that the financial institutions using those models turned out to be grossly undercapitalized and were hit by massive losses that should not have been experienced as predicted by the models. Even worse, financial institutions find it tantalizing to manipulate their models to produce results that make everyone happy (Moosa, 2008, 2010).

Once more, Thomson tries to identify levels of correlated risks that would give rise to systemic concerns. According to him, thresholds that would make groups of institutions systemically important include: (i) the probability that an economic or financial shock would decapitalize institutions accounting, in aggregate, for 35 per cent of financial system assets or 20 per cent of banking assets; and (ii) potential for economic/financial shock to decapitalize institutions accounting, in aggregate, for 15 per cent of financial system assets or 10 per cent of banking assets. But assets are a measure of size, which means that the correlation criterion boils down to size.

6.5   Concentration as a determinant of systemic importance

The underlying idea is that the presence of dominant firms in key financial markets or activities can give rise to systemic importance if the failure of one of these firms could materially disrupt or lock up the market. This is size relative to the market, therefore it is size. Concentration is measured by the size of the firm's activities relative to the contestability of the market. That is, concentration is less likely to make a financial institution systemically important if, other things being equal, the activities of a distressed institution can be easily assumed by a new entrant into the market or by the expansion of an incumbent firm's activities. Hence, it is logical to adjust concentration thresholds to account for contestability. Concentration, it seems, is some sort of a modified measure of size.

According to Thomson, thresholds for concentration that would render a financial institution systemically important include any institution (on a consolidated basis) that: (i) clears and settles more than 25 per cent of trades in a key financial market; (ii) processes more than 25 per cent of the daily volume of an essential payments system; and (iii) is responsible for more than 30 per cent of an important credit activity. Thomson, therefore, is suggesting arbitrary measures that pertain to size.

6.6   Conditions/context as a determinant of systemic importance

The underlying idea behind conditions/context is that in certain states of nature or under some macro-financial conditions, the effect of failure may not be independent of these conditions. In other words, regulators are reluctant to allow the official failure (closure) of a distressed financial institution under particular economic or financial market conditions if its solvency could be resolved under more normal conditions. Hence, conditions/context is a source of systemic importance. Thomson admits that institutions that might be made systemically important by conditions/context are probably the most difficult to identify in advance, but he argues that stress testing and scenario analysis can be used to identify them. As a result, a group of institutions that would not pose a systemic threat under normal economic or financial market conditions become systemically important.

LTCM as an example

Joseph Haubrich (2007) notes that the New York Fed's reluctance to allow the failure of Long-Term Capital Management resulted largely from the fragility of financial markets at that time—due to the Asian crisis and Russian default. This might explain, in part, why LTCM was treated as systemically important, whereas Amaranth (which was more than twice as big) was not. However, there is no indication whatsoever that the failure of LTCM under the conditions prevailing in 1998 or 1995 or whenever would have been that serious (due to size). We know that, for some reason, the New York Fed fought to find a better deal for the LTCM management than the deal offered by the Warren Buffett consortium.

It is not obvious to me how the systemic effect of LTCM would have been different under the better deal that pleased its management and preserved some of the wealth that they should have lost due to poor judgment on their part. How that could have made a difference for the whole financial sector because of the prevailing conditions is something I cannot comprehend. What I can comprehend, however, is that the Fed should have treated LTCM the same way as the much bigger Lehman Brothers was treated nine years later.

Another example would be intervention to prevent the bankruptcy of Bear Stearns by merging it (with generous assistance) into JP Morgan in early 2008, whereas Drexel Burnham Lambert was allowed to file for bankruptcy in 1990. But then why is it that Lehman Brothers was allowed to go down, given that it was operating under more distressed conditions than those under which LTCM was operating?

Assessing conditions/context

Thomson suggests two sets of criteria that can be used to judge firms as systemically important because of conditions/context. First, is there a probability that economic or financial conditions will materialize that produce the state of nature where a firm or a group of firms becomes systemically important? Second, are the thresholds for systemic importance (which presumably would be based on those used to classify SIFIs according to contagion, concentration and correlation) met during normal market conditions? We have seen that these criteria eventually revert back to size. Then, how is it possible to estimate the probability that certain conditions make firms systemically important? This is so hazardous that it renders the quantification of the criterion of conditions/context totally unreliable.

6.7   A classification scheme

Thomson (2009) suggests a classification scheme, whereby financial institutions can be placed into five categories according to their systemic importance, with regulatory implications such that more stringent regulatory measures are applied to institutions that are more systemically important. Within each category, every financial institution would be subject to equivalent regulatory treatment and intensity of supervision.

Categories 1–3 of the five categories include financial institutions that are considered as systemically important on the basis of: (i) size and concentration, (ii) interconnectedness, and (iii) correlated risk exposures and conditions/context. Thus, Thomson once more recognizes size as the main determinant of systemic importance. Category 4 includes large financial institutions that are not systemically important but whose failure could have economically significant implications for regional economies, while Category 5 encompasses all other institutions, primarily community financial institutions. What I cannot understand is Category 5. Institutions placed under this category are big but they are only important for regional economies. These institutions do not have a nation-wide or perhaps state-wide presence, in which case they cannot be that big. Then I cannot understand the difference between categories 4 and 5, as both have the word "regional".

Having classified financial institutions under the five categories, Thomson argues, progressive systemic mitigation measures are implemented to prevent the rise of a TBTF or TSITF situation—that is, to prevent the need for a bailout. The suggestion is that Category 5 institutions would be subject to a basic level of safety-and-soundness regulation and supervisory oversight. Category 4 institutions would not face any special capital surcharges or activity restrictions that might apply to categories 1–3, but they would be subject to additional reporting requirements and be expected to implement risk management systems and more sophisticated risk controls than Category 5 institutions.

At a minimum, Thomson suggests, Category 3 institutions should be subject to periodic stress tests and be required to have contingency plans in place. For Category 2 institutions, it is necessary to establish regulatory reporting requirements that allow for inter-bank/inter-firm exposures, direct and indirect, to be tracked and measured. For Category 1 institutions, two more types of regulatory treatment need to be added to those faced by Category 2 institutions: enhanced market discipline and a system of double indemnity for shareholders, which could be an effective device for providing socially compatible incentives for those institutions.

Alternative classification schemes

An alternative but related system of classification is suggested by the President of the Cleveland Fed, Sandra Pianalto (2009), which she calls "tiered parity". Under this classification scheme, financial institutions are separated into three categories "based upon their complexity". But this system is essentially the same as what is proposed by Thomson, except that categories 4 and 5 are combined into tier 3, while categories 2 and 3 are combined to form tier 2. Hence the criterion of complexity goes with size. It is size all over again.

A research paper of Standard & Poor's (2007) suggests yet another classification scheme. The system contains three categories: (i) high systemic importance, (ii) moderate systemic importance, and (iii) low systemic importance. High systemic importance covers top-tier deposit takers, institutions that have a strategic role in the economy and significant systemic implications of default and payment or exchange systems that are critical to the economy. Moderate systemic importance covers second-tier retail deposit takers and institutions that could recover from an isolated problem, those that provide credit and liquidity to the market and those whose potential systemic implications of default would be manageable on the national level. Low systemic importance covers institutions with minor retail deposit market share, those whose bankruptcy would have a limited effect on retail customers and minor potential systemic implications of default.

6.8 So, does size matter?

We have seen that no matter what alternative criterion is suggested, in the final analysis we revert back to size. And even if another criterion can be used to determine the probability of systemic failure, the extent of the failure (in terms of potential losses) is determined by size. Goodhart and Huang (2005) put forward a model of lender of last resort predicting that the central bank would only rescue banks that are above a threshold size. Yes, size does matter in the sense that the failure of a big financial institution is more harmful than the failure of a small one. Other criteria such as interconnectedness, complexity, correlation and conditions/context are either irrelevant or follow on from size. However, the statement "size does matter" needs to be qualified, so that it is not taken to mean that the failure of a big financial institution is not allowed as a rule or that the decision whether or not to bail out a financial institution depends on size only.

Caveats

The first caveat is that the failure of a big financial institution is no doubt harmful but it is not necessarily catastrophic. World financial history shows examples of swift recovery from the failure of financial institutions, individual big ones and a group of small ones. In the Great Depression, more than 5000 U.S. banks failed, but the banking system and the economy recovered eventually, be it because of World War II or for other reasons. Not a shred of evidence indicates that saving these institutions would have made a significant difference, since saving them would have imposed constraints on the ability of the government to allocate funds to productive activities. As a long as there is a minimal coverage by deposit insurance, banks (small or big) should be allowed to fail.

The second caveat is that there is no exact correspondence between size and the incidence of bailout or government-supported acquisitions. Cherry picking is not a function of size. LTCM was a small financial institution compared to Lehman Brothers, yet it was saved while Lehman was allowed to go down. Likewise, Lehman Brothers was twice as big as Bear Stearns, yet it was allowed to go down while Bear was saved by government intervention. The Fed, it seems, used carrots and sticks to facilitate the acquisition of Merrill Lynch by the Bank of America, but the deal to acquire Lehman Brothers by BOA was called off without a blink from the Fed.

Political power

If it is not size, then it could be one of the criteria stipulated by Thomson as the determinants of systemic importance. But we have seen that these factors eventually boil down to size. This leaves political power and connections, which are not independent of size (size yields both market and political power). The rescue of Merrill Lynch and Bear Stearns, but not Lehman Brothers, cannot be explained only in terms of potential systemic effect. A more plausible explanation may be the ability of the financial institution in question to convince the government to be sympathetic. Political connections would be vital for this purpose. Again, this is not to say that there is a one-to-one correspondence between size and political power.

It is not a secret that Goldman Sachs is the most politically connected and powerful financial institution although it is less than half the size of the Bank of America and Citigroup. And it seems that Goldman is politically powerful in more than one way. In a piece that has the provocative title "You're Not Worthy, But Goldman Is", Michael Crokery (2009) reported that Goldman had received large dosages of swine flu vaccines, while some New York City hospitals and clinics were running out of the vaccine. Lewis (2009a) makes the sarcastic remark that Goldman owns the executive branch outright. He writes:

> Every time we hear the phrase 'the United States of Goldman Sachs' we shake our heads in wonder. Every ninth-grader knows that the U.S. government consists of three branches. Goldman owns just one of these outright; the second we [Goldman] simply rent, and the third we have no interest in at all.

So, size is important because it yields political power. It is a necessary but not a sufficient condition to obtain the TBTF or WOBO status. It may be that too politically connected to fail (TPCTF) is a more realistic expression than TBTF. In October 2009 a commentator on community.timeson-line.co.uk wrote, as the U.K. got more and more into trouble with its public finance: "[Gordon] Brown saved banks to save his own skin. It was a mistake that we'll all be paying for many years". Another observer wrote:

> Sometime in the future it will be plain to see that saving banks was actually the wrong thing to do. Banks have gone bust before, so why not this time? I think you'll find the answer was a political consideration not a financial one.

Size does matter

Size does matter as it is conducive to obtaining political power. Sometimes TBTF becomes too interconnected to fail, too complex to fail, and too international to fail, but the problem remains size. Even if a financial institution is highly interconnected its failure will not be that harmful if the amounts involved are small. So, how do we prevent financial institutions from becoming TBTF? This is an issue that will be dealt with in a subsequent chapter.

7
Why Too Big to Fail is Too Outrageous to Accept

7.1 Any argument for TBTF?

It is interesting that those who support and oppose regulation argue against TBTF—that is, against the taxpayers' money-supported bailout of faltering financial institutions. Those advocating regulation say that financial institutions should be regulated in such a way as to avoid having to pay to save a TBTF institution. Those who oppose regulation, including believers in *laissez faire* finance, argue that the TBTF problem is caused by regulation and that if the government steps aside there is always a private-sector solution to the failure of financial institutions, that at the right price those institutions will find a buyer and the problem will be solved. Free marketeers argue that intervention to bail out financial institutions creates moral hazard of monstrous dimensions. Both parties, I think, are right.

There is only one argument for TBTF, the argument of systemic risk and failure. Mishkin (2006) expresses this idea as follows:

> When they [big banks] fail, it can lead to systemic risk in which the whole banking system is threatened. The failure of a large institution not only can cause immediate failures of its counterparties in both banking and the rest of the financial system, but can also lead to a crisis of confidence that may spill over to other banks and financial institutions, leading to a cascade of failures and financial crisis. Given the potential costs to the economy from a large bank failure, governments are very reluctant to let large banking institutions fail.

As we are going to see, those who put forward a doomsday scenario in the event of not saving a big bank typically use the word "cascading", as it makes the scenario sound more frightening.

No support in history or economics

There is no support in history for the proposition that the failure of one institution could bring about havoc on the entire financial system and the economy (they said that about Herstatt but it turned out to be a hoax). The same is true of the failure of a large number of small financial institutions (for example, the 5000 U.S. banks that collapsed in the 1930s and the 150 plus U.S. banks that collapsed in 2009). It is true that the world financial system was shocked by the failure of Lehman Brothers, but the outcome was not as catastrophic as we would have been led to believe, had the decision to save Lehman been taken. Conversely, had the U.S. government chosen to let Merrill Lynch go under, the outcome would have been adverse but manageable.

When a financial institution fails, the resulting losses are typically shared by a large number of investors and creditors who would have been making good returns in previous years. Then some managers who had been accumulating huge personal fortunes lose their jobs and most likely find others. Where small employees lose their jobs, it would be better to spend bailout money on creating new jobs for these people and paying them unemployment benefits. A failed institution will disappear because of serious errors of judgement, so what?

Walter (2004) argues that "while business failure is often exceptionally disruptive for the firm's managers and employees, it is beneficial for the society since it ensures that business resources are not devoted to inefficient enterprises". Some would argue that the failure of a financial institution puts thousands of people on the unemployment roster. But this is a feature of capitalism—called "creative destruction"—which is the idea that it is only by older, less-fit incumbents quitting the scene that newer, more energetic ones can take their place, just as old forests must burn to allow new shoots to take hold.

Kaufman (2001) makes the interesting remark that Adam Smith would be "deeply troubled by recent trends toward consolidation, particularly in the financial sector, and the emergence of 'too-big-to-fail' as an argument for government to weaken the discipline of the market". While Adam Smith believed firmly in *laissez faire* and that economic efficiency would be enhanced when market participants take on the amount of risk they desire while competing for profit, he also believed that firms must be left to bear the consequences of failure. Thousands of companies go bankrupt or slim down every year, making thousands of people redundant. Gup (2004b) points out that during the period 1985–1999 between 37,000 and 67,000 U.S. businesses per year filed for bankruptcy, about 70 per cent of which resulted in liquidation.

The financial sector should not be immune from the consequences of this feature of capitalism.

No valid argument for and plenty against

As far as I am concerned, there is no argument whatsoever for government bailout and TBTF. I also believe that it is a hoax to envisage catastrophic systemic losses resulting from the failure of badly managed financial institutions. Engaging in a TBTF policy is hazardous, as Ben Bernanke makes clear when he says (Gapper, 2009):

> The belief of market participants that a particular firm is considered too big to fail has many undesirable effects. For instance, it reduces market discipline and encourages excessive risk-taking by the firm. It also provides an artificial incentive for firms to grow in order to be perceived as too big to fail. And it creates an unlevel playing field with smaller firms, which may not be regarded as having implicit government support.

Too big to fail is too much to stomach. Let us, therefore, examine the arguments against TBTF, including those stated by Bernanke.

7.2   Argument 1: The difficulty of determining TBTF institutions

As we have seen from the discussion in the previous chapter, there is no objective way of determining which financial institution is worthy of the TBTF status and therefore government bailout, both pre- and post-failure. This creates the kind of environment that encourages lobbying for personal gains. The same environment is conducive to the triumph of institutions that have political power and intimate relations with the government, perhaps because of the exchange of personnel.

7.3   Argument 2: Diversion of resources away from more beneficial uses

As we know from very basic microeconomics, limited government resources have an opportunity cost. The opportunity cost of the money spent to bail out failed financial institutions is using it for other purposes such as the creation of jobs in the productive sectors of the economy. At the end of October 2009, it was announced that one reason for the emergence of the U.S. economy from recession (if we can call one quarter of positive growth a recovery) was the effect of the fiscal stimulus. Since

I am a believer in the potency of fiscal policy, I would argue that if the money assigned to financial institutions had been spent instead on crumbling physical infrastructure, the recovery might have been even stronger. We have learned from the Great Depression and World War II that fiscal stimulus does work. On this issue, Eliot Spitzer (2008) writes:

> In that case, vast sums now being spent on rescue packages might have been available to increase the intellectual capabilities of the next generation, or to support basic research and development that could give us true competitive advantage, or to restructure our bloated health care sector, or to build the type of physical infrastructure we need to be competitive.

In reference to the bailout of Citigroup, Lewis and Einhorn (2009) explain the diversion of resources succinctly by writing:

> Three hundred billion dollars is still a lot of money. It's almost 2 percent of gross domestic product, and about what we spend annually on the departments of Agriculture, Education, Energy, Homeland Security, Housing and Urban Development and Transportation combined.

They also argue that the dollars spent on failed institutions at the top of the financial system should be diverted to the individuals at the bottom. Specifically, they recommend that bailout money should be used to (i) repair the social safety net, and (ii) transform the bailout of the banks into a rescue of the borrowers.

According to the Bank of England, governments and central banks in the U.S. and Europe have committed some $14 trillion to support financial institutions, which is about 25 per cent of world GDP. Because of this kind of spending, and declining tax revenue as a result of the global recession, the public finances of many countries have been wrecked (Ford and Larsen, 2009). Acharya *et al* (2009) argue that the TBTF designation is "incredibly costly because it touches, somewhat paradoxically, a moral hazard in the form of a race to become systemic, and, when a crisis hits, results in wealth transfers from taxpayers to the systemic institution".

But it is not only government resources at stake, as TBTF imperils the health of the economy in other ways. If big or complex financial institutions keep their TBTF status, they will continue to divert lenders' money away from more deserving industries. According to Volz and Wedow (2009), a further aspect of misallocation is that "a bank seeking

TBTF subsidy will dedicate resources to grow beyond its socially optimal size". Penas and Unal (2004) and Kane (2000) provide evidence for this proposition.

7.4   Argument 3: Boosting rent-seeking unproductive activities

Rent seeking implies the extraction of uncompensated value from others without making any contribution to production. Rent-seeking activities yield pecuniary returns but do not produce goods or services. Examples include gaining control of land and other pre-existing natural resources and capturing special monopoly privileges. More specific examples are a farm lobby that seeks tariff protection or an entertainment lobby that seeks expansion of the scope of copyright. Other rent-seeking activities are associated with efforts to cause redistribution of wealth by, for example, shifting the tax burden or government spending allocation.

Rent seeking often takes the form of lobbying for regulation. A related concept is "regulatory capture", which refers to collusion between firms and the government agencies assigned to regulate them, which is seen as enabling extensive rent-seeking behaviour, especially when regulators must rely on the firms for knowledge about the market. The concept of rent seeking has been applied to corruption by bureaucrats who solicit and extract bribes in return for applying their legal but discretionary authority to award legitimate or illegitimate benefits to clients.

The moral hazard of rent seeking can be considerable. If "buying" a favourable regulatory environment is cheaper than building more efficient production, a firm will choose the first option, reaping incomes entirely unrelated to any contribution to total wealth or well-being. This results in a sub-optimal allocation of resources (money spent on lobbyists and counter-lobbyists rather than on research and development, improved business practices, employee training, or additional capital goods) which retards economic growth. Claims that a firm is rent seeking often accompany allegations of government corruption, or the undue influence of special interests. Given the characterization of rent-seeking activities and the related examples, it seems that big financial institutions are at the forefront of these activities. By lobbying for the TBTF status, financial institutions allocate resources to (i) rewarding bureaucrats, (ii) fostering a favourable public impression, and (iii) boosting size and complexity.

Goldman: The king of rent-seeking activities

Whenever the term "rent seeking" is mentioned, the name "Goldman Sachs"—dubbed the "vampire squid of investment banks"—invariably crops up. In an article entitled "Goldman Critics vs. Little Goldmans", Chidem Kurdas (2009) defends Goldman by arguing that (i) investment banking is profitable, and if it does not happen in the U.S. it will happen elsewhere; (ii) Goldman paid back public money that the government insisted it takes when the failure of Lehman Brothers paralysed the markets; and (iii) there is no problem with bonuses as they are like retained earnings. This is actually the first time that I hear that Goldman was forced to take taxpayers' money in what sounds like a gesture of goodwill towards taxpayers (who would have been really disappointed if their beloved Goldman had refused to accept the "gift"). I am not sure how the government could have forced Goldman to take the money, had they said "no". Then, how is it that bonuses are like retained earnings? While retained earnings are used instead of borrowing to finance the firm's operations, bonuses are used to finance the luxury life style of bonus recipients.

In a response to these claims, a commentator argues that Kurdas seems oblivious to the fact that a principal source of Goldman's profit is rent-seeking through intimate connections with top Treasury and Fed officials. Another commentator agrees with the rent-seeking proposition, arguing that there is evidence for the "cosy" relationship with the government: "the Paulson/Goldman Moscow meeting, the exclusive AIG/Treasury/Goldman negotiations in which Goldman had a $20 billion stake, Paulson's phone logs from his Goldman days showing contact communication with Bush and Bernanke, and Goldman front-running trades with special NYSE access". Yes, the U.S. government has a love affair with Goldman.

It is refreshing, therefore, to learn that the SEC decided in April 2010 to charge Goldman with fraud. Goldman was accused of "deceiving clients by selling them mortgage securities designed by a hedge fund [called Abacus] run by John Paulson who made a killing betting on the housing market's collapse" (Zuckerman *et al*, 2010). Let me rephrase that: the clients were sold securities that would benefit them only if the housing market kept on rising, while the hedge fund and Goldman bet on the collapse of the market. While some Goldman sympathizers claim that the bank was hedging its position, I can only wonder why it is that the clients were not advised to hedge their positions too. This is the problem of asymmetric information, which is one reason why financial institutions are regulated to protect customers. As far as I am concerned, what Goldman did was fraud, pure and simple. In London, the FSA announced in late April 2010 that Goldman would be investigated. Thanks God for the global financial crisis that has made Goldman incapable of "getting away with murder".

7.5   Argument 4: TBTF creates significant moral hazard

The term "moral hazard" refers to the danger that relieving a person or a company from the effects of bad economic decisions will cause them to think that future behaviour is risk free, since the bailout will always be there. When the government pours billions of dollars into failed financial institutions deemed too big to fail, it implicitly guarantees these institutions against failure in the future. The tendency to engage in high-risk behaviour is reinforced by the possibility of gains on the upside (reward for bearing risk) while the downside is protected. Moral hazard is one of the most basic concepts in economics. If someone pays you for your accidents, you will be less careful in trying to avoid them. Insurance companies understand this proposition fairly well, and this is why most insurance contracts include customer deductibles and limited coverage. It is not clear at all why policymakers appear to have missed this important lesson, or perhaps they pretend that they are unaware of it.

Moss (2009) points out that by rushing to help financial institutions during the global financial crisis, the government has created the "mother of all moral hazards", implicit rescue guarantees as far as the eye can see. He also argues that "the extension of implicit guarantees to all systemically significant institutions takes moral hazard in the financial system to an entirely new level". Burnside *et al* (2000, 2001a, 2001b) have shown analytically how moral hazard can explain financial crises.

Although Mishkin (2006) believes that TBTF is not as big a problem as it is portrayed, he admits that it boosts the moral hazard problem for big banks. He illustrates the problem as follows:

> The too-big-to-fail policy increases the moral hazard problem for big banks. If a deposit insurance agency like the FDIC were willing to close a bank and pay off depositors only up to the $100,000 insurance limit, large depositors would suffer losses if the bank failed. Thus they would have incentives to monitor the bank's activities closely.... However, once large depositors know that a bank is too big to fail, they have no incentive to monitor the bank... The result of the too-big-to-fail policy is that large banks are likely to take on greater risks, thereby making bank failures more likely.

Only a few central bankers and regulators give the moral hazard problem the importance it deserves. In his comments of 29 October 2009, Mervyn King said that "bailouts created the biggest moral hazard in history" (Conway, 2009). During that same week, John Gieve, a former deputy governor of the Bank of England, warned that the government has created moral hazard in the banking system that could prove dangerous when the economy recovers. In particular, he mentioned the handing over by the British government of billions of pounds to the Royal Bank of Scotland and its agreement to insure the bank against billions of pounds worth of potential losses on loans. He also argued that the safety net under banks could "make the next cycle much worse" when the economy recovers.

The dimensions of moral hazard

Moral hazard has more than one dimension. The creditors of big financial institutions who expect the government to protect their loans have little incentive to monitor the behaviour of these institutions or to select institutions that are prudent in their decisions. On the other hand, realizing that they face reduced monitoring from creditors and knowing that the government will bail them out if they fail, big financial institutions take on excessively risky projects and generally act less responsibly than they would if they had to shoulder the full burden of their behaviour. The result is squandered resources and more of the behaviour that leads to failure. The more extensive the protection the government offers to uninsured creditors, the more massive will be the moral hazard problem it creates.

Moyer and Lamy (1992) suggest another dimension of the moral hazard problem, which has an implication for the structure of the banking industry. The implication is that the TBTF status provides an incentive for big banks to maintain lower capital ratios than small banks. This tendency is reinforced by the Basel II Accord on capital adequacy (see Chapter 9 for a thorough discussion of this issue).

Another dimension of the moral hazard problem has been recognized by Dowd (1999), who argued that the rescue of LTCM in 1998 subjected the Fed to a "moral hazard over which it has no control". He pointed out that the LTCM bailout indicated that the Fed would accept responsibility for the "safety" of U.S. hedge funds, despite the fact that it had no legislative mandate to do so. Moreover, the Fed accepted that responsibility even though it had no regulatory authority over hedge funds and even though the chairman of its board explicitly declared that it should not have any such authority. The Federal Reserve thus maintained the extraordinary position that it should have responsibility for hedge funds but no power over them, which is a pretty good deal for hedge funds. This state of affairs allows large hedge funds to take risks that the Federal Reserve cannot control, yet the Fed picks up the tab if the funds get themselves into difficulties.

7.6   Argument 5: Financial burden on future generations or hyperinflation

To finance bailouts, the government may follow one or a combination of three courses of action: raise taxes, borrow and print money. If the government cannot raise taxes for the time being, it may resort to borrowing money by issuing bonds and selling them to domestic and foreign investors. In the future, interest payments and the repayment of principals have to be financed somehow, and one way to do that is to make future generations pay via higher taxes. But future generations have nothing to do with the malpractices of a minority of the current generation, a situation that is similar to what the employed non-drinkers found themselves in when they had to pay for the drinking of unemployed alcoholics (recall the anecdote in Chapter 1).

If the government finances bailouts by making the central bank print more money, hyperinflation may be the consequence. Hyperinflation is a phenomenon of continuously and rapidly rising prices that results mainly from excessive printing of money. This phenomenon has been experienced, with devastating effects, by a number of countries, the most recent case being that of Zimbabwe. It is wrongly claimed by the proponents of TBTF that failure to bailout a failed big bank may result in the failure of the payment system. While there is no evidence to suggest that something like this could happen, experience shows that hyperinflation does destroy the payment system as it renders the domestic currency incapable of performing the functions of store and measure of value.

7.7   Argument 6: Saving a minority at the expense of the majority

The minority and majority in this argument are financiers and the rest of the society, respectively. We are told that relationships are typically two-sided, where the parties give and take and share the underlying costs and benefits. Not this relationship, though. Financiers have the upper hand, pocketing bonuses and fat salaries when things are going well, but expecting taxpayers to maintain their bonuses and salaries when things go wrong. It is "heads you lose, tails I win" situation in favour of financiers, involving a reverse-Robin Hood wealth transfer from the prudent to the profligate. By referring to a murder in New York City while many bystanders did nothing to rescue the victim,

Taleb and Triana (2008) make parallels with the global financial crisis and the resulting bailouts:

> We have just witnessed a similar phenomenon in the financial markets. A crime has been committed. Yes, we insist, a crime. There is a victim (the helpless retirees, taxpayers funding losses, perhaps even capitalism and free society). There were plenty of bystanders. And there was a robbery (overcompensated bankers who got fat bonuses hiding risks; overpaid quantitative risk managers selling patently bogus methods).

I have a problem with the word "saving" in "saving a minority", because it is not entirely accurate. You save someone who is threatened with death, injury or financial adversity. But "saving" financiers means maintaining their lavish life style and financing the refurbishment of their summer and winter holiday homes by people who might have lost their jobs. Even worse, bailouts may amount to saving criminal behaviour that causes bank failure. Sprague (1986) reveals the results of a 1986 FDIC survey, which concluded that criminal misconduct by insiders was a major contributing factor in 45 per cent of bank failures. The relationship between the financial sector and the rest of society is certainly asymmetric. Why on Earth have we allowed this moral deterioration?

7.8 Argument 7: Rewarding recklessness and hampering market discipline

The doctrine of too big to fail has serious consequences for long-term financial stability. If the financial system is to be stable, individual institutions must be given incentives to make themselves financially strong. Rescuing an institution in difficulties sends out the worst possible signal, as it leads others to think that they, too, will be rescued if they get into trouble. That weakens their incentive to maintain their own financial health and makes them more likely to be in trouble. Bailing out a weak financial institution may help to calm markets in the short run, but it undermines financial stability in the long run. Volz and Wedow (2009) believe that the TBTF problem emerges for the very reason that the expectation of a bailout reduces the incentive to extend adequate market discipline, which enables managers to pursue riskier operations that may ultimately raise the overall risk in the financial system.

Consider, for instance, investment banks. The willingness of the government to help investment banks may be viewed as evidence of their indispensability. But what this willingness really underscores is how badly these institutions have managed their business in recent years. Because investment banks are typically highly leveraged, they must be exceptionally good at managing risk, and they need to insure that people trust them enough to lend them huge sums of money against very little collateral. For this reason, one would expect investment banks to be rigorous about balancing risk against reward and about earning and keeping the trust of customers and creditors. Instead, investment banks have taken on spectacular amounts of risk without acknowledging the scale of their bets to the outside world, or even (it now seems) to shareholders.

By sheltering the lenders of big institutions from market discipline, the government encourages the finance industry to take debt to unsustainable levels. Because of the TBTF doctrine, the lenders' critical role in disciplining the financial system (by refusing to lend to risky institutions) has gone. The doctrine is a direct inducement to large institutions to act irresponsibly. Eliot Spitzer (2008) writes:

> It is time we permitted the market to work: This means true competition with winners and losers; companies that disappear; shareholders and CEOs who can lose as well as win; and government investment in the long-range competitiveness of our nation, not in a failed business model of financial concentration and failed risk management that holds nobody accountable.

LTCM, once more

In his evaluation of the rescue of LTCM, Dowd (1999) argues that "if the Fed wishes to encourage institutions to be strong, it should make an example of those that fail". In that context, LTCM provided the Federal Reserve with an ideal opportunity to make such an example and send out the message that no firm (no matter how big, interconnected or whatever) could expect to be rescued from the consequences of its own mistakes. Other firms would have taken note and strengthened themselves accordingly, and financial markets would have been more stable as a result. "Throwing LTCM to the wolves would have strengthened financial markets, rather than weakened them", Dowd argues. He also points out that in theory, companies in a capitalist economy are free to stand or fall on the results of their own business decisions. If they do fall, investors who chose to buy their shares or bonds will lose out. Risk is supposed to keep everyone focused on making better decisions. Is not this what we call "risk management"?

Dowd argues forcefully against the extension of TBTF protection to hedge funds, pointing out that the worst consequence of the LTCM affair was the damage done to the credibility and, more importantly, the moral authority of Federal Reserve policy makers as they encouraged their counterparts in other countries to proceed with the necessary but difficult and painful process of economic liberalization. James Leach, Chairman of the House Committee on Banking and Financial Services, was absolutely right when he pointed out (Leach, 1998):

> The LTCM saga is fraught with ironies related to moral authority as well as moral hazard. The Federal Reserve's intervention comes at a time when our government has been preaching to foreign governments, particularly Asian ones, that the way to modernize is to let weak institutions fail and to rely on market mechanisms, rather than insider bailouts.

Allan Sloan (1998) put the same argument more colourfully in *Newsweek*:

> For 15 months, as financial markets in country after country collapsed like straw huts in a typhoon, the United States lectured the rest of the world about the evils of crony capitalism—of bailing out rich, connected insiders while letting everyone else suffer. U.S. officials and financiers talked about letting market forces allocate capital for maximum efficiency. Thai peasants, Korean steelworkers and Moscow pensioners may suffer horribly as their local economies and currencies collapse—but we solemnly told them that was a cost they had to pay for the greater good... . Cronyism bad. Capitalism good. Then came the imminent collapse of Long-Term Capital..., the quintessential member of The Club, with rich fat-cat investors and rich hotshot connected managers. Faster than you can say "bailout," crony capitalism U.S. style raised its ugly head... . John Meriwether and the rest of the guys who ran the fund onto the rocks got to keep their jobs.

As long as financial institutions operate under market rules, the overriding principle is that there can be no TBTF and bailout. Whoever picks profits in good times must be prepared to cough out losses in bad times.

7.9 Argument 8: TBTF is a source of poor performance

Moyer and Lamy (1992) believe that TBTF policy can have a negative effect on the efficiency of banks. The results of research conducted on the banking troubles of the 1980s show that large banks under-performed small- and medium-sized banks because of the perceived TBTF protection following the rescue of Continental Illinois in 1984. Boyd and Gertler (1994) found that "the reason why medium-sized banks outperformed large banks is that large banks are less risk-sensitive as a consequence of the TBTF distortion".

Stern and Feldman (2004) argue that the TBTF problem "can lead the firm to operate in a cost-inefficient manner relative to firms subject to competition". Bartel and Harrison (1999) believe that public support for firms appears to explain their inefficiency better than formal ownership by government. Stern and Feldman go as far as arguing that TBTF protection has played a major role in recent crises.

7.10   Argument 9: TBTF creates distortions

It has been found that TBTF protection has two effects: it creates size distortion in the banking industry and it tends to accentuate the risk distortion created by deposit insurance. Some empirical studies have found that economies of scale exhaust at a fairly modest bank size ($200 million in assets), which means that the existence of large banks may be the consequence of a TBTF distortion (Ennis and Malek, 2005). Another study found that in September 1984, after the Comptroller of the Currency testified before Congress that certain banks were TBTF, the equity value of those banks rose significantly relative to the rest of the industry (O'Hara and Shaw, 1990).

Volz and Wedow (2009) examine the potential distortion of prices in the market for certificates of deposit. Their findings show that prices are distorted due to the size effect that arises from the TBTF status and the resulting perception by investors of the likelihood of bailout if required. Specifically they find that a one percentage point increase in size reduces the spread on CDs by about two basis points. They also refer to the stock price distortions arising when a bank becomes large enough to warrant a bailout if necessary. Likewise, Flannery and Sorescu (1996) found that small banks paid higher spreads on subordinated debentures. An explanation for this result can be found in O'Hara and Shaw (1990) who point out that the interest rates a bank pays for its deposits, CDs and non-deposit borrowing reflect the possibility of bankruptcy. TBTF implies the removal of the coverage limit in the deposit insurance scheme, which is effectively a subsidy or wealth effect in favour of TBTF banks. Morgan and Stiroh (2005) found that the naming of 11 banks as too big to fail in 1984 led rating agencies to raise their ratings on new bond issues of TBTF banks relative to those of other, unnamed banks.

Mishkin (2006) presents some examples of TBTF distortions: (i) mergers undertaken by large banks result in an increase in market value, but this is not the case for small banks; (ii) the cost of deposits is lower for larger banks; and (iii) credit ratings are higher for large banks than for small but otherwise similar banks.

7.11 Argument 10: TBTF makes big institutions even bigger

We have seen from the discussion in Chapter 4 that bailout money has made big institutions even bigger and more powerful. One observer notes that "whether it's a government institution or a private institution I have always believed the continual move to consolidate power to be negative", and he wonders: "Haven't we been breaking up monopolies for this reason" and "Didn't the founders divide our government into three branches and seek to limit its power" (Word Press, 2008). Nothing much is said about the dangers of this kind of action to empower a failed system.

The proposition that TBTF has a negative impact on competition in financial markets is advocated, surprisingly, by Alan Greenspan. He is quoted by McKee and Lanman (2009) as arguing that TBTF banks "have an implicit subsidy allowing them to borrow at lower cost because lenders believe the government will always step in to guarantee their obligations". This, he argues, "squeezes out competition and creates a danger to the financial system".

7.12 Argument 11: Boosting the financial sector even further

The too big to fail problem has been central to the degeneration and corruption of the financial system over the past two decades. For one thing, TBTF enhances the ability of financial institutions to impose brain drain on the productive sectors of the economy. And, according to Seidman (2009), "a society that has too much of its energy, smarts and capital flowing... is, by definition, underinvesting in the rest of the economy". We have seen that the financial sector is already far too big for the efficient working of the economy and this causes misallocation of resources. TBTF makes bad things even worse.

7.13   Arguments against for all tastes

An observer has suggested arguments against TBTF that are suitable for all political perspectives (https:llselfevident.org/?p=720). This is what he said:

- For a fiscal conservative, TBTF is bankrupting the nation.
- For a social conservative, TBTF creates oligarchy, which is not a family value.
- For a liberal, no amount of regulation can contain the threat posed by TBTF.
- For a moderate, the *status quo* is a disaster waiting to happen.
- For a populist, there is no need to say anything.

TBTF, as he puts it, is financiers against everybody else. It is a fight that financiers are winning. Therefore (and these are my words) TBTF must go.

8
Dealing with the Menace of TBTF

8.1 Why TBTF should be tossed in the dustbin

In April 2009 the chairperson of the FDIC, Sheila Bair, gave a speech at the Economic Club of New York, in which she suggested that the notion of too big to fail "should be tossed in the dustbin". I could not agree more. To curtail the influence of financiers and the disproportionate size of the financial sector, TBTF must go. To stop the diversion of scarce resources from productive to parasitic activities, TBTF must go. To curtail rent-seeking unproductive activities, TBTF must go. To minimize the incidence of moral hazard, TBTF must go. To reduce the financial burden on future generations imposed by the malpractices of a small subset of the current generation, TBTF must go. To stop the reverse-Robin Hood transfer of wealth from the hard working majority to the minority of financial elites, TBTF must go. To stop rewarding recklessness, TBTF must go. To impose market discipline on financial institutions, TBTF must go. And to avoid other negative consequences of applying the TBTF doctrine, it must go. Too big to fail may be too problematic to address, but it must be addressed. According to Kay (2009b), it is "incompatible with democracy" and "it also destroys the dynamism that is the central achievement of the market economy".

Johnson (2009) describes a bank that is too big to fail as a "financial weapon of mass destruction", arguing that "a weapon of mass destruction cannot be allowed to fall in unsafe hands". As a firm believer in world peace, I would rather see a world that is free of weapons of mass destruction than a world where we just hope that these weapons will not fall in unsafe hands. By the same token, I would rather see a world that is free of TBTF financial institutions.

8.2 The million dollar question

There is therefore an impressive list of reasons why the TBTF doctrine should be tossed in the dustbin, but most people think that the million dollar question is how to do that. I believe that the question is not so tricky as to be priced at one million dollars. The answer is not difficult to find, but the problem is finding the political will to implement desperate measures at desperate times. The ideology that has been prevailing for some three decades makes such desperate measures seem extremely unorthodox, anti-market, socialist, leftist, perhaps even communist. But having experienced the pain inflicted by the global financial crisis, most people are changing their minds to the extent that there has been renewed interest in Keynes, Minsky and, yes, in Marx. It is acceptable for these people to be labelled anti-marketeers, socialist, and lefty by the free marketeers (who have proved to be wrong) as long as measures are taken to overcome the menace of TBTF. Even some regulators are thinking this way as they have been in the line of fire, accused of contributing to the emergence of the global financial crisis for lack of strong regulation and robust supervision.

The outspoken regulator

Take, for example, the (brave) comments made by Mervyn King (the governor of the Bank of England) in October 2009, confirming him as the most outspoken regulator against the orthodoxy of free marketeers (Seagar, 2009). To start with, King recognizes explicitly the fact that "people will pay the cost of the recent financial crisis for generations". Then, he calls for banks to split up so that their retail arms are separated from riskier investment banking operations, thus effectively calling for the return of the Glass-Steagall Act or the implementation of a new version thereof. He also criticizes the banking industry's failure to reform despite "breathtaking levels of taxpayer support".

King told business leaders in Edinburgh on 21 October 2009 that "the current regulatory arrangements are impractical" and that "it was hard to see why support could not be limited to retail, or utility, banking". He also told them that "anyone who proposed guarantees to retail depositors and other creditors, and then suggested that such funding could be used to finance highly risky and speculative activities, would be thought rather unworldly", adding that "this is where we now are". Ironically, King's comments came as several banks, including those that survived only because of government bailouts, were prepared to pay out billions of pounds in bonuses (business as usual, it seems). One important message that comes out of King's comments is that banks should be split up to prevent them from becoming TBTF. He even suggested that if banks were reluctant to split, the financial sector would end up with "ever increasingly detailed regulatory oversight", which would prove costly for the industry.

Unfortunately, the Treasury is less unorthodox than King, rejecting the idea of splitting up banks. Unfortunately also, it is unlikely that the separation of investment and commercial banking will happen under King's watch, according to some observers. And unfortunately, it seems that King's prediction of "increasingly detailed regulatory oversight" may not materialize because financiers are still too powerful to be dictated to (TPTBDT). When in mid-2009 the British Chancellor of the Exchequer (Finance Minister) co-chaired an inquiry with Win Brischoff, the chairman of the failed Lloyds Bank, he declared that it was "important to constrain any new regulations in response to the crisis that might change the City's international competitiveness".

Means justifying ends

So, what can be done to defeat the TBTF doctrine? To start with, forget about the possibility that financial institutions will change their bad habits or indulge in socially responsible self-regulation. All they are interested in is business as usual: a "quick buck" leading to a fat bonus. To put an end to the TBTF doctrine, measures should be taken that are regarded as unorthodox and radical by the prevailing ideology. Orthodox or unorthodox, all necessary means are to be considered and actually employed towards this end.

I have never believed in "means justifying ends", or the so-called principle of consequentialism that an action is judged (in terms of morality and appropriateness) by its consequences (Anscombe, 1958). I have always believed in deontology (deontological moral theories), the doctrine that the appropriateness, or otherwise, of an action forms the character of the action itself. On this occasion, and for a good reason, I will flip flop and argue from a consequential standpoint that a morally appropriate action is the one that produces a good outcome (good for the majority). Getting rid of the weapon of mass destruction called TBTF is certainly a good reason. What is even better is that consequentialism in this case justifies measures that will make the vast majority of people better off and a few people slightly worse off, which could even pass as a (modified) Pareto improvement.

The unorthodox and desperate measures that I am advocating here have been suggested by some politicians, some regulators, some journalists and observers, some economists and the majority of ordinary people writing in blogs to comment on current affairs. To rid the world of the TBTF menace, I would summarize these measures as follows:

1. Preventing financial institutions from growing too big. If that does not work, or if it only works to a certain extent, then measures should be taken to make it expensive for them to grow.
2. Imposing the kind of regulation that reduces the incidence of failure.
3. If a financial institution is on the verge of failing and the situation is desperate, then it should be allowed to fail. Even better, this institution should be assisted to fail by means of financial euthanasia.

The first two measures are preventive. By reducing the incidence of failure, it will not be necessary to invoke the TBTF doctrine. The third measure is meant to establish the credibility of the government as adopting a strict no-bailout policy. This will in turn reduce the incidence of failure, as TBTF institutions become less inclined to take on excessive risk. These points are discussed in the rest of this chapter.

8.3   Fighting the obesity of financial institutions

If a financial institution is TBTF, then it is TBTS (too big to save) and TBTE (too big to exist). Therefore, financial institutions should be prevented from growing excessively big. This is a "no-brainer", as one observer describes the proposition in comments that were made on a website (www.community.timesonline) in response to the October 2009 comments of Mervyn King against TBTF institutions. This is how he put it:

1. As the government seems unable to control them (that is, financial institutions), they will probably get into trouble again.
2. If they get too big and get into trouble, taxpayers will have to bail them out again.
3. We haven't got any money to bail them out again.
4. Therefore, they can't be allowed to get too big.

In particular, I like the idea of relating size to the probability of getting into trouble, which is a valid proposition, because of the complacency resulting from big size and the moral hazard produced by the TBTF status. For some, a big institution cannot, or cannot be allowed to, fail. But the government (taxpayers) may not have the money to fund salvage operations, and if it does why not instead use this money, for example, to build a dam or a highway? Our objective should be to do what it takes to create a financial sector consisting of small to medium size financial institutions, which was the model prevailing prior to the advent of big firms.

Breaking up big financial institutions into smaller entities means that the demise of one would not threaten to bring down the rest. Big institutions can be split vertically, by activities or products, and horizontally by a given activity among several independent entities. This idea boils down to enforcing competition policy in financial services, and to this end legislation should be in place to (i) split up existing financial institutions, and (ii) prevent small ones from getting excessively big.

Radical thinkers?

Splitting up existing oversized financial institutions is what Mervyn King, among others, advocates. Some free marketeers describe as "a new wave of radical thinkers" those intellectuals who advocate the breaking up of large financial institutions. According to Carmassi *et al* (2009), the so-called "radical thinkers" include de Grauwe (2008), Buiter (2009), Kay (2009c), Phelps (2009) and Stiglitz (2009). Strange that a free marketeer like Alan Greenspan is also "radical" because he is now calling for the breaking up of large banks. He is quoted by McKee and Lanman (2009) as saying that "U.S. regulators should consider breaking up large financial institutions considered too big to fail". This is a rather delightful change of heart by Greenspan.

How to break them up

Splitting up existing financial institutions can be done in a number of ways, starting with the re-privatisation of the financial institutions that are owned in whole or in part by the government as a consequence of bailouts. Ideally, big financial institutions should be sold in medium-size pieces, divided regionally or by type of business. Where this proves impractical (for the desire to sell these institutions quickly) they could be sold whole, provide that they will be broken up within a short time. This line of reasoning is consistent with a proposition put forward by Hubbard *et al* (2009) to split a failed financial institution in two: a bad institution that takes on the toxic assets and another without them. The bad part will bring with it lenders who would take losses based on the collapsed value of the assets. The good part could meet remaining obligations and raise new funds. It could then free itself from government administration, as in any corporate exit from bankruptcy.

Anti-monopoly laws can be used to break up big financial institutions that are still owned by the private sector. Johnson (2009) suggests that what is needed is to overhaul anti-monopoly legislation that was put in place more than a hundred years ago to combat industrial monopolies. This legislation, he argues, was not designed to address market power in the financial sector. Then, of course, we can reinstate the Glass-Steagall Act or a modified version thereof. Indeed, President Obama's endorsement of the so-called "Volcker Rule" is in the spirit of restoring some version of the Glass-Steagall Act (Scheer, 2010). A retrospective implementation of the legislation whereby commercial banking is separated from investment banking ensures that existing institutions combining the two functions will be split up and that no merger takes place between a commercial bank and an investment bank. This will have the added advantage of avoiding conflict of interest, which was a reason why the Glass-Steagall Act was instated in the 1930s.

A related measure involves changing the laws governing the operations of bank holding companies and universal banking. It may be necessary to revise the legislation governing the operations of bank holding companies so as to separate commercial banking from other financial services such as insurance, fund management and brokerage. Regulating mergers and acquisitions is also necessary for this purpose. Lanchester (2009) argues that mergers destroy value, as was made vividly evident by the Royal Bank of Scotland, which was once hailed as the king of mergers and acquisitions (as we have seen, a major reason for the destruction of the RBS was its acquisition of ABN Amro, which had invested heavily in toxic assets). A merger or acquisition should not violate the Glass-Steagall Act, anti-monopoly laws and any law preventing the marriage of commercial banking and other financial services. A proposed merger or acquisition must be approved by regulators only if it does not violate these laws and only after a demonstration by the applicant that the merger/acquisition will produce synergy gains. Regulators must put restrictions on mergers and acquisitions if the resulting product is an institution that can claim to be TBTF and if they lead to more concentration and more market power for some institutions.

Advantages of small size

Reducing the size of financial institutions has other advantages, because big financial institutions are problematical, as we saw in Chapter 4. It may, however, be useful to recap on some of the drawbacks of big institutions and the positive aspects of small size. Small institutions are easier to manage, and they are less likely to fail. Even when they do, disposing of them is easy. Small institutions have less tendency to bear risk and less market and political power. A market structure where the players are numerous small institutions is more conducive to competition. Small financial institutions have the advantages of paying attention to local needs, flexibility and transparency. Big financial institutions are less flexible, harder to manage, involve more self-dealing by employees and have greater agency problems. They cannot effectively adapt to the economic needs of local communities. Oversized institutions disproportionately influence public policy, as evidenced by the fact that they draw much of their power from being too big to fail. The dominance of do-it-all big institutions is the antithesis of specialization and the law of comparative advantage. We saw in Chapter 4 how two Swiss banks got into trouble by attempting to branch out of their areas of expertise. Economies of scale and scope often turn out to be diseconomies of scale and scope.

In introductory microeconomics we are told that average costs decline with size because of (i) savings due to mass production, (ii) specialization of factors of production (labour and machinery), and (iii) experience. But it is unlikely that specialization and experience advantage would be realized if the corporate objective is to chase economies of scope. Furthermore, diseconomies of scale may result because of bureaucracy-driven inefficiency, the problem of motivating a large work force, and greater barriers to innovation and entrepreneurial activity. There is also an increased principal agent problem, arising from misalignment of the objectives of shareholders (owners) and those of the management. Then, there is the argument that innovation and radically new business comes, not from large established and dominant companies but rather from new companies (for example, Microsoft and Google). Kay (2009b) justifies the proposition that innovation does not come from existing large firms to their "bureaucratic culture".

Separate and make them smaller

Carmassi *et al* (2009) argue that legally separating commercial and investment banking activities or prohibiting banks from undertaking particular activities would not be necessary, which is advantageous considering the enormous hurdles involved in implementing such a separation for large cross-border banking groups. This ideology-driven view overlooks the fact that desperate measures are needed in desperate times. This may seem like a crude and arbitrary step, but it is the best way to limit the power of individual institutions in a sector that is essential to the economy as a whole.

Some proponents of financial deregulation argue against fighting the obesity of financial institutions. For example, Matthew Rognline (2009) writes:

> I'm skeptical of proposals that we eliminate systemic risk (and dampen moral hazard) by preventing firms from becoming "too big to fail." First of all, I agree with Paul Krugman when he notes that there isn't some convenient size beneath which banks don't pose a threat to the system. I'm a big advocate of much strengthened financial regulation. One argument I don't buy, however, is that we should try to shrink financial institutions down to the point where nobody is too big to fail. Basically, it's just not possible.

Rognline further argues that what he calls "shrink the banks philosophy" rests on some shaky assumptions about the nature of financial crises: (i) it is always the failure of a big financial institution that marks the point at which the system starts to fall apart; and (ii) the distribution of risk among many small financial institutions demands less government intervention to prevent crises. He reaches the conclusion that replacing one large institution with 20 small ones does very little if the 20 institutions fail in exactly the same way.

Rognline seems to be missing the point. It is not about whether the crisis starts with the failure of a large or small financial institution. What matters is whether or not an institution is big enough to claim the TBTF status. I agree with the proposition put forward by Rognline that the failure of one big institution and a number of small institutions may be equivalent (at least in terms of the loss size), but there is a big difference with respect to the issue under consideration here. A big financial institution can claim the TBTF status whereas any of 20 small ones cannot do that. If, for example, Bank of America rather than Lehman Brothers had filed for bankruptcy in 2008, would this have prevented AIG from claiming TBTF protection? The bottom line is that no financial institution should be in a position to claim the TBTF status.

Stern and Feldman (2009) distinguishes between "static" and "dynamic" challenges to the "make-them-smaller" reform. The static challenge involves the determination of criteria to identify institutions that need to be made smaller. The argument here is that size may not be indicative of systemic importance. This is an issue that we discussed in Chapter 6 and concluded that other criteria of systemic importance boil down to size. The dynamic challenge pertains to the ability of regulators to keep institutions below the size threshold over time. The argument is that it is not easy to prevent institutions from growing big following the initial breakup. It is also not difficult if we recall the cancerous growth of the RBS, for example. Most of the growth in the financial sector happens through mergers or leveraged acquisitions. By regulating mergers and acquisitions, growth can be controlled. Stern and Feldman (2009) acknowledge the advantages of the shrinking-financial-institutions policy: (i) size can be easily measured, (ii) implementation of this policy is straightforward, and (iii) the ease of regulating small institutions. In the spirit of the policy, they advocate the following measures: (i) imposing special deposit insurance assessments for TBTF banks to allow for spillover-related costs, (ii) retaining the national deposit cap on bank mergers, and (iii) modifying the merger review process for large banks to provide better focus on the reduction of systematic risk.

On the other hand, Johnson (2009) defends the idea of small institutions. He writes:

> The better policy is to return to an era of vibrant competition among multiple, smaller entities—none so essential to the entire structure that it is indispensable. The concentration of power—political as well as economic—that resided in these few institutions has made it impossible so far for this crisis to be used as an evolutionary step in confronting the true economic issues before us. But imagine if instead of merging more and more banks together, we had broken them apart and forced them to compete in a genuine manner. Or, alternatively, imagine if we had never placed ourselves in a position in which so many institutions were too big to fail. The bailouts might have been unnecessary.

In response to Johnson, Kevin Drum (2009) argues that the size of individual financial institutions is not the problem, but rather it is the size and interconnectedness of the financial sector as a whole. He also argues that the lobbying power of financial institutions is a product of the profitability and large size of the financial sector. To reduce the lobbying power of the financial sector as a whole, we must reduce the size and profitability of the whole industry. In a response to Drum, a commentator argues that "big banks are a concern over and above the big banking industry". The *Wall Street Watch Report* suggests that "there are minimum scale effects to play in that [TBTF] game where you can buy insurance from politicians to use the taxpayers' revenue power to truncate their losses" (http://motherjones.com/kevin-drum).

Senator Bernard Sanders, the Vermont independent, has suggested that the Treasury Department should break up all financial institutions whose failure could cause a major disruption to the financial system (https://self-evident.org/?p=720). Based on the notion that "if an institution is too big to fail, it is too big to exist", Mr Sanders proposed the enactment of the "Too big to Fail, Too Big to Exist Act", which directs the Treasury Secretary to compile a list of financial institutions that are TBTF with the objective of breaking them up one year after the legislation has been signed into law.

Some would argue that breaking up financial institutions will produce "efficiency costs". In other words it would be bad to lose financial supermarkets and revert back to the financial equivalent of corner shops. Notwithstanding the possibility that the proclaimed efficiency advantages may in fact be inefficiency costs, sensible people would rather do their financial shopping in several corner shops as opposed to a supermarket if they are required (as taxpayers) to pay the bonuses of the executives of failed financial supermarkets. I cannot see anything wrong in doing my banking, insurance, fund management and brokerage with different institutions. We tell finance students that diversification reduces risk (the do-not-put-all-your-eggs-in-one-basket "doctrine"). Yet some of the people who believe in these principles and preach them advocate universal banking because it is convenient to do financial shopping in one place.

Naturally, bankers would argue that "big is not only beautiful but also essential for a modern economy". In November 2009, Josef Ackermann, the CEO of Deutsche Bank, declared: "the idea that we could run modern economies with mid-sized savings banks is totally misguided" (Ford and Larsen, 2009). Not many would buy this argument, not even corporate customers. The presence of a large number of small banks allows customers to pick and choose until they converge on the best deal. After all, it is typically the case that commercial and investment banking operations (such as lending and securities underwriting) involve syndicates of banks to spread risk. This is why we have syndicated loans and new issues lead managers, co-managers and underwriters. The fact of the matter is that bankers (like Mr Ackermann) have lucrative personal incentives to pursue size for its own sake. But then why is that a regulator like Ben Bernanke declares in front of an Independent Community Bankers of America Conference (in March 2010) that "big firms are still needed to keep the global economy humming?" (Cooke, 2010). Old habits (and beliefs) die hard, I suppose. This kind of attitude constitutes an appeasement of financiers who are trying hard to preserve the *status quo*.

Obama versus the fat cats

It is refreshing to see the brave move by President Obama to curb the tendency of financial institutions to grow bigger and assume excessive risk. On 21 January 2010, Mr Obama put forward a proposal to "limit the growth and risk-taking by financial institutions". The plan would prohibit banks from running proprietary trading operations—that is, gambling own money as opposed to that of customers—or investing in hedge funds, and participating in private equity funds. This move would particularly affect Goldman Sachs and JP Morgan, both of which have proprietary trading desks and private equity units. They also have the status of bank holding companies, which means that they can borrow from the Federal Reserve and accept retail deposits.

In his statement, Mr Obama said: "Never again will the American taxpayer be held hostage by banks that are too big to fail". Some observers interpreted the plan to mean that some of the largest U.S. banks will be broken up to prevent them from growing big. Surprisingly, the British Conservative Party was welcoming of the Obama move. The then Shadow Chancellor (now Chancellor), George Osborne, said: "this is a welcome move by President Obama that accords very much with our thinking". The deputy leader of the Liberal Democrats, Vince Cable, called on the (British) government to "get on with breaking up the banks", arguing that "Britain is much more dependent on banks than America is and we are therefore much more vulnerable to banking crashes". This move will be confronted by more rent-seeking unproductive activities so that banks can maintain their privileges. But Obama was brave enough to challenge the fat cats. He said: "If these guys [financiers] want a fight, it is a fight I am willing to have". In one of his weekly radio addresses in April 2010, Obama acknowledged the fact that "special interests are waging relentless campaign to thwart even basic, common-sense changes" (www.azfamily.com/news/national/91199914.html). Unfortunately, however, the U.S. financial reform legislation of July 2010 (the Dodd-Frank Act) does not go far enough to tackle the problems of size and propriety trading.

Make it expensive to grow

If, for some reason, it is not possible to curb big size, regulators can make it expensive for financial institutions to grow big. We use taxes to regulate externalities, so why not do that to regulate this kind of externality? Taxation in this case could be either an actual payment or in terms of capital requirements—that is, making the regulatory capital ratio a function of size. *The Economist* (2009m) suggests that breaking up financial institutions can be problematical, suggesting the alternative of "minimum capital ratios rising as they [financial institutions] get bigger or embrace more risk".

8.4   Appropriate and effective regulation

In addition to the regulatory measures implicit in the preceding discussion of how to combat size, regulation should cover not only capital but also leverage, liquidity, derivatives trading, executive pay, and taxation.

To start with, we should forget about Basel II, as the global financial crisis has demonstrated that the Accord is weak and inadequate. It has many loopholes and, contrary to what is sometimes claimed, an early implementation would not have prevented the global financial crisis or reduced its severity (Moosa, 2010). We should not choose to introduce cosmetic changes to Basel II, which is what the Basel Committee tries to do (see Chapter 9). This is because "successive failures of regulators at large cost over the last three decades made it clear that fine tuning the system is not likely to work" (Boone and Johnson, 2010).

Deregulation as a cause of the global financial crisis

Free marketeers tend to rule out financial deregulation as a cause of the global financial crisis, putting most of the blame on monetary policy. For example, Taylor (2009) argues that the financial crisis was caused, prolonged and worsened dramatically one year after it began by specific government actions and interventions (specifically referring to monetary policy). In a study of the causes of the global financial crisis, Carmassi *et al* (2009) suggests that lax monetary policy is to blame and that many "alleged" causes are simply symptoms of these policy errors. They put the blame on the abundance of liquidity in world capital markets, fed by large payment imbalances, notably a large and persistent current account deficit in the U.S. financed by ample flows of capital from emerging and oil-exporting countries. These "global" imbalances, they claim, fostered an unsustainable explosion of financial assets and liabilities. They conclude that the recommended corrective action is remarkably simple: "there is no need for intrusive regulatory measures constraining non-bank intermediaries and innovative financial instruments".

While I agree with the proposition that lax monetary policy played a big role in igniting the global financial crisis, over-emphasizing this role is nothing short of travesty. To allow non-bank financial institutions to do what they want while concentrating on commercial banks is a step backwards that should not be envisaged in view of the damage inflicted on all of us by investment banks and hedge funds. Moss (2009) argues that "by focusing attention almost exclusively on government error, it gives the impression that government can't solve any problems". Moss also points out that the global financial crisis is "the product of a mistaken regulatory philosophy" and that "in too many cases, regulators chose not to use tools they already had, or they neglected to request new tools to meet the challenges of an evolving financial system". Posner (2009) attributes the meltdown to market failure, arguing that "the movement to deregulate the financial industry went too far by exaggerating the resilience—the self-healing power—of laissez-faire capitalism". Posner also emphasizes the need for a "more active and intelligent government to keep our capitalist economy from running off the rail". Wyplosz (2009) rules out any role for greed and financial innovation and puts the blame totally on the lack of regulation. While he is right in putting the blame on lack of regulation, he is wrong in ruling out the role of financial innovation and greed.

Stern (2009b) puts the blame on improper regulation, arguing that "the risk-taking of large, complex financial institutions is not constrained effectively by supervision and regulation nor by the market place". He further writes:

> If this situation goes uncorrected, the result will almost surely be inefficient marshalling and allocation of financial resources, serious episodes of financial stability and lower standards of living than otherwise. Certainly, we should seek to improve and strengthen supervision and regulation where we can.

Carmassi *et al* (2009) also (and correctly) attribute the global financial crisis to the credit boom, leverage and financial innovation, including the explosion of securitization and derivatives, as well as the "originate to distribute" model of banking. This statement is inconsistent with their call to leave "innovative financial instruments" alone, a call that does injustice to the victims of collateralized debt obligations and credit default swaps. The key point is that if innovation was instrumental in allowing the growth of leverage, then regulation is needed, but this is not what they (that is, Carmassi *et al*) call for. Instead, they offer several policy changes intended to reduce the prevalence of bank bailouts by affecting the root cause they identify as motivating bailouts in the first place, which is the likelihood of spillover effects.

Among other changes, they recommend that policymakers use stress testing and contingency planning to identify the likely effects of a major bank's failure on the economy, as a means of reducing the uncertainty of spillovers. Other recommendations include introducing policy that would provide liquidity more rapidly to creditors when failure occurs, closing faltering banks before they can impose larger losses on creditors, requiring deposit coinsurance, and altering existing payment systems to limit the amount that banks owe each other through the system. Some of these points are fine, but stress testing once more? Stress testing is a faulty procedure that instils complacency. Bailing out the creditors of a failed institution rather than the institution itself is still a taxpayer-funded bailout that should not be allowed.

Free banking as an option

One option suggested for limiting the moral hazard problem created by TBTF protection is that of free banking. Under a free banking system, banks are unregulated, and there is no central bank in charge of issuing currency. Proponents of free banking believe that in a free banking system, banks are highly stable and may be less prone to runs that can bring about their failure (see, for example, Dowd, 1993, 1996a, 1996b; Glasner, 1989; Horwitz, 1992; Rockoff, 1975; Sechrest, 1993; Hayek, 1976; Friedman, 1960).

Free banking enthusiasts suggest that the relatively unregulated banking industries of Scotland, Sweden and Switzerland (before the advent of central banks) provide some historical support for their position. Carmassi *et al* (2009) argue that if banks, in the context of such a system, are less prone to failure than they are in the current system, it may be worth investigating free banking as a means of limiting the costs of TBTF protection. While there are some merits in the arguments for free banking, such as the market discipline argument, contemporary bankers typically demand the kind of deregulation that would take them as close as possible to free banking and yet seek TBTF protection when they are in trouble. This is simply double dipping. The fact of the matter is that banks are too important to be left to bankers (or banksters, as Lanchester (2009) calls them) and that proper regulation, rather than the dismantling of regulation altogether, is more conducive to financial stability.

Specific regulatory measures

I will not go into the details of the kind of regulation to be imposed on financial institutions. What I can say is that regulation should be appropriate, effective, tough and dependent on the degree of systemic importance (size). The rationale for differential regulation is discussed by

Thomson (2009) who justifies it in terms of economic efficiency and equity. For instance, economic efficiency dictates that regulation increases to the point where the cost of the last increment thereof is equal to the benefit of imposing regulation. In this respect, Thomson argues, "it is likely that the cost of complying with additional regulations is inversely related to an institution's size and complexity", hence "as institutions become larger and more complex, increased regulation and more intensive supervision may be consistent with economic efficiency". There are equally compelling arguments for progressively intensive or intrusive regulatory treatments on the grounds of equity as we move up the systemic category ladder. One such argument is that of the "level playing field": to the extent that systemic importance confers competitive advantages on an institution, equity concerns would dictate a system of gradual regulatory measures to remove (or at least minimize) the advantages of being (or becoming) systemically important.

Take, for example, the ingredients of regulatory reform suggested by Boone and Johnson (2010). These "simple and harsh" measures include the following:

1. Capital requirements need to be raised to about 15–25 per cent of assets.
2. Simple rules need to be in place to restrict leverage.
3. Complex derivatives involving hard-to-measure risk need to have very high capital requirements behind them.
4. All financial institutions have to be small enough so that they can fail without causing major damage to the economy.
5. A sensible tax system is needed that creates a punitive disincentive to size.

In a comment on the piece by Boone and Johnson, two more measures are suggested:

1. Full disclosure of an institution's derivative exposure, both in terms of profit and loss and in terms of counterparties' credit ratings.
2. Regulators should have the authority to impose regulatory measures on financial institutions whose credit standards fall below the regulator's safety and soundness standards.

Regulatory proposals

In response to the global financial crisis, regulatory changes have been proposed by economists, politicians, journalists and business leaders.

Even anti-regulation and pro-deregulations gurus, such as Alan Greenspan, call for regulatory changes. Greenspan (2009) suggests that banks should have what he calls a "stronger capital cushion", and that regulatory capital requirements should be a function of size. His successor as the Fed Chairman, Ben Bernanke (2008), proposes the establishment of resolution procedures for closing troubled financial institutions in the shadow banking system. Joseph Stiglitz (2008) is more worried about leverage, and justifiably so. He proposes to restrict the leverage that financial institutions can assume. Furthermore, Stiglitz (2009) recommends that executive compensation be more related to long-term performance and calls for reinstating the Glass-Steagall Act. Simon Johnson recommends the breaking up of TBTF institutions (Randall, 2009). Warren Buffett is more concerned with mortgages, suggesting a minimum down payment of at least 10 per cent and income verification (Reuters, 2009). Eric Dinallo (2009) wants to ensure that financial institutions have the necessary capital to support their financial commitments, and he calls for the regulation of credit derivatives by trading them on well-capitalized exchanges to limit counterparty risk. Raghuram Rajan (2009) wants financial institutions to maintain sufficient "contingent capital", which means that they should pay insurance premiums to the government during boom periods in exchange for payments during downturns. Other suggestions include the establishment of an early-warning system to detect systemic risk, imposing "haircuts" on bondholders and counterparties prior to using taxpayers' money in bailouts, and the nationalization of insolvent banks.

Stern (2009a) proposes the use of what he calls "systemic focused supervision", which is put forward as a preventive measure to circumvent the TBTF problem. It is designed to reduce spillovers, and consists of three pillars: (i) early identification, (ii) enhanced prompt corrective action, and (iii) stability-related communication. Early identification is a process to identify material exposures among large financial institutions and between these institutions and capital markets. Enhanced prompt corrective action requires supervisors to take specified actions against a bank as its capital falls below specific triggers. The third pillar of communication requires regulators to convey information to creditors about efforts pertaining to the first two pillars. The problem I see here is in Pillar 2 that is concerned with capital only. What about liquidity, the effects of which were pronounced during the global financial crisis?

Regulating leverage, liquidity and financial innovation

Tough regulatory measures should cover not only capital requirements but also leverage and liquidity. High leverage (debt to equity or assets to equity) indicates lower capacity to absorb losses. There are already some encouraging signs from Basel that the Basel II Accord is being revised by introducing provisions to deal with leverage and liquidity. Financial "innovation" should be regulated because many of the financial instruments that are allegedly used to avoid risk are merely forms of gambling.

Certain financial innovation may have helped financial institutions circumvent regulation. For example, off-balance sheet financing affects the capital cushion reported by institutions. Even some free marketeers admit that "in financial markets there is a constant game whereby banks and other agents innovate to circumvent regulation and boost returns by taking greater risks" (Carmassi *et al*, 2009). It would be a good idea to restrict the trading of derivatives to organized exchanges as opposed to over-the-counter markets. Opaque financial products should be outlawed (no more options on options on futures on swaps). Joseph Stiglitz is quoted by *The Economist* (2009n) as saying that the use of derivatives by the world's largest banks should be outlawed. Perhaps it is a good idea to create a law enforcement agency that is the financial equivalent of the DEA in the U.S.

In May 2009, the Obama administration sought new authority over derivatives, asking Congress to move quickly on legislation that would allow oversight of many kinds of exotic derivatives, including credit default swaps. U.S. Treasury Secretary, Timothy Geithner, announced that "the measure should require swaps and other types of derivatives to be traded on exchanges... and backed by capital reserves". The idea is simple: just like banks are required to hold capital in case loss events materialize, issuers of derivatives should set aside capital just in case they are called upon to pay. Recall that AIG did not have the funds necessary to cover defaults that required payment to the holders of CDSs. A measure like this would make it more expensive for issuers to participate in the derivatives market, but it is a price worth paying because the measure would force derivatives out in the open, reducing the role of shadow banking systems (Labaton and Calmes, 2009).

In April 2010 a new draft legislation on financial regulatory reform was announced, requiring real-time reporting of derivatives trades to both regulators and the public (Cameron, 2010). The objective of this kind of legislation is to repeal some provisions of the Commodity Futures Modernization Act, which was adopted in December 2000 to deregulate the trading of derivatives. Ironically, the Act was endorsed at the time by the then Treasury Secretary, Lawrence Summers. When the Chairman of the Commodity Futures Trading Commission, Brooksley Born, proposed to bring new derivatives under regulation, as some older types of derivatives, it was rejected by Summers who told Congress that "the parties to these kinds of contract are largely sophisticated financial institutions that would appear to be eminently capable of protecting themselves from fraud and counterparty insolvencies". Yes, that is the same Larry Summers who is now President Obama's economic advisor and who sounds rather hawkish when it comes to enhancing regulation.

Regulating executive pay

As far as executive pay is concerned, Johnson (2009) suggests that "caps on executive compensation, while redolent of populism, might help restore the political balance of power and deter the emergence of a new oligarchy". One advantage of this measure is to curtail the power of the financial sector to inflict brain drain on the rest of the economy. As Johnson puts it, "Wall Street's main attraction—to the people who work there and to the government officials who were only too happy to bask in its reflected glory—has been the astounding amount of money that could be made". This is one way to deprive the financial sector of its undeserved status as the jewel in the crown of the economy.

Some economists object to the intervention of governments in the decisions of private firms in matters of executive compensation (for example, Wyplosz, 2009). However, Wyplosz points out that "macro-prudential regulation will push banks to develop incentive packages that are more encouraging of long-term behaviour". Then what about giving shareholders a say in what executives pay themselves? I am sure that shareholders would not mind receiving dividends as opposed to exec-utives receiving bonuses. Some would argue that outright pay caps are clumsy, especially in the long run, and that they are too easily thwarted. And some argue that pay caps would deprive financial institutions of talent (the alleged brain drain argument). I would say that what the finance industry needs is honesty, while talent should be left for NASA. I must emphasize, once more, that "honest but dumb" will not suffice. What I mean is that the basic finance needed to support real economic activity can do without people who are good at solving partial differential equations. Advising a client on how to cover exposure to foreign exchange risk is not as mentally demanding as the calculations required to make sure that a space shuttle will not burst in flames upon re-entry into the Earth's atmosphere. Using complex mathematics to design betting devices (derivatives) is simply an extravaganza with potentially fatal consequences.

As an alternative to pay caps, the FDIC has published (as a public circulation paper) a proposal to curb excessive risk within remuneration packages. The paper includes a broad set of questions designed to solicit information on the types of structures that should be encouraged, and on whether and how employee compensation should be factored into risk-based pricing systems. In defence of the proposal, the FDIC chairperson, Sheila Bair, cited a "broad consensus of academic studies", arguing that "improperly designed compensation structures can misalign incentives and induce risk-taking". She also argued that "the recent crisis has shown that compensation practices that encourage excessive risk can create significant losses in the financial system and deposit insurance fund". Bair made it explicit that the proposal was targeting the formulation of compensation structures rather than just capping the end-product of pay levels (McElroy, 2010).

Penny Cagan, managing director of credit and operational risk at Algorithmics, believes that the FDIC's proposal is better than what she calls "kneejerk reactions that have been coming from governments". In particular, she objects to the imposition of heavy taxes on bonuses that will result in "an increase in base compensation, which could remove pay consideration from the risk and reward equation altogether and make the financial sector less competitive" (Benyon, 2010). Here we go again: any measure that makes the executives of financial institutions less well-off hurts the competitiveness of the financial sector (I am not sure how that happens). The U.S. Comptroller of the Currency, John Dougan, agued against what he called the "premature release of the document by the FDIC".

Taxing financial institutions

In a speech to the G20 finance ministers in St Andrews (Scotland) on 8 November 2009, Gordon Brown defended the idea of imposing a tax on financial transactions, a contemporary version of the Tobin tax. Part of the proceeds, he suggested, could be diverted to a fund run by the IMF to support bank bailout in the future, or diverted to assist growth in developing countries, while part of the tax revenue could be used to help the budget deficit. That was a big "flip-flop" by a politician who, as the Chancellor of the Exchequer, described the idea of financial tax as "having big problems" and "very substantial drawbacks" (*The Economist*, 2009a). Lord Turner, the head of the FSA, has been arguing on similar lines and for that he was criticized by Boris Johnson, mayor of London, who described Turner as "crackers" for suggesting taxing the City. Gordon Brown, too, showed no enthusiasm for the idea when Turner suggested it in August 2009. But, as Turner and others have repeatedly stressed, the only condition for introducing a financial transaction tax is that everyone does it, so there would be no loss of competitiveness for anyone. This again was stressed by Brown: "Britain would move only if the rest of the world moved too", he said. However, an international agreement on financial tax is easier to contemplate than to be reached.

The idea of a financial transactions tax has been attacked on the grounds that it is impractical and that it will damage the financial system's liquidity. However, if financial transactions are conducted mainly on organized exchanges, a transactions tax would be simple and easy to administer. Yet another objection is that a financial transactions tax will reduce the volume of transactions, and therefore make business inefficient. In fact, it is the opposite that is true: the size of the financial sector has exploded, which means that it is efficient to reduce it. Hutton (2009) makes the cynical remark that "it is efficient for individual bankers, who have the chance to make fortunes—but inefficient for the rest of us". Commenting on the possibility of imposing a financial transactions tax, Hutton says that "it can't be ruled out" and that "I never thought to live to see the day".

A special kind of tax, called "financial crisis responsibility fee", has been suggested by President Obama who declared in January 2010 that he wanted "to recover every single dime the American people are owed for bailing out the economy" (Calmes, 2010). The idea behind this tax is to recover about $117 billion of bailout losses. This tax would apply to banks, thrifts and insurance companies with more than $50 billion in assets, starting after 30 June 2010. By exempting small banks from the tax, the proposal divided the industry lobby and left less popular banks on their own. Mr Obama's proposal has been endorsed by Germany and the U.K. (Saltmarsh, 2010). About the same time, a group of House democrats called for a 50 per cent tax on bonuses exceeding $50,000 at banks that took bailout money. However, the administration has opposed taxing bonuses in the past, arguing that shareholders should determine corporate pay policy. Mr Obama made the remark that his tax could have the same effect by forcing banks to reduce bonuses.

Naturally, financiers oppose the idea of special taxes on financial institutions. Bob Kelly, Chairman and CEO of The Bank of New York Mellon, said the tax would be bad policy for the country on an international front by putting U.S. banks at a disadvantage in regions without a similar fee. Additionally, he hinted that tax could force banks to cut staff in order to avoid passing on fees. "I always worry about the unintended consequences of really material actions, and the things that may result from that", he said. The tax would also affect banks' aggressiveness in pursuing mergers and acquisitions. "There are a lot of things that need to be thought through here that are not good for the industry or the country", Kelly said (*Wall Street Letter*, 2010). This is the language of fear all over again. I would imagine that reducing banks' aggressiveness in pursuing mergers and acquisitions would be good, but I am not sure how the tax would do it. Wall Street opposed the idea, using the twisted logic that it is more appropriate for the American people, not financial institutions, to bear the cost of the bailout (how convenient!). This twisted logic is used by executives as they give themselves big bonuses, which is why outraged observers want to be even harsher on these executives. One observer suggests that "if a bailout is required, the present assets and compensation over the prior five years of the top X percent of earners at the bailed out institutions must be forfeited first to pay for the bailout" (*The Baseline Scenario*, 2010).

Towards the end of April 2010, the IMF came up with a proposal to impose fees and taxes on financial institutions. In a document entitled *A Fair and Substantial Contribution by the Financial Sector*, the IMF suggests two kinds of taxes. One is called a "financial stability contribution", which is a fee that financial institutions would pay in a fund to help weak financial institutions (or payments could go straight to general government revenue). The other is called a "financial activities tax", which would be imposed on profits and pay. The IMF proposal was applauded by Alistair Darling, the former British Finance Minister, who declared that "the recognition that banks should make a contribution to the society in which they operate is right" (Reuters UK, 2010). It is refreshing to realize that even the IMF is no longer as enthusiastic about *laissez faire* finance as it has always been (probably due to pressure from member governments).

There is a problem with a particular aspect of tax proposals, that of using the proceeds to bail out failed financial institutions in the future. On the surface, this sounds good: make them pay for their failure rather than put the burden on taxpayers. However, such a measure will not kill moral hazard (and the TBTF problem). It may even boil down to a transfer of funds from well-managed financial institutions to recklessly-managed ones. I am more in favour of sending the proceeds straight to general government revenue and/or a fund used for development assistance.

The reform and consumer protection act

Some of the talked about measures of regulation are embodied in the Wall Street Reform and Consumer Protection Act crafted by the U.S.

House Financial Services Committee in December 2009. The Act includes major provisions dealing with consumer protection, financial stability, executive compensation, derivatives, predatory lending, credit rating agencies, hedge funds, and insurance. The following are some of these provisions:

- The creation of the Consumer Financial Protection Agency (CFPA) to be in charge of protecting ordinary people from "abusive financial products and services". A related provision requires the strengthening of the SEC to enhance its ability to protect investors and regulate financial markets.
- The creation of an inter-agency oversight council to identify and regulate financial institutions that are so large, interconnected or risky that their collapse would put the entire financial system at risk.
- Giving shareholders a "say on pay", an advisory vote on pay practices including executive compensation and "golden parachutes". The Act also enables regulators to ban inappropriate or imprudently risky compensation practices.
- Regulating OTC derivatives.
- Regulating mortgages, predatory lending, credit rating agencies, hedge funds, and the insurance industry.

On 15 March, 2010 the Democrat chairman of the Senate Banking Committee, Chris Dodd, unveiled a new banking regulation bill that would give the Fed the power to write new regulations for banks including those with assets of more than $10 billion, as well as for all mortgage-related businesses and large non-bank financial firms, such as insurance companies. Naturally, the anti-regulation lobby resists any such move. The plan to reinforce the powers of the Federal Reserve for a complete regulatory oversight across the entire U.S. economy has been criticized as heralding "the beginning of a new form of government in the United States, an ultra-powerful banking dictatorship controlled by a small gaggle of shadowy and corrupt elitists". It is even argued that this measure "goes a step further than the centrally planned economies of the Soviet Union or Communist China, in that the Federal Reserve is not even accountable to the U.S. government" (Watson and Watson, 2009). Do you see the language of fear here? You mention the word "regulation" and you get the word "communist" in return. If accountability of the Fed is the problem, the solution is simple: nationalize it. There is nothing communist about the government running the central bank.

In July 2010 the Dodd-Frank Act was passed to "promote the financial stability of the United States by improving accountability and
transparency in the financial system, to end 'too big to fail', to protect American taxpayers by ending bailouts, to protect consumers from
abusive financial services practices, and for other purposes". Thanks
mainly to effective lobbying by bankers, the Act is a watered down
version of the original proposals.

8.5 Allowing failing financial institutions to fail

Finally, if they have to fail, let it be. Kay (2009b) correctly argues that
"it is both better politics and better economics to deal with the [TBTF]
problem by facilitating failure than by subsidizing it. Likewise, Sheila
Bair, the head of the FDIC is quoted by Jordan (2009) as saying that
"big financial institutions that take too many risks and become insolvent should be allowed to fail, with their shareholders and bondholders
wiped out and top management getting the boot". Bair also said that
"if investors and executives think government will bail out such companies, a vicious circle of dangerous risk-taking results". Instead, she
said, "the government should set up an orderly system to resolve such
problem firms, allowing their financial functions to continue while
replacing management, eliminating shareholder value and taking other
steps to restore them to order". Kaufman (2003) suggests that "bank
regulators appear to be able to resolve insolvent large banks efficiently
without either protecting uninsured deposits through invoking 'too big
to fail' or causing serious harm to other banks or financial markets".

The proposition that failing institutions should be allowed to fail is
in line with the reasoning of Stern and Feldman (2004) who believe
that "the root of the TBTF problem lies in creditors' expectations...
when uninsured creditors of large, systemically important banks expect
to receive government protection if their bank fails". It is the lack of
credibility on the part of the government that causes the problem and
provides the incentive for excessive risk taking. By allowing failing
institutions to fail consistently, the government will gain the credibility that solves the problem.

The language of fear

In every case of government bailout, a typical argument is put forward
that allowing a big institution to fail brings about havoc in the financial
sector and the economy as a whole. Wolf (2009) tells an anecdote from
just after the failure of Lehman Brothers in September 2008. When Ben

Bernanke was asked "what if we don't do anything", he replied "there will be no economy on Monday". During a town hall meeting on 27 July, Bernanke made similar remarks as he said the following (*Money Really Matters*, 2009):

> The problem we have is that in a financial crisis if you let the big firms collapse in a disorderly way, they'll bring down the whole system. When the elephant falls down, all the grass gets crushed as well.

The irony here is that regulators construct a doomsday scenario only when it suits them. They let Lehman Brothers go down although it was twice as big as Bear Stearns, but this is what the Federal Reserve said to justify the bailout of Bear (Board of Governors of the Federal Reserve System, 2008):

> A bankruptcy filing would have forced the secured creditors and counterparties of Bear Stearns to liquidate the underlying collateral, and given the illiquidity of markets, those creditors and counterparties might well have substantial losses. If they had responded to losses or unexpected illiquidity of their holdings by pulling back from providing secured financing to other firms and by dumping large volumes of illiquid assets on the market, a much broader financial crisis would have ensued with consequent harm to the overall economy.

In the first major case of a TBTF bailout, that of Continental Illinois, a doomsday scenario was drawn by Charles Conover, the then Comptroller of the Currency. Conover (1984) declared:

> Had Continental failed and been treated in a way in which depositors and creditors were not made whole, we could very well have seen a national, if not an international, financial crisis, the dimensions of which were difficult to imagine. None of us wanted to find out.

Then the Chairman of House Banking Committee, Congressman St Germain, argued that "had the Continental Illinois been allowed to fail... all those people [would have been] put out of work and all those corporations out of money" (Kaufman, 2004). This is the same St Germain as in the deregulatory Garn-St Germain Act of 1982, which means that an enthusiastic free marketeer justified government intervention to save a failed private-sector business. In a subsequent testimony a former governor of the Fed, John LaWare, went as far using the Chernobyl disaster as an analogy for financial failure (what a joke!). LaWare (1991) declared:

It is systemic risk that fails to be controlled and stopped at the inception that is a nightmare condition that is unfair to everybody. The only analogy that I can think of for the failure of a major international institution of great size is a meltdown of a nuclear generating plant like Chernobyl. The ramifications of that kind of failure are so broad and happen with such lightning speed that you cannot after the fact control them. It runs the risk of bringing down other banks, corporations, disrupting markets, bringing down investment banks along with it... We are talking about the failure that could disrupt the whole system.

Likewise, a doomsday scenario would be used by the management of a failed institution and regulators alike to bail out the institutions (or else). For example, some would argue that finance is deeply interconnected, so that even a moderately large player can take down the system if it implodes. Those who argue along these lines would say that it was the failure of Lehman Brothers (not Citigroup or Bank of America) that brought the world to the brink. This claim is far-fetched because the world came to the brink as a result of the collective malpractice of financiers. Saving Lehman in any shape or form could not have changed the course of the global financial crisis.

Back to AIG

When the U.S. government was considering what to do about AIG, the management of the failed company claimed that any failure by the government to bail it (or them) out would have "catastrophic" consequences. This is the same management that, in the words of O'Rourke (2009), adopted financial practices that "displayed a shameful level of arrogance and irresponsibility" and the same management that was unable to "practice even the most basic risk management". In an AIG (2009) document dated 26 February 2009—and marked "strictly confidential" although it is freely available on the internet—the following consequences of the failure were envisaged:

- The failure of AIG would have a cascading impact on a number of U.S. life insurers.
- State insurance guarantee funds would be quickly dissipated, leading to runs on the insurance industry.

- Given AIG's size relative to other U.S. insurance companies, there is no ability for an "arranged marriage" of AIG with other U.S. insurance companies.
- The government's unwillingness to support AIG could lead to a crisis of confidence over other large financial institutions.
- The loss of confidence is likely to be particularly acute in countries that have large investments in U.S. companies and securities and whose citizens may suffer significant losses as a result of the failure of AIG's foreign insurance subsidiaries.
- This could lead directly to a decrease in the attractiveness of U.S. government securities and a consequent increase in borrowing costs for the U.S. government.
- It is questionable whether the economy could tolerate another shock to the system that a failure of AIG would produce.
- The failure of AIG could create a "chain reaction of enormous proportions", given the extent and interconnectedness of AIG's business.
- The failure of AIG would have a devastating impact on the U.S. and global economy.
- Potential unemployment for a large portion of the 116,000 employees, including 50,000 employees generating annual U.S. salaries totalling $3.5 billion.
- Adverse impact on AIG's 74 million policyholders worldwide. Existing policy holders could be unable to obtain cover from other insurance companies.
- Possible outcomes for which the Treasury would need to be prepared to respond include: (i) fall in the value of the dollar, (ii) increase in Treasury borrowing costs, and (iii) doubts about the ability of the U.S. to support its banking system.
- AIG has $1.6 trillion in notional derivatives exposures. Unwinding of portfolios in an AIG failure would likely cause enormous downward pressure on valuations across a wide range of associated asset classes.
- And there is more that I will just overlook.

Notice the language of fear: "cascading impact", "crisis of confidence", "chain reaction of enormous proportions", and "devastating impact". This kind of language is used only by the agents of apocalypse. If these claims were true then the people who caused the problem should be tried for crimes against humanity (on the contrary, they got their bonuses out of taxpayers' money).

But these claims are false, as there is no way the failure of one firm can cause this kind of damage to the world economy. They make it sound more catastrophic than a massive earthquake (and people survive and flourish even after massive earthquakes). I will not dignify AIG's claims by commenting on them individually. What is most ludicrous, however, is the claim that the failure of AIG would bring about dollar depreciation. If my memory serves me right, I recall that the dollar soared in value in the fourth quarter of 2008, when problems at AIG started to surface to become public knowledge, then it started to depreciate following the bailout. If anything, currency depreciation may result from bailing out a failed institution if the bailout is financed by printing money (Stern and Feldman, 2004).

I do not believe that it would have been catastrophic (a really big word) to let AIG's partners in derivative transactions (which are mainly buyers of credit default swaps) take substantial losses (this is business, is it not?). They took a gamble, and it did not work. The alternative to bailout would have been to allow (or force) AIG to file for bankruptcy, in which case AIG's creditors (including its derivative counterparties) would obtain the company's assets. They would end up with a certain recovery rate on their claims (say 20 per cent), bearing the losses them-selves. They could afford it, and if they could not then bad luck. In a Congressional hearing held in July 2009, Dean Mahoney suggested allowing financial institutions to go through bankruptcy proceedings, so that costs may be appropriately passed to creditors rather than tax-payers (US Fed News Service, 2009). Governments do not compensate people for losses in the stock market, so why compensate rich com-panies (and the rich people who mismanage them) for their gambles? This is like opening loss compensation offices in the casinos of Las Vegas. By the way, I have often wondered why governments bail out institutions but not markets.

Let us assume for the sake of argument that it was legitimate to be worried about AIG's counterparties, including major U.S. and foreign banks, some of which would deplete their capital. The question is why pay AIG to pay these counterparties? It only made it easy for AIG executives to get their bonuses, having just blown up the world. It is important to understand that the government can also employ inter-mediate approaches between fully backing AIG's derivative obligations and no backing at all. For example, the government could place AIG in Chapter 11, but commit to providing supplementary coverage that would make up any difference between the value that creditors would get from AIG's reorganization and, say, an 80 per cent recovery rate. Such an approach could allow setting different "haircuts" for different classes of creditors. The government, for example, might elect not to provide such supplementary coverage to executives owed money by AIG. Letting AIG's derivative counterparties take a significant "haircut", however, should not lead to a crisis.

It is not only big institutions that portray doomsday scenarios to claim TBTF bailout. Even unknown small-medium institutions do it from time to time. In late 2001 a medium-size broker-dealer firm based in Minneapolis, MJK Clearing, experienced severe financial difficulty. The management of the firm argued with the Federal Reserve Bank of Minneapolis that its failure would spill over and severely impair around 200,000 retail customers, several brokerage firms involved in the stock-lending deal that initially caused the problem, and a variety of small brokerage houses. MJK's lawyer claimed the TBTF status and urged the Fed to provide financial assistance. It was subsequently demonstrated that the alleged spillover effect was exaggerated, and no assistance was provided (Stern and Feldman, 2004). If, instead, the Fed had chosen to go for a rescue operation, we would have been told that failure to do so would be destructive for the State of Minnesota and the U.S. economy as a whole.

Inflated figures

What I would like to see from a failing institution using alarming language is a list of how much each counterparty would lose as a result of its failure. There is no point in talking about the trillions of dollars of losses that would be incurred by counterparties all around the world. Deals involving derivatives, for example, produce inflated, frightening but unrealistic figures. For example, the notional value of outstanding credit default swaps at one time was $36 trillion, but this figure counts all guaranteed debt—the equivalent, in home insurance, of the total value of houses covered rather than the premium paid (*The Economist*, 2009n). Interest rate swaps provide another good example. The value of outstanding contracts is measured in terms of notional values, which means nothing because interest payments represent a tiny fraction of notional values. For example, AIG claimed an impending disaster that could result from the unwinding of $1.6 trillion of positions on derivatives. This figure, however, is the notional amount involved, not the actual payments that would have been a fraction thereof.

Furthermore, the word "loss" could mean anything or nothing, as Davis (2009) explains. When asset prices collapse, what is lost is "paper wealth" that was created by the increase in asset prices on the perception of some market participants that those assets were worth more.

Loss also depends on which price level is used as a benchmark. Quiggin (2009) refers to "notional losses" resulting from the wiping out of the "spurious gains of previous years". The only real losers in a TBTF fiasco are taxpayers.

When they ask for money, let them fail

Moss (2009) suggests that creating a receivership process would allow an efficient handling of failed companies. He also suggests that all systemic institutions would get limited support during a period of economic turbulence, but if this turns out to be inadequate, then they are going to be taken into the receivership process and liquidated or restructured. However, he argues, once these firms are getting to a point where they look like they might fail, the government needs to keep away and let the firm fail. It is not the taxpayers' responsibility to bail out big institutions that keep failing time and time again. Moss goes as far as saying that "everybody in government needs to show some respect for the hardworking Americans that vote them into office and not do things that benefit the few at the expense of the many".

Lewis and Einhorn (2009) argue strongly for "other things the Treasury might do when a major financial firm assumed too big to fail comes knocking, asking for free money". One thing is "let it fail". They write:

> Not as chaotically as Lehman Brothers was allowed to fail. If a failing firm is too big to fail for that honour, then it should be explicitly nationalized, both to limit its effect on other firms and to protect the guts of the system. Its shareholders should be wiped out, and its management replaced. Its valuable parts should be sold off as a functioning business to the highest bidders.... The rest should be liquidated in calm markets.

Back to LTCM

Consider once more the case of LTCM, where the language of fear was used by the regulators to describe the situation (the same do-it-or-else story). In his testimony to the House Banking and Financial Services Committee, Alan Greenspan said the following (Federal Reserve Board, 1998):

> In situations like this, there is no reason for central bank involvement unless there is a substantial probability that a fire sale would result in severe, widespread and prolonged disruption to financial

market activity.... It was the FRBNY's judgment that it was to the advantage of all parties—including the creditors and other market participants—to engender if at all possible an orderly resolution rather than let the firm go into disorderly fire-sale liquidation following a set of cascading cross defaults.

Then take this comment from President McDonough of the Federal Reserve Bank of New York (House Committee on Banking and Financial Services, 1998, p. 38):

I think that you have to start with the notion that we were really very convinced that the American people would suffer in a way that is not appropriate for them to suffer if LTCM failed.

He added:

The reason I thought it was appropriate or recommended that we get the Federal Reserve Bank of New York involved was because [sic] we were in such a chaotic market situation that the risk to the real economy, the real people, was sufficiently high.

The American people suffering from the collapse of a parasitic hedge fund? For a while I thought that the subject under consideration was the 2005 hurricane (Katrina) or the 2010 oil spill in the Gulf of Mexico, two disasters that inflicted suffering on the people of Louisiana. Then I realized that this statement was made in the late 1990s, many years before the occurrence of these disasters. It is ironic that, having said what he said about the necessity of saving LTCM, Mr Greenspan declared: "I say nothing is too-big-to-fail", and Mr McDonough followed by saying: "I couldn't agree more". However, Mr Greenspan added: "there is an issue here of too-big-to-liquidate-quickly". Yet another "too good to believe" or "too outrageous to accept" concept.

The LTCM case is analysed brilliantly by Dowd (1999). He wonders what might have happened if LTCM had failed, and whether or not the Federal Reserve's fears were plausible. The underlying arguments for bailouts were that (i) financial markets were in a particularly fragile state in September 1998; (ii) LTCM was a big player that was heavily involved in derivatives trading; and (iii) it had significant exposures to many different counterparties, and many of its positions were difficult and costly to unwind. These were the justifications for why the Fed was nervous about the prospect of LTCM's failing. Dowd, however, argues that financial markets could have absorbed the shock of LTCM's failing without going into the financial meltdown that Federal Reserve officials feared. He supports his argument as follows:

- Although many firms would have taken large hits, the amount of capital in the markets is in the trillions of dollars. It is therefore difficult to see how the markets as a whole could not have absorbed the shock, given their huge size relative to LTCM. "The markets might have sneezed, and perhaps even caught a cold, but they would hardly have caught pneumonia", as Dowd puts it. A pebble falling in the ocean cannot cause a tsunami.
- When firms are forced to liquidate positions in response to a major shock, there are usually other firms willing to buy at the right price. Sellers may have to take a loss to liquidate, but buyers can usually be found (ask Warren Buffett who was willing to buy LTCM at a fair price). Competition for good buys usually puts a floor under sellers' losses.
- Market experience suggests that the failure of even a big derivatives player usually has an impact only on the markets in which that player is very active. Worldwide market liquidity has never been threatened by any such failure. It follows, then, that the failure of LTCM might have had a major negative impact on some of the derivatives markets in which the fund was active, but it would not have caused a global liquidity crisis.
- Even in those rather extreme and unusual markets where liquidity might be paralysed in the immediate aftermath of a major shock, participants have every reason to resume trading as soon as possible. Time and time again in the 1990s, derivatives markets exhibited remarkable ability to absorb major shocks and return quickly to normal. There is no reason to suppose that market response would have been much different if LTCM had failed.
- Major developments in derivatives risk management mean that most firms' "true" exposures are now only a small fraction of what they might otherwise appear to be. The Federal Reserve's nightmare scenario, a mass unwinding of positions with widespread freezing of markets, is far-fetched even in the fragile market conditions of the time.

Some empirical studies have been conducted to quantify the impact of the LTCM fiasco on the U.S. financial system, producing results that undermined the proposition of significant systemic effect. An event study examined the response of four banks that later attended the rescue meeting at the New York Fed. Kho *et al* (2000) concluded:

> Our analysis shows that the market distinguished well between exposed and non-exposed banks when an event occurs.... There is therefore no basis for concerns that markets react similarly across banks and that banks have to be protected from markets. Our evidence raises important questions especially for those who emphasize the importance of U.S. systemic risks as a motivation for bailouts.

The results of the Kho *et al* study suggest that markets understood that while the LTCM saga hurt exposed banks profits, their solvency was not under any threat. Likewise, Furfine (2006) found no evidence for the proposition that investors restricted their lending to the nine banks that eventually participated in the LTCM rescue.

They should write wills

One suggestion that has been put forward with respect to the idea of letting badly-run institutions fail if necessary is for an institution to have a will, a bankruptcy contingency plan that would lay out how it would resolve itself quickly and efficiently. Such a plan would require financial institutions to track and document their exposure much more carefully and in a timely manner. Furthermore, regulators must inspect the balance sheets and identify the institutions that cannot survive a severe downturn. These institutions should face a choice: write down your assets to their true value and raise private capital within a specified period of time or be taken over by the government. The government would write down the toxic assets of the institutions taken into receivership and transfer those assets to a separate government entity, which would attempt to salvage whatever value is possible for the taxpayer. Once these institutions have their balance sheets cleansed, and they are in a position to lend safely, they regain the trust of lenders and investors. They can then be sold off.

One of the provisions of the Wall Street Reform and Consumer Protection Act deals with this issue. It calls for establishing "an orderly process for dismantling large, failing financial institutions in a way that ends bailouts, protects taxpayers and prevents contagion to the rest of the financial system". But irrespective of how, failing institutions should be allowed to fail without fear of a catastrophe. People are resilient, and if they can survive natural disasters and prosper in the aftermath, they can certainly survive and prosper following the collapse of a financial institution, be it AIG, LTCM or whoever.

9
Forget about Basel II

9.1 Basel II in the aftermath of the global financial crisis

In Chapter 5 it was argued that deregulation has been one reason why the financial sector has a super size and an undeserved status. In Chapter 8 it was suggested that effective and appropriate regulation is needed as part of the solution to the TBTF problem. While some regulatory measures were discussed briefly in Chapter 8, this chapter is devoted to the argument that international banking regulation, represented by the Basel accords, is neither appropriate nor effective. In evaluating the Basel accords, alternative regulatory measures are suggested in a general form.

Following the onset of the global financial crisis, a controversial issue has arisen as to whether or not the Basel II Accord could have prevented the crisis or reduced its impact. To the architects of Basel II, who reside in the beautiful Swiss city of Basel, the Accord could have done wonders, had it been implemented earlier. For example, the Chairman of the Basel Committee, Nout Wellink (2008), argues that Basel II "would have helped prevent the global credit crisis from occurring" and that "it was a misunderstanding to say that Basel II would have allowed the risky practices among banks that triggered the crunch". Although he admits that "Basel II adopts the models that failed to perform in the recent turmoil", he claims that "rules do not allow banks to use the credit pricing models that failed to perform". He further argues that Basel II would provide impetus for banks to produce "forward-looking approaches to assessing, managing and holding adequate capital for risk". Bearing these views in mind, one can only wonder how Basel II could have dealt with the malpractices of AIG (which is an insurance company that is not covered by the Accord) and with the extreme funding model of Northern Rock.

Long before the crisis struck, some economists and observers expressed concern about Basel II as a piece of banking regulation. For example, Rodriguez (2002) expressed the view that "it is not clear that the new framework [Basel II] will guarantee the safety and soundness of the international banking system or protect taxpayers from the moral hazard created by implicit or explicit government deposit insurance". I would definitely agree with this statement, except that I would replace "deposit insurance" with "bailout".

In the aftermath of the crisis, observers were prompt in casting a big shadow of doubt on Basel II. In the 28 February 2008 issue of *Financial Times*, Harald Benink and George Kaufman declared that "turmoil reveals inadequacy of Basel II", suggesting that the Accord should not be implemented, if at all, without first making a number of important changes. Two questions in particular have been raised: (i) Does Basel II adequately address key issues related to financial risk management?, and (ii) Is the full implementation of Basel II an effective remedy for current and future disturbances in financial markets? A suggested answer is that "Basel II does not address all the regulatory issues that figure in the lessons learned from current market events" (Caruana and Narain, 2008).

The crisis has highlighted two additional, more basic questions about Basel II. The first of these questions is whether or not the style of capital regulation incorporated in the Accord is fundamentally misguided. The second question is that even if the basic Basel II approach has promises as a paradigm for domestic regulation, is the effort at extensive international harmonization of capital rules and supervisory practices useful and appropriate? (Tarullo, 2008). The mood has certainly changed as a result of the crisis, as critics have shifted from attacking the technical and methodological details of Basel II to attacking its very concept. The death of Basel II was declared in an editorial of *OpRisk & Compliance* (2008) entitled "Basel II is Dead, Long Live Basel III".

9.2 The Basel Accords

In 1988, the Basel Committee on Banking Supervision (BCBS) established a global standard for measuring capital adequacy for banks, which has become known as the Basel I Accord (also known as the 1988 Accord). The objectives of Basel I were: (i) to establish a more "level playing field" for international competition among banks, and (ii) to reduce the probability that such competition would lead to bidding down of capital ratios to excessively low levels. Basel I sought to develop a single risk-adjusted capital standard that would be applied throughout the world.

Basel I was adopted by a large number of countries over a relatively short period of time. The most important feature of Basel I is the provision that a bank must hold capital that varies according to the perceived credit risk of the bank's loan portfolio. Before that, regulators had focused on simple (but perhaps more appropriate and more effective) leverage ratios calculated by using total assets as the base—that is, the value of assets is not adjusted for risk. Under Basel I, individual assets were divided into four basic credit risk categories, according to the creditworthiness of the counterparty, and each category was assigned a weight ranging from 0 (risk-free assets) to 100 per cent (most risky assets). Banks were required to hold as capital an amount of no less than 8 per cent of their risk-weighted assets.

In response to the criticism of the Basel I Accord and to address changes in the banking environment that the 1988 Accord could not deal with effectively, the BCBS decided to create a new capital accord, Basel II. The new Accord was intended to deal with market innovations and a fundamental shift towards more complexity in banking. Following the publication of the first round of proposals for revising the capital adequacy framework in November 1999, the BCBS subsequently released additional proposals in January 2001 and April 2003 and conducted quantitative impact studies pertaining to these proposals. This consultation process has produced the revised framework that was published in June 2004, subsequently further revised frameworks appeared in November 2005 and June 2006. While retaining the key elements of the Basel I Accord, including the general requirement that banks ought to hold a regulatory capital ratio of at least 8 per cent of their risk-weighted assets, Basel II provides a range of options for determining capital requirements, allowing banks to use approaches that are most appropriate for their operations.

The Basel II Accord is portrayed as providing a more sophisticated measurement framework for evaluating capital adequacy in banks. A proclaimed significant innovation of Basel II is the greater use of internal models for risk assessment and the calculation of regulatory capital. But this is a privilege that is only granted to big banks (again, the word "big" crops up). It is also portrayed as the means to circumvent the shortcomings of Basel I and accomplish the following objectives: (i) to promote the safety and soundness of the financial system; (ii) to enhance competitive equality; (iii) to establish a more comprehensive approach to risk; and (iv) to equate economic capital and regulatory capital (by allowing banks to use their internal models), which would eliminate incentives for regulatory capital arbitrage. As we are going to find out, all of these claims are questionable.

9.3   Basel II as a form of capital-based regulation

The idea behind capital regulation is that a firm that is adequately capitalized remains solvent if it is hit by a big loss event. While this argument is acceptable at face value and in general terms, the problem with the capital adequacy provisions of Basel II is that they distract attention away from simple but effective leverage ratios. The problem is not capital requirements *per se* but risk-based capital requirements, which are calculated from risk-weighted assets. Studies conducted, among others, by Avery and Berger (1991), Furlong and Keeley (1989), Keeley (1980), and Keeley and Furlong (1990) revealed that there is an inverse relation between risk-based capital requirements and bank risk taking.

Another justification for regulatory capital is that it makes banks more careful and provides an incentive to avoid excessive risk for fear of significant losses (Hawkins and Turner, 2000). For this proposition to be valid, capital ratios must be set to very high levels. When capital ratios are not high (which is typically the case because the business will not be viable), taking excessive risk by banks is still attractive. This is because if a risky strategy is followed, banks reap all the upside whereas the downside is limited to capital. More importantly, however, is that this argument seems to overlook the fact that decisions about risk assumption are made by managers, not by shareholders (hence, the agency problem resulting from the separation of management and ownership). Managers have much less to lose than shareholders (collectively) when things go wrong.

9.4   Basel II: The wrong kind of regulation

Basel II is a piece of micro-prudential regulation, which is directed at the stability of individual financial institutions, whereas macro-prudential regulation deals with the stability of the financial system as a whole. Unlike micro-prudential regulation, which ignores the systemic importance of institutions as indicated by size, the degree of leverage, and interconnectedness with the rest of the system. Wyplosz (2009) suggests that systemically important institutions should be subject both to micro-prudential and macro-prudential regulation—the latter can be implemented by adjusting the micro-prudential capital ratio by a coefficient corresponding to their systemic risk.

For most countries, the adoption of Basel II by itself means that better public policy structures are forgone, thus increasing both the likelihood and cost of financial instability (Kaufman, 2005). There is also the proposition that holding capital against risk may provide a false sense of security, which provides disincentive for fostering adequate controls (Doerig, 2003). A related view is that "the problem with using risk capital to act as a deterrent... is that it creates a form of moral hazard" (McConnell, 2006).

Basel II allows banks (at least big banks) to determine their own capital, which amounts to regulating banks in the same way as they are managed. This cannot be right because while regulators are concerned about the systemic effect of a catastrophic loss event hitting one bank, bank managers are more concerned about the risk-return trade-off associated with the day-to-day running of the business (Rebonato, 2007). This means that the "novel" objective of aligning regulatory capital with economic capital (which implies running the bank the same way as regulating it) is way off the mark. Banks should not be regulated in the same way as they are managed because of differences between the roles and objectives of regulators and shareholders. The role of regulators is to protect the soundness of the financial system, in which case the holding of excess capital may be desirable. From the managers' (shareholders') perspective, excess capital is not available for income generation, which reduces return on equity, and hence it is not desirable (McConnell, 2006). The opponents of regulation argue that regulators do not take into account the fact that risk creates value and that by attempting to avoid systemic risk in the name of the general public, they end up making the financial system more unstable. This is why they suggest that sustained and diversified profitability is a "precondition" for the protection of customers (Doerig, 2003). Irrespective of the soundness of this view, there are indeed differences between how regulators and managers think and between their "utility functions" as a whole.

Basel II has been compared with the U.S. regulatory systems of structured early intervention and resolution, and prompt corrective action. The conclusion reached in this respect is that Basel II compares poorly in terms of maintaining a safe and sound banking system. As a matter of fact, Basel II may do damage by encouraging some large banks to put pressure on their regulators to reduce the capital ratio (Kaufman, 2005). The process of quantifying risk can create a "false sense of precision and a false impression that measurement has by necessity resulted in management". Managers may wrongly think that risk has been addressed, in which case they may reduce their vigilance, creating an environment where losses are more likely to occur (Sheedy, 1999).

9.5   The treatment of liquidity and leverage

The role played by liquidity and leverage in the global financial crisis has been conspicuous. Northern Rock and Bear Stearns collapsed because the Rock was extremely illiquid, thus inducing a run on its deposits, while Bear was leveraged 32 to 1 when it collapsed. Low liquidity hampers business and may induce a run on bank deposits. High leverage means that the effect of an adverse market movement will be amplified, causing the destruction of the underlying firm. Numerous hedge funds were wiped out by the crisis because they are typically highly leveraged. Basel II does not deal with the mismatch of the maturities of assets and liabilities. Wyplosz (2009) argues that "one of the significant lessons of the crash of 2007/08 is that the risk of an asset is largely determined by the maturity of its funding". He points out that Northern Rock might have survived with the same assets if the average maturity of its funding had been longer.

Figures 9.1–9.3 illustrate the situation of declining liquidity and rising leverage during the global financial crisis. Figure 9.1 shows a liquidity index measured as the number of standard deviations from the mean. The index is calculated as an unweighted average of nine liquidity measures such as interbank market liquidity. The collapse of liquidity during

Figure 9.1   Index of Liquidity (Standard Deviations away from the Mean)

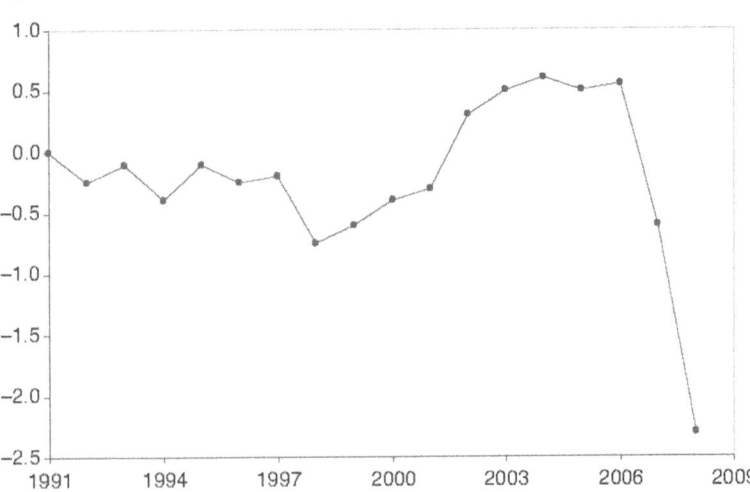

Data Source: Financial Stability Report, October 2008. Based on data provided by Bank of England, Bloomberg, Chicago Board Options Exchange, Debt Management Office, London Stock Exchange, Merrill Lynch, Datastream

Figure 9.2   Debt/GDP Ratio in the U.S. and E.U.

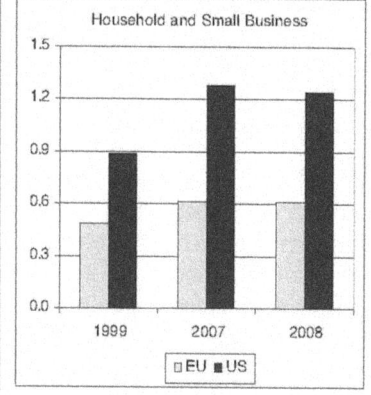

Data Source: European Central Bank and Federal Reserve

the crisis is conspicuous. Figure 9.2 illustrates the rising debt/GDP ratio in the U.S. and E.U. for the whole economy and some sectors. In 2008 the debt/GDP ratio in the E.U. was 4.7. Figure 9.3 shows the leverage of U.S. and E.U. banks measured as the ratio of total liabilities to net tangible equity. The upward trend is obvious.

The importance of liquidity

The importance of liquidity has been highlighted by a number of economists and observers. Harper and Thomas (2009) argue that "when liquidity in the wholesale capital markets dries up, no level of capital may be adequate to ward off potential insolvency". Referring to the global

Figure 9.3   Leverage of U.S. and E.U. Banks (Liabilities/Net Tangible Equity)

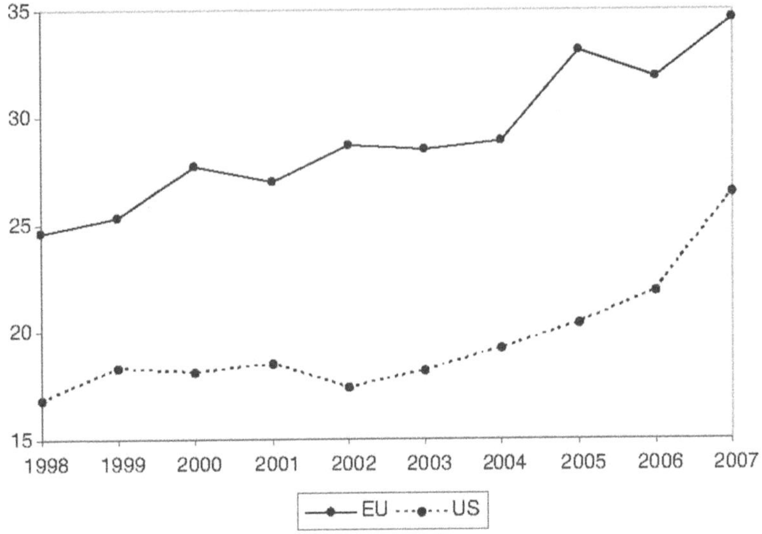

Data Source: Carmassi *et al* (2009)

financial crisis, they argue that "even well-capitalised banks—including the major Australian banks—have struggled to obtain adequate funds at times during the crisis". Goldstein (2008) points out that "much of the crisis has been about liquidity", arguing that "large banks in some G-7 countries have reduced significantly the share of narrow liquid assets, like treasuries, in their total assets". The practice, according to Goldstein, has been "just-in-time" borrowed liquidity for major players instead of an adequate reserves of own liquidity. A similar view is put forward by Kaufman (2009) who points out that the public perception of liquidity has changed from one based on assets (what you could sell) to one based on liabilities (ease of borrowing). Goldstein attributes the unpopularity of higher liquidity to the effect of limiting leverage and asset growth, thus reducing the rate of return when things are going well. The lack of liquidity risk management is indicated by (i) many banks failed to take into account the basic principles of liquidity risk management when liquidity was plentiful; (ii) many banks did not consider the amount of liquidity they might need to satisfy contingent obligations; and (iii) many banks viewed severe and prolonged liquidity disruptions as implausible (Lekatis, 2009).

In the aftermath of the global financial crisis, national regulators started to take measures to force financial institutions to boost their liquidity. In October 2009, the FSA announced the introduction of new liquidity rules requiring British banks and securities firms to increase their holdings of cash and government bonds by £110 billion and cut their reliance on short-term funding by 20 per cent in the first year following the implementation of the new rules. According to the *Financial Times*, if the FSA ramps up the requirements in subsequent years, as expected, financial institutions may have to increase their holdings of easily-liquidateable assets by some $370 billion. Alternatively, they will have to cut their reliance on short-term funding by 80 per cent.

The importance of leverage

Measures of leverage and capital adequacy are related. While leverage is measured in terms of the ratio of assets to shareholders' equity (capital), capital adequacy is measured in terms of the ratio of capital to assets. Thus a high capital ratio implies low leverage, and vice versa. This relation, however, gets distorted when the capital ratio is calculated on the basis of risk-adjusted assets. The leverage ratio is more objective, easier to calculate and easier to understand than the risk-based capital ratio. Regulation should be based on leverage, particularly that the leverage ratio is indicative of capital adequacy.

Leverage is motivated by the desire to maximize profit, particularly when interest rates are low. While there is substantial empirical evidence for a negative relation between leverage ratios and bank insolvency, there is no such evidence on how bank insolvency is related to risk-based capital ratios (Evanoff and Wall, 2001). Koos Timmermans, the chief risk officer at the Dutch bank ING, is quoted by *The Economist* (2008d) as saying that three types of leverage helped propel the boom and have now accentuated the bust: (i) financial institutions loaded up on debt to increase return on equity when asset prices were rising; (ii) financial institutions were exposed to product leverage via complex instruments such as CDOs, which needed a slight deterioration in value for losses to escalate rapidly; and (iii) they indulged in liquidity leverage, using structured investment vehicles (SIVs) or relying too much on wholesale markets to exploit the difference between borrowing cheap short-term money and investing in long-term high yield assets.

Eichengreen (2008) suggests that investment banks were so highly-leveraged that regulators will now insist, for the sake of stability, on some reduction in investment banks' leverage. He also suggests that regulators will attempt to calibrate capital requirements not just to the riskiness of a bank's assets but also to the riskiness of its funding. This, he argues, "is another lesson of the crisis and of Northern Rock in particular".

In a nutshell, measuring and monitoring the leverage ratio (the ratio of total assets to shareholders' equity) is rather easy and makes more sense than using a "sophisticated" model to measure the risk-adjusted capital ratio as required by Basel II. The latter produces an arbitrary number that means absolutely nothing. Furthermore, regulating (limiting) leverage will have another advantage: controlling the growth of financial institutions, which has been put forward as one of the measures required to solve the TBTF problem.

Dealing with the problem of excessive leverage is essential for financial stability and should form an integral part of any financial reform. Morris (2008) argues that "any program to restore confidence in American markets must start with the banks" such that "loans to very highly leveraged parties should carry penalty capital charges" and that "absurdities like prime broker loans to hedge funds that do not disclose balance sheets should simply stop". This proposition involves the link between capital adequacy and leverage in the sense that an increase in capital reduces the leverage ratio.

9.6   The use of internal models

Internal models are invariably based on the value at risk (VAR) methodology. The value at risk, also called capital at risk, is a number representing the maximum amount that can be lost on a particular position, asset or portfolio in a given period of time, with a given probability. If, for example, daily value at risk with a probability of 5 per cent is X, this means that on any day, the probability of the loss exceeding X is 5 per cent. It also means that such a loss could only happen on five out of every 100 days, and that the underlying bank can be 95 per cent certain that the loss will not exceed X on any day.

The risk models used by financial institutions failed miserably in predicting the losses incurred by them as a result of the global financial crisis. These models created some sort of complacency as they predicted that losses of the magnitudes actually endured by financial institutions could only happen once every few billion years. That is not to mention that the development of these models cost banks millions of dollars. Following "normal" banking practices, this cost is naturally recovered in multiples from customers via higher fees and commissions. This is what Taleb and Triana (2008) say about the risk models used by financial institutions (with particular reference to the Merton-Scholes models used by LTCM until its demise in 1998):

> Almost everyone in risk management knew that quantitative methods—like those used to measure and forecast exposures, value complex derivatives and assign credit ratings—did not work and could provide undue comfort by hiding risks. Few people would agree that the illusion of knowledge is a good thing. Almost everyone would accept that the failure in 1998 of Long Term Capital Management discredited the quantitative methods of the Nobel economists involved with it (Robert Merton and Myron Scholes) and their school of thought called "modern finance". LTCM was just one in hundreds of such episodes. Yet a method heavily grounded on those same quantitative and theoretical principles, called Value at Risk, continued to be widely used. It was this that was to blame for the crisis.

When the crisis was surfacing in the second half of 2007, David Viniar, the CFO of Goldman Sachs, declared that Goldman was experiencing "25-standard deviation moves, several days in a row". This claim is preposterous, as Bonner (2007) commented that these events were supposed to happen once every 100,000 years, concluding "either that or Goldman's models were wrong". This argument is valid, except that Bonner got the number (100,000) wrong. Dowd *et al* (2008) demonstrated that a 25-sigma event would happen, according to models assuming normally distributed returns, once every 1.309×10^{135} years (compare this with the age of Planet Earth (4.5×10^9 years) or the age of the universe (15×10^9 years)). In reality, however, extreme events (the so-called low-frequency, high-severity events) are quite common. The need to recapitalize banks after the onslaught of the crisis reveals that the internal models of many banks performed poorly and underestimated exposure to risk significantly, which reflects the difficulties associated with accounting for low-frequency, high-severity losses.

Proclaimed novelty

The proclaimed Basel II "novelty" of allowing banks to use their own models is simply ludicrous according to some observers. On the Naked Capitalism website (www.nakedcapitalism.com), some bloggers wrote on 28 February 2008 things like "having banks to decide [on capital] is laughable" and that "what kind of idiots would let the banks determine their own capital requirements (by allowing them to rig their own risk models)". Rodrik (2010) argues that allowing large banks to use their internal models is tantamount to allowing them to police themselves, which is hazardous, as made clear by the global financial crisis. A problem with this approach is that by using their own models, banks are tempted to be too optimistic about their risk exposure in order to minimize required regulatory capital and maximize return on equity. In this sense, therefore, Basel II creates perverse incentives to underestimate risk.

Regulatory capture

Another problem arising from the use of own models is that regulators must approve and validate these models. This is a problem because regulators should not indulge in this kind of activity, let alone the fact that they are unlikely to have the expertise to execute the task effectively. The European Shadow Financial Regulatory Committee (2003) points out that the supervisors' important role in validating risk models is conducive to "regulatory capture", as well as the possibility that supervisors will be held politically responsible for bank failure. Regulatory capture implies that "the regulator fails to keep an arm's length relation with the industry but tends to incorporate the interests and objectives of the regulated firms in its own objectives" (Wihlborg, 2005). Evaluating and approving models amounts to regulatory capture, as regulators are pushed to believe that they would be responsible for bank failure if it materializes. Furthermore, regulators typically do not have the expertise to evaluate internal models because high-flying quants would rather work for banks as model developers than for regulatory bodies as model evaluators (they get more money working for banks).

Manipulation of models

Because banks do not like holding too much capital and because regulators do not have adequate skills to check and validate models, banks will be tempted to manipulate their models and change the underlying assumptions in numerous ways until they converge on the model that makes everyone happy. Monte Carlo simulations can be used to demonstrate the sensitivity of the calculated capital charge to model assumptions (see Moosa, 2008, for an illustration). The temptation of picking the model that gives the lowest capital charge is irresistible.

The hazard of "sophisticated" models

"Sophisticated" risk models can be hazardous because they create a sense of complacency (the attitude of "we know the risk and we are ready for it because we have a powerful model"). However, these models can be completely inadequate. Wood (2008) raises the question whether or not the industry's models are any good, quoting a high-profile quant as saying that "a lot of them [the models] are disastrous" and that "modeling is currently in terribly, terribly bad shape". Wood points out that "practitioners and regulators alike will argue that models do what they say on the tin", but in private "they're more willing to admit to doubt and frustration". Furthermore, Richard Pike, product director with software vendor Ci3 in Dublin is quoted by Wood as saying that "many of the industry's risk managers claim to be happy with the numbers their models produce but if you ask them to guarantee that it's correct then, no – they can't". A problem with the models used by financial institutions is that they ignore history and human nature, and this is why business schools should teach students financial history before risk modelling (Kaufman, 2009).

In a Ci3 survey published in the October 2007 issue of *OpRisk & Compliance*, complaints aimed at the internal models included the following: (i) they do not capture the risk of tail events, (ii) they are not forward-looking, and (iii) they encourage too great a focus on measuring rather than managing risk. Richard Pike mentions the value at risk system at one bank, which is supposed to generate a number that would be the bank's maximum loss 19 days out of 20. In August 2007, that same bank exceeded the maximum loss 16 times. Pike attributes the poor performance of the model to the "pure quantification approach". He puts it succinctly by saying "you make so many assumptions in the mathematics and if these assumptions are incorrect, the model is practically useless" (Wood, 2008).

A critique of the VAR methodology

The VAR methodology has been criticized severely as a measure of risk (for example, Danielsson *et al*, 2001; Hubner *et al*, 2003). It is arguable that VAR can be misleading to the extent of creating unwarranted complacency. Moreover, VAR is a number that itself is measured with some error or estimation risk, which means that the VAR results must be interpreted with reference to the underlying statistical methodology. More importantly, however, is that the VAR approach cannot cope with sudden and sharp changes in market conditions, because it neglects the possibility of large discrete jumps in prices. Losses resulting from catastrophic events are overlooked due to dependence on symmetric statistical measures that treat upside and downside risk in the same way. *The Economist* (2008e) describes VAR as a "staple of the risk-management toolkit", but argues that "the trouble is that it is well-nigh useless at predicting catastrophe".

Shojai and Feiger (2010) suggest the following shortcomings of the VAR methodology: (i) while VAR is based on the assumption that there is no change in portfolio composition, this composition changes continuously; (ii) while VAR can be used to determine the number of loss events that fall beyond the accepted confidence level, it cannot be used to determine the magnitude of loss; (iii) VAR fails to account for the interrelationships between financial institutions; and (iv) VAR relies on data that is backward looking, incomplete and fails to account for the important events that financial institutions really need to look out for.

The global financial crisis and the large losses that hit financial institutions regularly cast a big shadow of doubt on the usefulness of VAR as a foundation of risk management. One problem with the concept of VAR is that it is typically used to estimate how bad things could get on the basis of data from the preceding three or four years, which means that predictions get more favourable the longer things go smoothly. Yet common sense tells us that the risk of a blow-up increases the further away we get from the last one. Therefore, VAR is "programmed to instill complacency", while "it acts as yet another amplifier when trouble does hit" (*The Economist*, 2008e). Also, VAR captures how bad things can get 99 per cent of the time, but the real trouble is caused by the outlying 1 per cent. Unfortunately, these outliers appear too often for comfort in the real world.

In the February 2008 issue of *Asia Risk*, Schachter (2008) describes a certain VAR model as a "straw man", which may be indicative of how smart the authors are but it is not a source of useful insight. Schachter further writes:

> This is the reverse thinking of "if I can build a model that has some correspondence with something observed, then the model must represent the underlying truth and its predictions must be valid". The fact that there may be other models that also fit those same facts, each with different implications, does not appear to enter into the authors' thinking.

Compare this line of reasoning with what a VAR guru said in defence of his "bread and butter". In a seminar held in Melbourne on 10 June 2008, Chris Finger (Head of Research at RiskMetrics, the inventors of VAR) labelled as "irresponsible" the critics of what he called "good VAR-based models".

Naturally, the slogans "blame it on misuse rather than the model itself" and "the models can be rectified" have also been used to defend VAR models. For example, Sheedy (2009) uses the second slogan, arguing that "the recent risk modelling problems were caused by the use of inappropriate risk models which are fixable rather than fundamentally flawed". She blames the failure of risk (VAR) models on the "failure to use them properly" and suggests that "the way to fix them is to use GARCH-based risk measures". As far as I know, the GARCH process (or one of its many sequels) has been incorporated in the VAR methodology for some time now, but no potential improvement has been seen (for example, Dowd, 2005). The inventor of the ARCH methodology, Robert Engle, has come up with a sequel to VAR, the so-called "conditional autoregressive value at risk" or CAVIAR (Engle and Manganelli, 1999). While CAVIAR (like anything else that Robert Engle comes up with) is marvelled at by academics, I have yet to hear from any practitioner that CAVIAR is worthy more than the paper it is written on, notwithstanding the enormous brain power used to develop the model.

Value at risk Basel-style

As if VAR models are not bad enough, the Basel-style VAR models are nothing short of a joke, as the Basel Committee requires "sophisticated" (meaning big) banks to calculate VAR at the 99.9^{th} percentile, which implies a 99.9 per cent confidence level that losses would not exceed the percentile. The use of the 99.9^{th} percentile is an "unrealistic level of precision" that would introduce moral hazard, thus encouraging managers to claim that risk has been fully mitigated rather than to address the serious issues underlying large loss events in particular (McConnell, 2006). The 99.9^{th} percentile makes the quantitative criteria of Basel II overly stringent (Jobst, 2007). This level of precision is unheard of even in experimental physics, which makes one wonder why the Basel Committee believes that the risk of losses can be measured more precisely than the thrust of a jet engine. It is perhaps easier to estimate the age of Planet Earth than to measure expected or unexpected loss, but again scientists do not claim that they aspire to estimate the age of the Planet to a 99.9 per cent degree of precision.

9.7   Risk sensitivity and procyclicality

The global financial crisis and consequent recession have demonstrated the procyclical nature of the banking industry. The credit squeeze exacerbated the recession and delayed recovery in both the real economy and financial markets. The Basel II Accord has been criticized severely because it is believed that the resulting risk-sensitive capital requirements enhance the procyclicality of the banking system. The underlying idea is that banking is a procyclical business, in the sense that banks tend to contract their lending activity in recessions and expand it in booms. This behaviour boosts the amplitude of the business cycle, making recessions more severe and booms more inflationary. Increased risk sensitivity of bank capital requirements may exacerbate the procyclical tendencies of the banking industry. Being constrained by risk-sensitive capital requirements, banks will be more unable to lend in recessions and more willing to do so in booms, because risk-sensitive capital requirements increase when the estimates of default risk are higher, and vice versa (Allen, 2004).

Counter arguments

The President of the BIS, who is naturally a Basel II enthusiast, believes that although some of the arguments that suggest procyclicality in Basel II have merit, the Accord on the whole has positive macro-economic implications (Caruana, 2005). He suggests that the extent to which capital requirements swing in response to economic conditions depends largely on the dynamic features of specific banks' rating systems and the probability of default. He also argues that a number of factors that are built into the framework are designed to ease some of the pro-cyclicality effects. The most important offset against the procyclical effects of Basel II, he argues, is the increased emphasis on effective risk management in the form of better control structures, sound corporate governance, and investment in technology, information systems and human capital. The problem with these arguments is that Basel II is not about risk management as such, but rather it is about compliance with regulatory requirements. And risk management practices cannot be harmonized, as they are institution-specific. One point remains valid, however: banking is a risk-sensitive business, which brings about a natural tendency towards procyclicality even in the absence of regulation. It is difficult to argue against the proposition that Basel II, as a form of capital-based regulation, boosts the procyclical tendencies of the banking business.

Risk-adjusted assets

The procyclicality of Basel II results from the calculation of capital ratios on the basis of risk-adjusted assets, which means that one of the proclaimed advances over Basel I (increased risk sensitivity) is counter-

Figure 9.4 Total and Risk-Weighted Assets of the Top Ten Publicly Traded Banks (trillion euros)

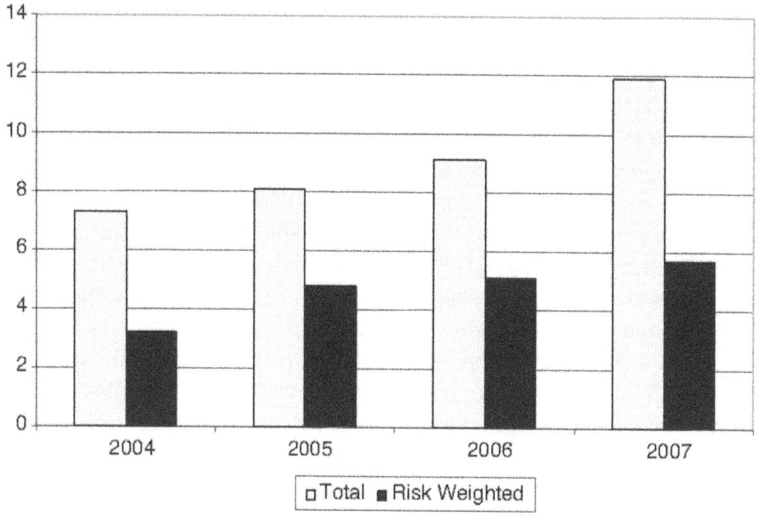

Data source: International Monetary Fund (2008)

productive. This is why some economists argue that procyclicality can be reduced by calculating capital ratios from total unadjusted assets. For example, it has been suggested that one way in which counter-cyclical elements could be introduced into regulatory capital require-ments is to make required capital a function of the change in assets, not the risk-weighted level (Goldstein, 2008). Figure 9.4 portrays the growth of total assets and risk-weighted assets of the top ten publicly traded banks, where the weights are those determined by the Basel Committee.

A remedy?

To remedy this problem, there have been frequent calls for the imple-mentation of countercyclical capital ratios. For example, Harper and Thomas (2009) advocate the introduction of countercyclical capital requirements, arguing that "countercyclical capital regulation may do as much if not more than monetary policy to forestall the formation of bubbles by acting directly on the capacity of lenders to increase their leverage". Wyplosz (2009) points out that the first proposal of the *Geneva Report*, which deals with how world leaders should think about financial regulation reform, is to make capital requirements countercyclical.

9.8   Reliance on rating agencies

There is a widespread and justified belief that, through malpractice, rating agencies played a major role in the materialization of the subprime crisis in 2007. This is because these agencies have been too generous in giving out top AAA ratings to securities backed by subprime loans to please paying clients (issuers of the securities). Rating agencies have also given a big villain of the crisis, AIG, AAA rating, which made it possible for the insurance giant to sell credit default swaps without having adequate funds to cover potential losses from default.

Reliance on the ratings of the rating agencies to determine the riskiness of assets sounds ludicrous in the post-crisis era. Even without the crisis, this reliance is misguided because rating agencies do not provide consistent estimates of creditworthiness. In the May 2008 issue of *OpRisk & Compliance* (p. 10), it is reported that "industry bodies such as the European Savings Banks Group, British Bankers' Association, and the European Banking Federation agree that the rating agencies have failed to deliver sufficient transparency regarding their methodologies or to demonstrate enough independence". It is also doubtful if the agencies had the expertise to assess the risk embodied in CDOs, even if they wanted to be objective. "They did not have a clue", said one observer who made this statement in a documentary entitled "Crash: the Next Depression", shown on the History Channel in June 2009.

Supervisory recognition

By giving them supervisory recognition, Basel II has enhanced a certain faith in rating agencies, allowing them a free hand and a significant contribution to the global financial crisis. This sounds ironic, given that two economists at the Bank for International Settlements, which is where the BCBS resides, argued against the use of the ratings of the rating agencies back in 2000. Hawkins and Turner (2000) suggested that "many would be wary of putting too much emphasis on the assessment of credit-rating agencies". To support their argument, they referred to the performance of the rating agencies during the Asian crisis. While the agencies did not downgrade most Asian countries before the crisis (when imbalances were developing), their downgrades in the midst of the crisis made it even worse. They concluded that "rating agencies were backward-looking rather than forward-looking in their assessments". For example, Enron was given an investment-grade rating on its debt until five days before the company applied for bankruptcy.

The former head of the FSA, Howard Davies, finds it rather strange that Basel II relies heavily on the work of the rating agencies when discussion is under way on the question of regulating these agencies and keeping them on leash (Davies, 2005). Yet, there has been little interaction between the Basel Committee and the bodies taking part in discussions on how to regulate the rating agencies (such as the European Commission and the SEC). Davies also believes that Basel II will deliver a significantly lower capital charge than what the rating agencies look for, at a time when banks are more influenced by the rating agencies than by Basel II.

Paying rating agencies

The practice of paying rating agencies by the issuers of the securities is seen as representing conflict of interest. Harper and Thomas (2009) argue against "setting up a new arm of bureaucracy to replace rating agencies". Rather, they suggest that issuers should pay fees to the regulators, who then distribute the fees to the credit rating agencies. It is not clear, though, what mechanism will be used to distribute the fees.

9.9   The implementation problems

The global financial crisis is truly global, having affected every country in the world. If the Basel II Accord was to provide the means for protecting financial institutions from insolvency and alleviate the effects of financial crises, we should expect some uniformity in the implementation of the Accord worldwide. In reality, however, Basel II is not (and perhaps cannot be) implemented uniformly, which creates problems. The BCBS gives so much latitude to individual countries that the capital charge will depend as much on supervisory implementation in each jurisdiction as it does on actual regulations" (de Fontnouvelle *et al*, 2005). The Accord will differ from one country to another in a way that has led Imeson (2006) to conclude that "it [Basel II] looks as though it will become another example of disunity among nations and a monument to discord".

The implementation of the Accord will be extremely difficult in certain countries, requiring, according to Davies (2005), "massive re-engineering of the regulating body and huge increases of staff". In other words, he argues, "the Capital Accord will involve a major cultural shift in regulation". This pertains particularly to emerging economies, an issue that Stan Fischer, the former chief economist of the IMF, deals with in detail.

Fischer (2002) argues that certain elements of Basel II will pose difficulties for banks and supervisors in emerging market economies because the Accord will likely affect the banks operating in emerging markets (local banks and internationally-active banks) differently. Furthermore, Fischer seems to be concerned about the ability of supervisory authorities in many emerging and developing countries to meet the standards set by Basel II. Davies (2005) raises a similar point, advocating a role for emerging economies at an earlier stage. He actually warns of the risk of adopting advanced approaches in emerging countries because of the belief that this is the global standard, although it is not appropriate for their banks at the current stage of development.

9.10   The exclusionary and discriminatory aspects of Basel II

The global financial crisis has hit financial institutions across the board: small and large, sophisticated and not-so-sophisticated, internationally active and not-so-internationally active, and those operating in emerging economies and otherwise. It has hit commercial banks, investment banks, hedge funds and other financial (and non-financial) institutions. Financial institutions incurred losses by being exposed to market risk, credit risk, operational risk, business risk and reputational risk. Yet, the Basel II Accord covers commercial banks only. It discriminates between large banks and small banks, between sophisticated and down-to-earth banks, and between internationally active and internationally inactive banks. And it ignores business and reputational risks. Perhaps what is more alarming is that these exclusions and double standards are typically motivated by convenience, not by substance.

Business and reputational risks

Consider business risk and reputational risk that are not covered by Basel II. Financial institutions incurred losses during the global financial crisis because they took positions on CDOs, believing that credit default swaps would provide adequate protection, an operation that involved business risk. This exposure, which resulted from severe errors of judgment, produced significant losses. As far as reputational risk is concerned, the financial institutions that endured market and credit losses during the crisis also suffered from dented (if not completely lost) reputation (for example, Northern Rock). Empirical studies of operational risk have shown that a firm can suffer a market value decline in the days surrounding the announcement of a large loss that is significantly larger than the loss itself. This is attributed by Perry and de Fontnouvelle (2005) to the indirect impact of reputational risk, because disclosure of fraudulent activity or improper business practices within a firm may damage the firm's reputation. Yet these risks are not recognized by Basel II (as they are excluded from the BCBS's definition of operational risk).

Commercial banks only

Another facet of the Basel II exclusionary design is that the Accord covers commercial banks only, while the main casualties of the crisis were investment banks and hedge funds. Requiring commercial banks only to hold regulatory capital against market, credit and operational risk makes them less competitive in this era of universal banking (so much for the objective of enhancing competitive equality). As a result of the crisis, Eichengreen (2008) expects some extension of regulation, including capital regulation, to investment banks. This, he believes, is "a consequence of the Bear Stearns rescue, which taught regulators... that these financial institutions are too intimately connected with other financial institutions to be allowed to fail". Excluding non-bank financial institutions from capital regulation raises a series of serious questions in relation to this issue. What are the measures designed to avoid potential systemic risk from NBFIs? Why care about systemic risk by banks while ignoring NBFIs? Why should banks be subject to a special operational risk capital charge? Does this not make banks less competitive?

Small and less sophisticated banks

Furthermore, Basel II discriminates against small banks, less sophisticated banks and internationally-inactive banks because the use of the "more sophisticated" approaches to the calculation of regulatory capital produces lower capital charges than those of small banks (which is what the BCBS claims). There is, therefore, something in common between the too big to fail doctrine and Basel II: while the doctrine says that big banks are too big to be allowed to fail, the Accord says that big banks are too sophisticated to use simple methods to calculate regulatory capital. In both cases, big banks have a privilege *vis-à-vis* small banks: government protection under the doctrine and the luxury of manipulating regulatory capital under the Accord.

Small banks may, therefore, feel that Basel II puts them at a competitive disadvantage *vis-à-vis* large banks, which makes them attractive potential takeover targets. However, large banks may (and do) complain that, unlike small banks, they have to spend a fortune on the development of internal models to measure regulatory capital under the advanced measurement approach (AMA) of Pillar 1 (see, for example, Moosa, 2007, 2008). Small banks may (and do) claim that the capital charge under the basic indicators approach (BIA) is too high, but the BCBS cannot reduce this number without enraging the large banks adopting the AMA. It is a real mess!

9.11   The one-size-fits-all problem

Basel II is viewed as a one-size-fits-all approach, which is unsatisfactory (Doerig, 2003). The crisis has shown that differences among financial institutions led to significantly different results. For example, Australian banks (at least most of them) were affected only slightly by the crisis while British and U.S. banks suffered severe losses. This is why Doerig (2003) argues that "a firm's scale, business mix, risk appetite and strategic objectives should influence its risk management hierarchy" and that "Basel II... is deliberately non-specific on what is appropriate for particular institutions".

Another aspect of standardization is the international harmonization of capital adequacy regulation. Research shows that when capital standards are harmonized across countries that have different rescue policies, the presence of international banks leads to a spillover effect from the country with a more forbearing policy to the other country (Acharya, 2000). This would boost the vulnerability of banks in the latter, forcing the authorities in that country to adopt a more forbearing policy. The outcome is a "regression to the worst regulation". Rodriguez (2002) argues that the international harmonization of banking regulation "prevents competition among different regulatory regimes and innovation in these regimes and makes it more difficult for domestic regulators to adapt the regime to the special circumstances of their own banking systems".

9.12   Basel II as a pure compliance exercise

Some observers suggest that preoccupation with Basel II and its complexity hurt financial institutions during the crisis because it is not a risk management exercise and because banks were concerned more with compliance than with actual risk management. Topping (2008) argues that "financial institutions with cross-border operations face a particularly daunting task in trying to comply with varied versions of Basel II".

In a report produced by KPMG (2005), it is argued that "Basel II... is perceived as being yet another regulatory compliance obligation", which brings with it the risk of non-compliance and the potential losses associated with it. As a result, the focus (as far as banks are concerned) has become on meeting the requirements rather than driving business value from the effort, given time and resource constraints. The complexity of Basel II is criticized because although the intention of its designers was to create a capital standard that can be implemented across jurisdictions in such a way that banks compete on a "level playing field", the many dimensions of bank risk make national and bank-specific discretion inevitable. Complexity does not necessarily make regulation more accurate, but it raises compliance costs and reduces banks' and supervisors' understanding of the underlying concepts and issues. The complexity of Basel II is "likely to make compliance costs prohibitively high". The Credit Suisse Group (2001) estimated compliance costs to average $15 million per bank for about 30,000 banks worldwide. One can only wonder if Basel II is feasible in terms of costs and benefits (it is not).

Risk (2008) quotes Andrew Kuritzkes, a managing director with Oliver Wyman, as saying that "the tremendous effort required in Basel compliance led to things like asset/liability risk, liquidity risk and business risk being crowded out. He points out that "given a bit more freedom, I'd argue that risk managers would have been more focused on risks outside the Basel II box and would have been better able to anticipate the kind of events that played out from July [2007] onwards". The challenges of implementing Basel II had taken regulators' eyes off business as usual, to which liquidity management supervision in banks should be central. Therefore, Basel II is a source of distraction for regulators as well (Business Mirror, 2008).

9.13 Concluding remarks

The global financial crisis has revealed the inadequacy of Basel II and the focus on capital-based regulation in general. Basel II provides the wrong kind of regulation and ignores liquidity and leverage, two factors that played prominent roles in the crisis. It allows the use of bank internal models, which the crisis has shown to be faulty. The Basel-style capital regulation makes things worse by boosting the procyclicality of the banking industry. Reliance on rating agencies to estimate capital charges is misplaced and ludicrous in the post-crisis era. The Accord cannot deal with financial crises adequately because it is exclusionary, discriminatory and represents a one-size-fits-all approach. It is simply a compliance exercise that has nothing much to do with risk management. The crisis has shown that under Basel II, banks could underestimate some important risks and overestimate their ability to deal with them. We should not forget that it was the Basel capital adequacy standards that led to the growth of the market for mortgage-backed securities, the conduit to the global financial crisis. And, as one observer put it, "the bureaucratic machinery of Basel II could become a classic case of the law of unintended consequences" (Coy, 2008).

The proponents of Basel II have been feverishly defending the Accord, going as far as claiming that an early implementation could have avoided the crisis. This is not surprising, given that the architects of Basel II and domestic regulators have invested time, money and their reputation in the Accord. However, not many people buy their arguments. In the post-crisis era, it has become rather difficult to defend the Accord. At the very least, the crisis has reinforced the view that Basel II is simply not viable in terms of costs and benefits.

Perhaps the way forward is Basel III, a new accord that circumvents the problems associated with Basel II. To do that, Basel III should: (i) have provisions to deal explicitly with leverage and liquidity; (ii) not allow the use of internal models; (iii) not have provisions that depend on the "wisdom" of the rating agencies; (iv) introduce countercyclicality in banking; (v) be simple, straightforward and easy to implement; and (vi) be more about risk management than about compensating creditors. This may be too much to expect from an international accord on banking regulation. Therefore, the way forward is perhaps to forget about Basel II.

10
TBTF: Where Do We Stand?

10.1 The costs and benefits of TBTF

There is only one (society-wide or economy-wide) perceived (or alleged) benefit that can be gained from bailing out financial institutions deemed too big to fail: avoiding a systemic collapse. However, the claim that the failure of one financial institution can cause systemic failure and significant economic destruction cannot be substantiated by resorting to history, economics or simple intuition. Corporate failure is an integral part of the so-called "creative destruction", which is a feature of capitalism that the TBTF doctrine is inconsistent with. Avoiding systemic failure is a perceived benefit only because regulators and the managers of failed institutions use the language of fear to warn that failure to bailout the underlying institution will cause misery for millions of people. It is all nonsense because humans are resilient. If people can outlive an earthquake or a tsunami, they can surely survive and flourish in the aftermath of the collapse of a bank, an insurance company or a hedge fund.

Now the costs. To start with, TBTF is a self-perpetuating problem. Bailing out one institution on one occasion gives the impression that all other institutions of comparable size, systemic importance or political connections will, or should, be rescued when they are about to go under. By indulging in this malpractice, the government creates moral hazard of significant dimensions. But there is more to the costs of TBTF than its self-perpetuation. The costs include a menu of the adverse consequences: diverting scarce resources from productive to parasitic activities, encouraging rent seeking, placing financial burden on future generations, rewarding recklessness and encouraging risk taking, and weakening the market discipline of financial institutions. TBTF-justified bailing out of financial institutions is incompatible with democracy and does not make economic sense, irrespective of which political and economic school of thought you belong to. It is also immoral, because it represents a reverse-Robin Hood transfer of wealth from the hard-working majority to the minority of financial elites. It is only because of moral deterioration that the TBTF problem has been allowed to persist for so long.

10.2   Circumventing the TBTF problem: Why and how?

The proposition that it is necessary to find a solution to the TBTF problem can be justified on the basis of the balance of costs and benefits. We know that the costs significantly outweigh the benefits, if any. This leaves us with the question of how to solve the problem. As we have seen, some people believe that the TBTF problem does not exist, or that it is not serious. That was a common line of thinking in the pre-crisis era, but not even the crisis has changed the views of the "true believers". Most people now recognize the seriousness of the problem, but some would argue that we have to live with it and keep on bailing out financial institutions deemed too big to fail. This is not right: the TBTF problem should and can be solved.

The solution to the TBTF problem is simple in principle, but it requires political will. To start with, a preventive action can be based on the proposition that if a firm is too big to fail, it is too big to exist. Financial institutions should be prevented from growing big, while existing big institutions should be squeezed to become smaller. It is not that something like this has not been done in the past (even in the distant past). In 1911 Standard Oil Company was broken up, a course of action that brought about benefits to the company and the economy at large. If breaking up a firm that does something useful (like Standard Oil) is beneficial, it would be prudent to break up a firm that produces useless derivatives for the sake of fees and commissions. One way to make financial institutions smaller is to make them specialized (hence, the need for some version of the Glass-Steagall Act).

Apart from breaking up big ones, financial institutions should be regulated across the board, the kind of regulation that does not give them a free hand to do as they please. The kind of malpractices of financial institutions that have led to the global financial crisis should be scrutinized and even prohibited if necessary. To eliminate moral hazard, discourage excessive risk taking and enhance the credibility of regulators, a failing financial institution must be allowed to fail. No room is to be left for financial institutions to use the language of fear to demand bailout money.

Regulation, including the reduce-size policy, coupled with willingness of the government to allow a failing financial institution to fail, is in essence what Stern and Feldman (2004) suggest to circumvent the TBTF problem. They point out that the government should reduce the tendency to renege on a no-bailout commitment. I would go even further, suggesting that this tendency should be eliminated altogether. They also suggest that measures should be taken to reduce spillovers from the failure of one financial institution to the rest of the financial sector. This can be done by introducing effective regulation, including the reduce-size policy, which Stern and Feldman are not keen on. As Authers (2009) puts it, "either Wall Street winners from the crisis must be forced to shrink until they are small enough to fail, or if they are too big to fail and carry an in effect government guarantee, government will have to regulate them more closely".

10.3   Regulation: The way forward

Financial institutions, it seems, are too important to be left to financiers, and this is why it is prudent to intensify regulation and reverse deregulation. Governments regulate aspects of our lives all the time. Law enforcement is regulation, and so are traffic lights. Contrary to what we have been led to believe, regulation is not a dirty word, particularly when it is used to the disadvantage of financiers. Anything should be done to get rid of the TBTF doctrine and free people from the politics of fear and the tyranny of financial markets.

One way forward is to forget about the international harmonization and unification of banking regulation and to leave every country to formulate its own regulation. This is what happened after the collapse of the Bretton Woods system of fixed exchange rates when countries were allowed to choose the exchange rate systems they deemed appropriate for their economies. After all, the global financial crisis has taught us big lessons on financial regulation. The BIS and Basel Committee could still provide a forum for regulators to consult, exchange views and compare notes.

Unfortunately, there seems to be some hostility to the idea of national regulation. When President Obama announced in January 2010 his intention to seek tough new rules for banks (on what they can and cannot do) he received unsympathetic reaction from the Europeans who perceived his initiative as a "unilateral move that would undermine international co-ordination of financial regulation" (Rodrik, 2010). The Managing Director of the IMF, Dominique Strauss Khan, reacted by saying that "reform of the global financial system should not be driven by what each country sees fit for itself". Rodrik (2010) argues against the international harmonization of regulation, suggesting that "the practical reality is that it cannot deliver the tough regulation, closely tailored to domestic economic and political requirements, which financial markets badly need in the aftermath of the worst financial upheaval the world economy has experienced since the Great Depression". Rodrik believes that "in a world of divided political sovereignty and diverse national preferences, the push for international harmonization is a recipe for weak and ineffective rules". This is why banks have some affection for international co-ordination. While regulatory diversity is costly for bankers, some degree of financial segmentation is a price worth paying for stronger and more appropriate regulation.

10.4 No more business as usual

It is imperative that we kill nostalgia for the good old days and the desire to return to business as usual for financiers and their supporters. Business as usual here means financiers demanding (and obtaining) big bonuses and bailout when they get in trouble; academics marvelling at the efficient market hypothesis, rational expectations, *laissez faire* finance, and their wonderful models; risk managers putting blind faith in methodologies and models such as value at risk; and regulators and policymakers defending deregulation in the name of free markets. As Morris (2008) succinctly puts it, "the breadth of the current crash suggests that we've reached the point where it is market dogmatism that has become the problem, rather than the solution".

Unfortunately, there are still strong voices calling for the return to business as usual in this sense. Some free-market gurus still argue for "the prosperity that we have been enjoying because of free markets and deregulation". For example, a Nobel Prize winner, Jagdish Bhagwati, has come out in full force against a fellow economist and Nobel Prize winner, Joseph Stiglitz, for pointing out that the financial crisis has revealed loopholes in untamed capitalism (Bhagwati, 2009). He writes:

> But Stiglitz made much-cited claim that the current crisis was for capitalism (and markets) the equivalent of the collapse of the Berlin Wall. Now, we know that all analogies are imperfect, but this one is particularly dicey. When the Berlin Wall collapsed, we saw bankruptcy of both authoritarian politics and an economics of extensive, almost universal, ownership of the means of production and central

planning. We saw a wasteland. When Wall Street and Main Street were shaken by the crisis, however, we witnessed merely a pause in prosperity, not a devastation of it.

Whose prosperity is Mr Bhagwati talking about? If it is the prosperity of financiers, then let it be. Just like you might be accused of communism if you advocate regulation, you might be accused of defending central planning (hence communism) if you to dare expose loopholes in untamed capitalism. I bet that Stiglitz, like almost everyone else, does not wish to live under communism, but he is conscious of the ramifications of the hubris and excesses associated with *laissez faire* capitalism. This reminds me of a news "anchor" on Foxtel who accused his interviewees bluntly of being "unpatriotic" and of "hating America" if they dared to say that they did not agree with something that George Bush did.

10.5   Basic finance without TBTF

A modern economy needs the finance industry. Banks and other financial institutions serve the real economy by pooling out the capital of savers and grant loans at the maturities required by borrowers, who would then invest the borrowed funds in factories and machines. The finance industry serves the economy by providing payment mechanisms and liquidity. It also provides the means for managing financial risk and a market for corporate control, allowing capital to be moved from inefficient businesses to more efficient ones. These functions can be performed without the extravaganza of financial engineering. Therefore, we should strive to go back to the basics of banking and finance.

We must also return to and embrace the principle of capitalism that a failing firm must vanish with no life support offered by the government and financed by taxpayers' money. Consider the wisdom in the following statement, made by an ordinary tax-paying citizen in private correspondence with the author:

> The other thing I feel strongly about is the old [proverb] "if you can't stand the heat, then get out of the kitchen"... In other words, any business, whether a lemonade stand or TBTF must simply shut up shop if it finds itself failing... survival of the fittest, or something. As a gardener I've learnt to rip out diseased plants rather than attempt to stake them. And if we find ourselves scavenging in the

gutters because a TBTF has been allowed to fail, then it's simply a hard lesson to be learnt by us all, but in the end progressive for society if we learn, as we must, from the experience.

I could not have said it more eloquently. It is rather refreshing to conclude with a statement like this, which summarizes the spirit of this book. What remains for me to say is one thing: the too big to fail doctrine is a myth that must go the way of the dinosaurs, and quickly.

References

Acharya, V.V. (2000) "Is the International Convergence of Capital Adequacy Regulation Desirable?", Mimeo, Stern School of Business, New York University.

Acharya, V.V., Philippon, T., Richardson, M. and Roubini, N. (2009) "The Financial Crisis of 2007–2009: Causes and Remedies", in Acharya, V.V. and Richardson, M. (eds) *Restoring Financial Stability*, New York: Wiley.

AIG (2009) "AIG: Is the Risk Systemic?", 26 February. Available at http://www.aig.com/aigweb/internet/en/files/AIG%20Systemic%20Risk2_tcm385-152209.pdf.

All Business (2005) "Fortune Magazine Names Bear Stearns 'Most Admired' Securities Firm". Available at www.allbusiness.com/banking-finance/financial-markets-investing-securities/5023640-1.html.

Allen, L. (2004) "The Basel Capital Accords and International Mortgage Markets: A Survey of the Literature", *Financial Markets, Institutions and Instruments*, 13, 41–108.

Angbazo, L. and Saunders, A. (1997) "The Effect of TBTF Deregulation on Bank Cost of Funds", The Wharton School, Working Paper No 97–25.

Anscombe, G.E.M. (1958) "Modern Moral Philosophy", *Philosophy*, 33, No 124, January.

Authers, J. (2009) "Return of the Banks' Golden Age is an Illusion", *Financial Times*, 18 July.

Avery, R.B. and Berger, R.B. (1991) "Risk-Based Capital and Deposit Insurance Reform", *Journal of Banking and Finance*, 15, 847–874.

Bank for International Settlements (2005) "Triennial Central Bank Survey of Foreign Exchange and Derivatives Market Activity in 2004", March.

Bank for International Settlements (2007) "Triennial Central Bank Survey of Foreign Exchange and Derivatives Market Activity in 2007", December.

Barnes, P. (2009) "AIG Apparently was Not 'Too Big to Fail'", *Fox Business*, 29 June. Available at www.foxbusiness.com.

Bartel, A. and Harrison, A. (1999) "Ownership versus Environment: Why are Public Sector Firms Inefficient?", NBER Working Papers, No 7043.

Bauer, P.W., Berger, A.N. and Humphrey, D.B. (1993) "Efficiency and Productivity Growth in U.S. Banking", in Fried, H.O., Lovell, C.A. and Schmid, S.S. (eds) *The Measurement of Productive Efficiency: Techniques and Applications*, Oxford: Oxford University Press, 386–413.

Beck, T., Demirguc-Kunt, A. and Levine, R. (2006) "Bank Concentration, Competition and Crises: First Results", *Journal of Banking and Finance*, 30, 1581–1603.

Beckner, S.K. (1996) *Back from the Brink: The Greenspan Years*, New York: Wiley.

Beiner, S. and Schmid, M.M. (2005) "Agency Conflicts, Corporate Governance and Corporate Diversification: Evidence from Switzerland", Working Paper, University of Basel.

Benston, C.J., Hunter, W.C. and Wall, L.D. (1995) "Motivation for Bank Mergers and Acquisitions: Enhancing the Deposit Insurance in Put Option versus Earnings Diversification", *Journal of Money, Credit and Banking*, 27, 777–788.

Benston, G.J. and Kaufman, G.G. (1996) "The Appropriate Role of Bank Regulation", *Economic Journal*, 106, 688–697.

Benyon, D. (2010) "Remuneration: It's Payback Time", *Risk.net*, March.

Berger, A.N. and Humphrey, D.B. (1991) "The Dominance of Inefficiencies over Scale and Product Mix Economies in Banking", *Journal of Monetary Economics*, 28, 117–148.

Berger, P.G. and Ofek, E. (1995) "Diversification's Effect on Firm Value", *Journal of Financial Economics*, 37, 39–65.

Berger, A.N., Hanweck, G.A. and Humphrey, D.B. (1987) "Competitive Viability in Banking: Scale, Scope and Product Mix Economies", *Journal of Monetary Economics*, 20, 501–520.

Berger, A.N., Hunter, W.C. and Timme, S.G. (1993) "The Efficiency of Financial Institutions: A Review and Preview of Research Past, Present and Future", *Journal of Banking and Finance*, 17, 221–249.

Berger, A.N., Strahan, P.E. and Demsetz, R.S. (1999) "The Consolidation of the Financial Services Industry: Causes, Consequences, and Implications for the Future", *Journal of Banking and Finance*, 23, 135–194.

Berger, A.N., Miller, N., Petersen, M., Rajan, R. and Stein, J. (2002) "Does Function Follow Organizational Form? Evidence from the Lending Practices of Large and Small Banks", NBER Working Papers, No 8752, January.

Berman, D.K. (2007) "Life is Beautiful When You are Too Big to Fail". Available at http://blogs. wsj.com/deals/2007/12/10.

Bernanke, B.S. (2006) "Modern Risk Management and Banking Supervision", Speech given at the Stonier School of Banking, Washington DC, 12 June. Available at www.federalreserve.gov/newsevents/speech/Bernanke20060612a. htm.

Bernanke, B.S. (2008) "Federal Reserve Policies in the Financial Crisis". Available at www.federalreserve.gov/newsevents/speech/bernanke20081201a. htm.

Bhagwati, J. (2009) "Feeble Critiques: Capitalism's Petty Detractors", *World Affairs*, Fall. Available at www.worldaffairsjournal.org/articles/2009-Fall/full-Bhagwati-Fall-2009.html.

Blommestein, H.J. (2009) "The Financial Crisis as a Symbol of the Failure of Academic Finance?" (A Methodological Digression), *Journal of Financial Transformation*, 27, 3–8.

Board of Governors of the Federal Reserve System (2008) "Monetary Policy Report to the Congress", 15 July.

Bonner, B. (2007) "25 Standard Deviations in a Blue Moon". Available at www.moneyweek.com.

Boone, P. and Johnson, S. (2010) "Changing the Rules, Not the Tax Bill", *Economix*, 14 January. Available at http://economix.blogs.nytimes.com/2010/01/14/ changing-the-rules-not-the-tax-bill/?pagemode=print.

Boyd, J.H. and de Nicolo, G. (2005) "The Theory of Bank Risk-Taking and Competition Revisited", *Journal of Finance*, 60, 1329–1343.

Boyd, J.H. and Gertler, M. (1994) "The Role of Large Banks in the Recent U.S. Banking Crisis", *Federal Reserve Bank of Minneapolis Quarterly Review*, Winter, 319–368.

Boyd, J.H. and Graham, S. (1991) "Investigating the Bank Consolidation Trend", *Federal Reserve Bank of Minneapolis Quarterly Review*, Spring, 3–15.

Boyd, J., Graham, S. and Hewitt, R.S. (1993) "Bank Holding Company Mergers with Non-Bank Financial Firms: Effects on the Risk of Failure", *Journal of Financial Economics*, 17, 43–63.

Brewer, E. and Jagtiani, J. (2007) "How Much Would Banks be Willing to Pay to Become 'Too-Big-to-Fail' and to Capture Other Benefits?", Federal Reserve Bank of Kansas City, Research Working Papers, No RWP 07-05.

Brunner, K. and Meltzer, A. (1963) "The Place of Financial Intermediaries in the Transmission of Monetary Policy", *American Economic Review*, 53, 372–382.

Buckley, P.J. and Casson, M.C. (1976) *Multinational Enterprise*, London: Macmillan.

Buiter, W. (2009) "Regulating the New Financial Sector", *Vox*, 9 March. Available at www.voeu.org/index.php?q=node/3232.

Burnside, C., Eichenbaum, M. and Rebelo, S. (2000) "Understanding the Korean and Thai Currency Crisis", *Federal Reserve Bank of Chicago Economic Perspectives*, Third Quarter, 45–60.

Burnside, C., Eichenbaum, M. and Rebelo, S. (2001a) "Government Guarantees and Self-Fulfilling Speculative Attacks", Unpublished Paper, September. Available at www.kellogg.northwestern.edu/faculty/rebelo/htm/sunspot-26march2003.pdf.

Burnside, C., Eichenbaum, M. and Rebelo, S. (2001b) "Prospective Deficits and the Asian Currency Crisis", *Journal of Political Economy*, 109, 1155–1197.

Business Mirror (2008) "Is Basel II Dead?", 2 November. Available at http://businessmirror.com.ph.

Calmes, J. (2010) "Taxing Banks for the Bailout", *New York Times*, 14 January.

Cameron, M. (2010) "Senate Ag Committee to Take OTC Derivatives Transparency to New Levels", *Risk*, 15 April.

Caminal, R. and Matutes, C. (2002) "Market Power and Banking Failures", *International Journal of Industrial Organization*, 20, 1341–1361.

Carmassi, J. Gros, D. and Micossi, S. (2009) "The Global Financial Crisis: Causes and Cures", Unpublished paper available at www.astrid-online.it/rassegna/02-09-2009/Carmassi_Gros-Micossi_Global-Financial-Crisis_Causes-and-Cures.pdf.

Carney, J. (2009) "Why Do Banks Grow Too Big to Fail?", *The Business Insider*, 8 August.

Caruana, J. (2005) "Implementation of Basel II", *Financial Markets, Institutions and Instruments*, 14, 253–265.

Caruana, J. and Narain, A. (2008) "Banking on More Capital", *Finance and Development*, 45. Available at www.imf.org/external/pubs/ft/fandd/2008/06/caruana.htm.

Chen, S.S. and Ho, K.W. (2000) "Corporate Diversification, Ownership Structure and Firm Value: The Singapore Evidence", *International Review of Financial Analysis*, 9, 315–326.

Cho, D. (2009) "Banks Too Big to Fail Have Grown Even Bigger", *Washington Post*, 28 August.

Chong, B.S. (1991) "Effects of Interstate Banking on Commercial Banks' Risk and Profitability", *Review of Economics and Statistics*, 73, 78–84.

Coase, R. (1937) "The Nature of the Firm", *Economica*, 4, 386–405.

Cohan, W.D. (2009) *House of Cards: A Tale of Hubris and Wretched Excess on Wall Street*, London: Allen Lane.

Congressional Budget Office (2009) "The Troubled Asset Relief Program: Report on Transactions Through December 31, 2008". Available at www.cbo.gov/ftpdocs/ 99xx/doc9961/01-16-TARP.pdf.

Conover, C.T. (1984) "Testimony: Inquiry Into the Continental Illinois Corp. and Continental National Bank: Hearing Before the Subcommittee on Financial Institutions Supervision, Regulation, and Insurance of the Committee on Banking, Finance and Urban Affairs, U.S. House of Representatives", 98th Congress, 2nd Session, 18–19 September and 4 October, 98–111.

Conway, E. (2009) "Mervyn King: Bail-outs Created 'Biggest Moral Hazard in History'", 20 October. Available at www.telegraph.co.uk/finance/economics/ 6389906/Mervyn-King-bailouts-created-biggest-bailouts-in-history.html.

Cook, C. (2008) "Peak Credit—the US Approach: 'Too Big to Fail'". Available at www.opencapital.net/papers/PeakCredit.pdf.

Cooke, K. (2010) "Bernanke: Too Big to Fail a 'Pernicious' Problem". Available at www.reuters.com/articles/idUSTRE62J0SM20100320.

Cordon, G. and Quinn, J. (2009) "Brown Calls for 'Social Contract'", *The Independent*, 7 November.

Cornett, M.M. and Tehranian, H. (1992) "Changes in Corporate Performance Associated with Bank Acquisition", *Journal of Financial Economics*, 31, 211–234.

Coy, P. (2008) "How New Global Banking Rules Could Deepen the U.S. Crisis", *Business Week*, 17 April.

Credit Suisse Group (2001) "The Basel Capital Accord Consultative Paper of January 16, 2000: Comments", 30 May.

Crokery, M. (2009) "You're Not Worthy, But Goldman Is". Available at http://blogs.wsj.com/deals/2009/11/06/you-are-not-worthy-but-goldman-is/.

Dabos, M. (2004) "Too Big to Fail in the Banking Industry: A Survey", in Gup, B.E. (ed.) *Too Big to Fail: Policies and Practices in Government Bailouts*, West Port (CT): Praeger.

Danielsson, J., Embrechts, P., Goodhart, C., Keating, C., Muennich, F., Renault, O. and Shin, H.S. (2001) "An Academic Response to Basel II", LSE Financial Markets Group, Special Paper No 130.

Dash, E. (2009) "If It's Too Big to Fail, Is It Too Big to Exist?", *New York Times*, 21 June.

Dash, E. and Creswell, J. (2008) "Citigroup Pays for a Rush to Risk", *New York Time*, 23 November.

Davies, H. (2005) "A Review of the Review", *Financial Markets, Institutions and Instruments*, 14, 247–252.

Davis, K. (2009) "Where Has All the Money Gone?", *Economic Papers*, 28, 217–225.

de Fontnouvelle, P., Garrity, V., Chu, S. and Rosengren, E. (2005) "The Potential Impact of Explicit Basel II Operational Risk Capital Charges on the Competitive Environment of Processing Banks in the United States", Unpublished Paper, Federal Reserve Bank of Boston, January.

de Grauwe, P. (2008) "The Banking Crisis: Causes, Consequences and Remedies, Centre for European Policy Studies", Policy Brief No 178.

de Nicolo, G. (2000) "Size, Charter Value and Risk in Banking: An International Perspective", *International Finance Discussion Papers*, No 689, Board of Governors of the Federal Reserve System.

Dehnad, K. (2009) "Efficient Market Hypothesis: Another Victim of the Great Recession", *Journal of Financial Transformation*, 27, 35–36.

Dinallo, E. (2009) "We Modernised Ourselves into This Ice Age", *Financial Times*, 30 March.

Doerig, H.U. (2003) "Operational Risks in Financial Services: An Old Challenge in a New Environment", Working Paper, Credit Suisse Group.

Dowd, K. (1993) *Laissez-Faire Banking*, London: Routledge.

Dowd, K. (1996a) *Competition and Finance: A New Interpretation of Financial and Monetary Economics*, London: Macmillan.

Dowd, K. (1996b) "The Case for Financial Laissez-Faire", *Economic Journal*, 1996, 106, 697–687.

Dowd, K. (1999) "Too Big to Fail? Long-Term Capital Management and the Federal Reserve", *Cato Institute Briefing Papers*, No 52, September.

Dowd, K. (2005) *Measuring Market Risk* (second edition), Chichester: Wiley.

Dowd, K., Cotter, J., Humphrey, C. and Woods, M. (2008) "How Unlucky is 25-Sigma?", *Journal of Portfolio Management*, Summer, 1–5.

Drum, K. (2009) "Big Banks, Big Banking Industry", 26 March. Available at http://motherjones.com/kevin-drum/2009/03/big-banks-big-banking-industry.

Eichengreen, B. (2008) "Securitization and Financial Regulation: Pondering the New Normal", Remarks delivered to the Fixed-Income Forum, Santa Barbara, California, 23 July.

Elsinger, H., Lehar, A. and Summer, M. (2006) "Systemically Important Banks: An Analysis for the European Banking System", *International Economics and Economic Policy*, 3, 73–89.

Engle, R.F. and Manganelli, S. (1999) "CaViaR: Conditional Value at Risk by Quantile Regression", NBER Working Papers, No 7341.

Ennis, H.M. and Malek, H.S. (2005) "Bank Risk of Failure and the Too-Big-to-Fail Policy", *Federal Reserve Bank of Richmond Economic Quarterly*, Spring, 21–42.

European Shadow Financial Regulatory Committee (2003) "Bank Supervisors' Business: Supervision or Risk Management", Statement No 16, Basel/Zurich.

Evanoff, D.D. and Wall, L.D. (2001) "SND Yield Spreads as Bank Risk Measures", *Journal of Financial Services Research*, 19, 121–146.

Federal Reserve Board (1998) "Testimony of Alan Greenspan before the Committee on Banking and Financial Services", 1 October. Available at www.federalreserve.gov/broaddocs/Testimony/1998/19981001.htm.

Feldman, R.J. and Rolnick, A.J. (1997) "Fixing FDICIA: A Plan to Address the Too Big to Fail Problem", Federal Reserve Bank of Minneapolis, Annual Report.

Ferguson, N. (2008) "Wall Street Lays Another Egg", *Vanity Fair*, December.

Ferrier, G.D. and Lovell, C.A. (1990) "Measuring Cost Efficiency in Banking: Econometric and Linear Programming Evidence", *Journal of Econometrics*, 46, 229–245.

Fischer, S. (2002) "Basel II: Risk Management and Implications for Banking in Emerging Market Countries", The William Taylor Memorial Lecture at the International Conference of Banking Supervisors, Cape Town, 19 September.

Flannery, M.J. and Sorescu, S.M. (1996) "Evidence of Bank Market Discipline in Subordinated Debenture Yields", *Journal of Finance*, 51, 1347–1377.

Foley, D. (2009) "The Economy Needs Agent-Based Modelling", *Nature*, 46, 685–686.

Ford, J. and Larsen, P.T. (2009) "How to Shrink the Banks", *Prospect*, No 165, 18 November.

Fox, J. (2009) *The Myth of Rational Market*, New York: Harper Collins.

Friedman, M. (1960) *A Program for Monetary Stability*, New York: Fordham University Press.

Furfine, C. (2006) "The Costs and Benefits of Moral Suasion: Evidence from the Rescue of Long-Term Capital Management", *Journal of Business*, 79, 593–622.

Furlong, F.T. and Keeley, M.C. (1989) "Capital Regulation and Bank Risk-Taking: A Note", *Journal of Banking and Finance*, 13, 883–891.

Galbraith, J.K. (1952) *American Capitalism: The Concept of Countervailing Power*, Boston: Houghton Mifflin.

Gapper, J. (2009) "The Case for a Glass-Steagall 'Lite'", *Financial Times*, 11 March.

Garnaut, R. (2009) "Economic Society of Australia Distinguished Fellow for 2009 Acceptance Speech", *Economic Papers*, 28, 184–185.

Gelinas, N. (2009) "Too Big to Fail Must Die", *City Journal*, Summer. Available at www.city-journal.org/2009/19_3_financial-institutions.html.

Genberg, H. (2009) "Data Requirements for Assessing the Health of Systemically Important Financial Institutions (SIFSs): A Perspective from Hong Kong", Paper Presented at the IMF-FSB Users Conference, Washington DC, 8–9 July.

Gilbert, R.A. (1984) "Bank Market Structure and Competition – A Survey", *Journal of Money, Credit and Banking*, 19, 617–645.

Glasner, D. (1989) *Free Banking and Monetary Reform*, Cambridge: Cambridge University Press.

Goldstein, M. (2008) "The Subprime and Credit Crisis", Paper based on transcript of speech presented at the Global Economic Prospects meeting, Peterson Institute for International Economics, 3 April.

Goldstein, S., McNulty, J. and Verbrugge, J. (1987) "Scale Economies in the Savings and Loan Industry Before Diversification", *Journal of Economics and Business*, 39, 199–207.

Goodhart, C. and Huang, H. (2005) "The Lender of Last Resort", *Journal of Banking and Finance*, 29, 1059–1082.

Greenspan, A. (2009) "We Need a Better Cushion Against Risk", *Financial Times*, 26 March.

Grocer, S. (2009) "Wall Street Compensation—'No Clear Rhyme or Reason'", *Wall Street Journal*, 30 July.

Gup, B.E. (1998) *Bank Failures in the Major Trading Countries of the World: Causes and Remedies*, West Port (CT): Quorum Books.

Gup, B.E. (2004a) "What Does Too Big to Fail Mean?", in Gup, B.E. (ed.) *Too Big to Fail: Policies and Practices in Government Bailouts*, West Port (CT): Praeger.

Gup, B.E. (2004b) "Enron: Not Too Big to Fail", in Gup, B.E. (ed.) *Too Big to Fail: Policies and Practices in Government Bailouts*, West Port (CT): Praeger.

Guzman, M. (2000) "Bank Structure, Capital Accumulation and Growth: A Simple Macroeconomic Model", *Economic Theory*, 16, 421–455.

Harada, K. and Takatoshi, I. (2008) "Did Mergers Help Japanese Mega-Banks Avoid Failure? Analysis of the Distance to Default Banks", *NBER Working Papers*, No 14518.

Harper, I. and Thomas, M. (2009) "Making Sense of the GFC: Where Did it Come From and What Do we Do Now", *Economic Papers*, 28, 196–205.

Haubrich, J.G. (2007) "Some Lessons on the Rescue of Long-Term Capital Management", Federal Reserve Bank of Cleveland, Policy Discussion Papers, No 19, April.

Hawkins, J. and Turner, P. (2000) "International Financial Reform: Regulatory and Other Issues", Paper Presented at a Conference on International Financial Contagion, Washington DC, 3–4 February.

Hayek, F.A. (1976) "Choice in Currency: A Way to Stop Inflation", Occasional Paper No 48, London: Institute of Economic Affairs.

Hetzel, R.L. (1991) "Too Big to Fail: Origins, Consequences, and Outlook", *Federal Reserve Bank of Richmond Economic Review*, November/December, 3–15.

Honohan, P. and Klingebiel, D. (2000) "Controlling Fiscal Costs of Banking Crises", World Bank Policy Research Papers, No 2441.

Horn, K. (2009) "The Serendipity of Genius", *Standpoint*, 7 October. Available at www.standpointmag.co.uk/node/2164/full.

Horwitz, S. (1992) *Monetary Evolution, Free Banking and Economic Order*, Boulder: Westview.

Hosono, K., Sakai, K. and Tsuru, K. (2007) "Consolidation of Banks in Japan: Causes and Consequences", NBER Working Papers, No 13399.

House Committee on Banking and Financial Services (1998) "Hearing on Hedge Fund Operations before the House Committee on Banking and Financial Services", 105th Congress, 2nd Session, Serial No 105–180.

House Committee on Banking and Financial Services (1999) "Hearing on the President's Working Group Study on Hedge Funds", 106th Congress, 1st Session, Serial Number 106–119.

Hubbard, G., Scott, H. and Zingales, L. (2009) "Banks Need Fewer Carrots and More Sticks", *Wall Street Journal*, 6 May.

Hubner, R., Laycock, M. and Peemoller, F. (2003) "Managing Operational Risk", in Mestchian, P. (ed.) *Advances in Operational Risk: Firm-wide Issues for Financial Institutions*, London: Risk Books.

Hughes, J.P. and Mester, L. (1998) "Bank Capitalization and Cost: Evidence of Scale Economies in Risk Management and Signaling", *Review of Economics and Statistics*, 80, 314–325.

Hughes, J.P., Mester, L.J. and Moon, C.G. (2001) "Are Scale Economies in Banking Elusive or Illusive? Evidence Obtained by Incorporating Capital Structure and Risk Taking into Models of Bank Production", *Journal of Banking and Finance*, 25, 2169–2208.

Humphrey, D.B. (1990) "Why Do Estimates of Bank Scale Economies Differ?", *Federal Reserve Bank of Richmond Economic Review*, 76, 38–50.

Hunter, W.C. and Timme, S.G. (1986) "Technological Change, Organizational Form and the Structure of Bank Productivity", *Journal of Money, Credit and Banking*, 18, 152–166.

Hunter, W.C. and Timme, S.G. (1991) "Technological Change in Large U.S. Commercial Banks", *Journal of Business*, 64, 339–362.

Hunter, W.C. and Wall, L. (1989) "Bank Mergers Motivations: A Review of the Evidence and Examination of Key Target Banking Characteristics", *Federal Reserve Bank of Atlanta Economic Review*, September, 2–19.

Hunter, W.C., Timme, S.G. and Yang, W.K. (1990) "An Examination of Cost Subadditivity and Multiproduct in Large U.S. Banks", *Journal of Money, Credit and Banking*, 22, 504–525.

Hutton, W. (2009) "Gordon Brown Backs Radical Plans to Transform Global Banking System", *The Observer*, 8 November.

Imeson, M. (2006) "Capital Accord or Capital Discord?", *The Banker*, March.

International Monetary Fund (2008) *Global Financial Stability Report*, April.

Jayaratne, J. and Strahan, P.E. (1998) "Entry Restrictions, Industry Evolution and Dynamic Efficiency: Evidence from Commercial Banking", *Journal of Law and Economics*, 49, 239–274.

Jensen, M. (1978) "Some Anomalous Evidence Regarding Market Efficiency", *Journal of Financial Economics*, 6, 95–101.

Jobst, A.A. (2007) "Operational Risk: The Sting is Still in the Tail but the Poison Depends on the Dose", *Journal of Operational Risk*, 2 (Summer), 3–59.

Johnson, S. (2009) "The Quite Coup", *The Atlantic*, May.

Jordan, S. (2009) "'Too Big to Fail' Idea Should End", FDIC Chief Says, *Tribune Business News*, 25 July.

Kane, E. (2000) "Incentives for Banking Megamergers: What Motives Might Regulators Infer from Event Study Evidence?", *Journal of Money, Credit and Banking*, 32, 671–701.

Kaufman, G.G. (2003) "A Proposal for Efficiently Resolving Out-of-the-Money Swap Positions at Large Insolvent Banks", Federal Reserve Bank of Chicago, Working Papers, No WP-03-01.

Kaufman, G.G. (2004) "Too Big to Fail in U.S. Banking: Quo Vadis?", in Gup, B.E. (ed.) *Too Big to Fail: Policies and Practices in Government Bailouts*, West Port (CT): Praeger.

Kaufman, G.G. (2005) "Basel II vs. Prompt Corrective Action: Which is Best for Public Policy?", *Financial Markets, Institutions and Instruments*, 14, 349–357.

Kaufman, G.G. and Scott, K. (2000) "Does Bank Regulation Retard or Contribute to Systemic Risk?", Mimeo, Loyola University Chicago and Stanford Law School.

Kaufman, H. (2001) "What Would Adam Smith Say Now?", *Business and Economics*, 36, 7–12.

Kaufman, H. (2009) *The Road to Financial Reformation: Warnings, Consequences, Reforms*, New York: Wiley.

Kay, J. (2009a) "Too Big to Fail? Wall Street, We Have a Problem", *Financial Times*, 22 July.

Kay, J. (2009b) "Why 'Too Big to Fail' is Too Much for Us to Take", *Financial Times*, 27 May.

Kay, J. (2009c) *The Long and the Short of It: A Guide to Finance and Investment for Normally Intelligent People Who Aren't in the Industry*, London: Erasmeus Press.

Keeley, M.C. (1980) "Deposit Insurance, Risk and Market Power in Banking", *American Economic Review*, 80, 183–200.

Keeley, M.C. and Furlong, F.T. (1990) "A Reexamination of Mean-Variance Analysis of Bank Capital Regulation", *Journal of Banking and Finance*, 14, 69–84.

Kho, B., Lee, D. and Stulz, R.M. (2000) "U.S. Banks, Crises and Bailouts from Mexico to LTCM", *American Economic Review* (Papers and Proceedings), 90, 28–31.

Kim, H.Y. (1986) "Economies of Scale and Economies of Scope in Multi-product Financial Institutions: Further Evidence from Credit Unions", *Journal of Money, Credit and Banking*, 18, 220–226.

Koehn, M. and Santomero, A.M. (1980) "Regulation of Bank Capital and Portfolio Risk", *Journal of Finance*, 35, 1235–1244.

KPMG (2005) "Managing Operational Risk Beyond Basel II", KPMG Financial Services.

Krugman, P. (2009) "Reagan Did It", *New York Times*, 1 June.

Kurdas, C. (2009) "Goldman Critics vs. Little Goldmans", ThinkMarkets, 20 October (with comments). Available at www.thinkmarkets.wordpress.com/2009/10/10/goldman-critics-vs-little-goldmans/.

Labaton, S. and Calmes, J. (2009) "Obama Proposes a First Overhaul of Finance Rules", *New York Times*, 14 May.

Laeven, L. and Levine, R. (2007) "Is There a Diversification Discount in Financial Conglomerates", *Journal of Financial Economics*, 85, 331–367.

Lanchester, J. (2009) "It's Finished", *London Review of Books*, 28 May. Available at www.lrb.co.uk/v31/n10/print//lanc01_html.

Landon, T. (2008) "What's $34 Billion on Wall Street?", *New York Times*, 27 January.

Lang, L.H.P. and Stulz (1994) "Tobin's q, Corporate Diversification and Firm Performance", *Journal of Political Economy*, 102, 1248–1280.

LaWare, J. (1991) "Testimony: Economic Implications of the 'Too-Big-to-Fail' Policy: Hearing before Subcommittee on Economic Stabilization of Committee on Banking, Finance and Urban Affairs", U.S. House of Representatives, 102d Cong., 1st Session, 9 May.

Lawson, D. (2009) "Fool's Gold: How an Ingenious Tribe of Bankers Rewrote the Rules of Finance, Made a Fortune and Survived a Catastrophe", by Gillian Tett, *The Sunday Times*, 3 May.

Le Compte, R.L.B. and Smith, S.D. (1990) "Changes in the Cost of Intermediation: The Case of Savings and Loans", *Journal of Finance*, 45, 1337–1346.

Leach, J.A. (1998) "The Failure of Long-Term Capital Management: A Preliminary Assessment", Statement to the House Banking and Finance Committee, 12 October. Available at www.house.gov/banking/1012981e.htm.

Leathers, C.G. and Raines, J.P. (2004) "Some Historical Perspectives on 'Too Big to Fail' Policies", in Gup, B.E. (ed.) *Too Big to Fail: Policies and Practices in Government Bailouts*, West Port (CT): Praeger.

Lee, E. (2007) "Understanding a Bank's Balance Sheet", *The Motley Fool*, 5 January. Available at www.fool.com/investing/general/2007/01/05/understanding-a-banks-balance-sheet.aspx.

Lekatis, G.J. (2009) "Basel II and Liquidity Risk after the Financial Crisis", *Ezine Articles*. Available at http://ezinearticles.com.

Lewis, M. (1989) *Liar's Poker*, New York: W.W. Norton and Company.

Lewis, M. (2009a) "Bashing Goldman Sachs is Simply a Game for Fools", Bloomberg Press, 27 July.

Lewis, M. (2009b) "The Man who Crashed the World", *Vanity Fair*, August. Available at www.vanityfair.com.

Lewis, M. and Einhorn, D. (2009) "How to Repair a Broken Financial World", *New York Times*, 4 January.

Linder, J.C. and Crane, D.B. (1992) "Bank Mergers, Integration and Profitability", Working Paper, Harvard Business School.

Lins, K. and Servaes, H. (1999) "International Evidence on the Value of Corporate Diversification", *Journal of Finance*, 54, 2215–2239.

Mason, P.M., Steagall, J.W. and Fabritiust, M.M. (1992) "Publication Delays in Articles in Economics: What to Do about Them", *Applied Economics*, 24, 859–874.

McAlister, P.H. and McManus, D.A. (1993) "Resolving the Scale Efficiency Puzzle in Banking", *Journal of Banking and Finance*, 17, 389–405.

McConnell, P. (2006) "A Perfect Storm—Why are Some Operational Losses Larger than Others?", Unpublished Paper, July. Available at www.gloriamundi.org/library_journal_view.asp?journal_id=7642.

McDonald, I.M. (2009) "The Global Financial Crisis and Behavioural Economics", *Economic Papers*, 28, 249–254.

McElroy, A. (2010) "FDIC Board Seeks Comments on Incorporating Employee Compensation Structures into the Risk Assessment System", *Bank Notes*, 34, 2.

McKee, M. and Lanman, S. (2009) "Greenspan Says U.S. Should Consider Breaking up Large Banks". Available at www.bloomberg.com/apps/news?pid= 20670001& sid=aJ8HPmNUfchg.

Mester, L.J. (1987) "A Multiproduct Cost Study of Savings and Loans", *Journal of Finance*, 42, 423–445.

Mester, L.J. (1989) "Testing for Expense Preference Behavior: Mutual versus Stock Savings and Loans", *Rand Journal of Economics*, 20, 483–498.

Mester, L.J. (1991) "Agency Cost Among Savings and Loans", *Journal of Financial Intermediation*, 3, 257–278.

Metais, E. (2009) "The Failure of Mergers-Acquisitions, Myth or Reality?", EDHEC Business School. Available at www.edhec-mba.com/jsp/fiche_pagelibre.jsp? CODE=0337090&LANGUE=1.

Mishkin, F.S. (1992) "An Evaluation of the Treasury Plan for Banking Reform", *Journal of Economic Perspectives*, 6, 133–153.

Mishkin, F.S. (1999) "Financial Consolidation: Dangers and Opportunities", *Journal of Banking and Finance*, 23, 675–691.

Mishkin, F.S. (2001) "Financial Policies and the Prevention of Financial Crises in Emerging Market Countries", NBER Working Papers, No 8087.

Mishkin, F.S. (2006) "How Big a Problem is Too Big to Fail? A Review of Gary Stern and Ron Feldman's Too Big to Fail: The Hazards of Bank Bailouts", *Journal of Economic Literature*, 44, 988–1004.

Mitchell, K. and Onvural, N. (1996) "Economies of Scale at Large Commercial Banks: Evidence from the Fourier Flexible Functional Form", *Journal of Money, Credit and Banking*, 28, 178–199.

Money Really Matters (2009) "Nothing is Too Big to Fail—Part I", 26 August. Available at www.moneyreallymatters.com/category/tags/citibank-bankruptcy.

Moosa, I.A. (2002) *Foreign Direct Investment: Theory, Evidence and Practice*, London: Palgrave.

Moosa, I.A. (2007) *Operational Risk Management*, London: Palgrave.

Moosa, I.A. (2008) *Quantification of Operational Risk under Basel II: The Good, Bad and Ugly*, London: Palgrave.

Moosa, I.A. (2010) "Basel II as a Casualty of the Global Financial Crisis", *Journal of Banking Regulation*, 11, 95–114.

Morgan, D.P. and Stiroh, K.J. (2005) "Too Big to Fail After All These Years", Federal Reserve Bank of New York, Staff Reports, No 220.

Morris, C.R. (2008) *The Trillion Dollar Meltdown*, New York: Public Affairs.

Moss, D. (2009) "An Ounce of Prevention: The Power of Public Risk Management in Stabilizing the Financial System", Harvard Business School, Working Paper No 09-087.

Moyer, R.C. and Lamy, R.E. (1992) "'Too Big to Fail': Rationale, Consequences, and Alternatives", *Business Economics* 27, 19–24.

Murray, J.D. and White, R.W. (1983) "Economies of Scale and Economies of Scope in Multiproduct Financial Institutions: A Study of British Columbia Credit Unions", *Journal of Finance*, 38, 887–902.

Murray, W.J. (2009) "United States: 'Too Big to Fail'?", Available at www.wnd.com/index.php?fa=PAGE.view&pageId=107749.

NECN.com (2008) "Govt. Agrees to Provide $85 billion Emergency Loan to AIG", 17 September. Available at www.necn.com/Boston/Business/Govt-agrees-to-provide-85-billion-emergency-loan-to-AIG/1221614810.html.

Norman, P. (2008) "The Role of 'Too Big to Fail' Status in Bank Merger Activity", PhD Dissertation, George Mason University.

Norris, F. (2008) "News Analysis: Another Crisis, Another Guarantee", *New York Times*, 24 November.

Noulas, A.G., Ray, S.C. and Miller, S.M. (1990) "Returns to Scale and Input Substitution for Large U.S. Banks", *Journal of Money, Credit and Banking*, 22, 94–108.

O'Hara, M. and Shaw, W. (1990) "Deposit Insurance and Wealth Effects: The Value of Being 'Too Big to Fail'", *Journal of Finance*, 45, 1587–1600.

O'Rourke, M. (2009) "Too Big to Fail?", *Risk Management*, May, 61.

OpRisk & Compliance (2008) "Basel II is Dead, Long Live Basel III", 28 November.

Palia, D. and Porter, R. (2003) "Contemporary Issues in Regulatory Risk Management of Commercial Banks", *Financial Markets, Institutions and Instruments*, 12, 2003, 223–256.

Patinkin, D. (1956) *Money, Interest and Prices*, Evanston (Ill): Row Peterson.

Penas, M. and Unal, H. (2004) "Gains in Bank Mergers: Evidence from the Bond Market", *Journal of Financial Economics*, 74, 149–179.

Perry, J. and de Fontnouvelle, P. (2005) "Measuring Reputational Risk: The Market Reaction to Operational Loss Announcements", Working Paper, Federal Reserve Bank of Boston, November.

Phelps, E. (2009) "Letter to the G-20 Leaders: Emerging from the Financial Crisis", 6th Annual Conference of the Center on Capitalism and Society at Columbia University, New York.

Philippon, T. (2007) "The Evolution of the US Financial Industry from 1860 to 2007: Theory and Evidence", Unpublished Paper, New York University.

Philippon, T. (2008) "The Future of Financial Industry", Stern on Finance. Available at http://sternfinance.blogspot.com/2008/10/future-of-financial-industry-homas. html.

Pianalto, S. (2009) "Steps Toward a New Financial Regulatory Architecture", Ohio Banker's Day Address, 1 April. Available at www.clevelandfed.org/For_the_Public_News_and_Media/Speeches/2009/Pianalto_20090401.cfm.

Posner, R. (2009) *A Failure of Capitalism*, Cambridge (MA): Harvard University Press.

Prospect (2009) "How to Tame Global Finance", 27 August.

Quiggin, J. (2009) "Six Refuted Doctrines", *Economic Papers*, 28, 239–248.

Rajan, R. (2009) "On the G20's Urge to Regulate", *The Economist*, 8 April.

Randall, M.J. (2009) "Economists Seek Breakup of Big Banks", *Wall Street Journal*, 22 April.

Rebonato, R. (2007) *The Plight of the Fortune Tellers: Why We Need to Manage Financial Risk Differently*, Princeton (NJ): Princeton University Press.

Reuters (2009) "FACTBOX: Highlights of Warren Buffett's annual investors' letter", 28 February. Available at http://www.reuters.com/article/idUSTRE51R16220090228? PageNumber=3&virtualBrandChannel=0.

Reuters UK (2010) "Darling Welcomes IMF Bank Tax Proposals", 20 April. Available at http://uk.reuters.com/article/idUKTRE63J55020100420.

Rhoades, S.A. (1986) "The Operating Performance of Acquired Firms in Banking Before and After Acquisition", Staff Economic Studies 149, Board of Governors of the Federal Reserve System.

Rhoades, S.A. (1990) "Billion Dollar Bank Acquisitions: A Note on the Performance Effects", Working Paper, Board of Governors of the Federal Reserve System.

Risk (2008) "Basel II Backlash", 1 January. Available at www.risk.net/public/showPage.html.

Rockoff, H. (1975) *The Free Banking Era: A Re-examination*, New York: Arno.

Rodriguez, L.J. (2002) "International Banking Regulation: Where's the Market Discipline in Basel II?", *Policy Analysis*, No 455, October.

Rodrik, D. (2010) "The Case Against International Financial Coordination". Available at www.project-syndicate.og/commentary/rodrik40/English.

Rognline, M. (2009) "Too Big to Fail?". Available at http://makeanysense.blogspot.com/2009/06/too-big-to-fail.html.

Roth, M. (1994) "Too-Big-to-Fail and the Stability of the Banking System: Some Insights from Foreign Countries", *Business Economics*, 9, 43–50.

Rothwell, J. (2009) "How "Too Big" Failed Us". Available at http://blogs.princeton.edu/14points/2009/04/how-too-big-failed-us.html.

Salmon, F. (2009) "Let us Hurt the American Financial Services Industry", 13 April. Available at http://blogs.reuters.com/felix-salmon/2009/04/13/lets-hurt-the-american-financial-services-industry/.

Saltmarsh, M. (2010) "U.S. Proposals for Taxes on Banks to Cover the Bailouts Gain Ground in Europe", *New York Times*, 22 March.

Santos, J.A.C. (2001) "Bank Capital Regulation in Contemporary Banking Theory: A Review of the Literature", *Financial Markets, Institutions and Instruments*, 10, 41–84.

Saporito, B. (2009) "How AIG Became Too Big to Fail", *Time*, 19 March.

Saunders, A. and Walter, I. (1994) *Universal Banking in the United States*, New York: Oxford University Press.

Schachter, B. (2008) "Kooky Science for Value-at-Risk", *Asia Risk*, March, 8.

Scheer, R. (2010) "Obama's Endorsement of the 'Volcker Rule' for Once Puts Him on the Side of Ordinary Americans". Available at www.cbsnews.com/stories/2010/02/03/opinion/main6170135.shtml.

Schmid, M.M. and Walter, I. (2006) "Do Financial Conglomerates Create or Destroy Economic Value?". Available at SSRN: http://ssrn.com/abstract=929160.

Scholes, M. (2000) "Crisis and Risk Management", *American Economic Review*, 90 (Papers and Proceedings), 17–21.

Seagar, A. (2009) "Financial Crisis will Burden a Generation of British People", *The Guardian*, 20 October.

Sechrest, L.J. (1993) *Free Banking: Theory, History and a Laissez-Faire Model*, Westport (CT): Quorom Books.

Seeling, S.A. (2004) "Too Big to Fail: A Taxonomic Analysis", in Gup, B.E. (ed.) *Too Big to Fail: Policies and Practices in Government Bailouts*, West Port (CT): Praeger.

Seidman, D. (2009) "Why I Don't Want the Recession to End Yet", *Business Week*, 20 July.

Sheedy, E. (1999) "Applying an Agency Framework to Operational Risk Management", Applied Finance Centre, Macquarie University, Working Paper 22.

Sheedy, E. (2009) "Can Risk Modeling Work?", *Journal of Financial Transformation*, 27, 82–87.

Shojai, S. and Feiger, G. (2010) "Economists' Hubris: The Case of Risk Management". Available at http://ssrn.com/abstratct=1550622.

Sloan, A. (1998) "What Goes Around", *Newsweek*, 12 October.

Smith, R. (1998) "Competition and Macroeconomic Performance", *Journal of Money, Credit and Banking*, 30, 793–815.

Solow, R. (2008) "Getting it Wrong", *The New Republic*, 10 September.

Soros, G. (2008) "The Worst Market Crisis in 60 Years", *Financial Times*, 22 January.

Spaventa, L. (2009) "Economists, Economics and the Crisis", *Vox*, 12 August.

Spindt, P.A. and Tarhan, V. (1992) "Are There Synergies in Bank Mergers?", Working Paper, Tulane University.

Spitzer, E. (2008) "Too Big Not to Fail". Available at www.slate.com/id/2205995/pagenum/all/.

Sprague, I.H. (1986) *Bailout: An Insider's Account of Bank Failures and Rescues*, New York: Basic Books.

Spring, M. (2008) "On Target: Is This Really a Bull Trap?", *Martin Spring's Private Newsletter on Global Strategy*, No 95, 5 April.

Srinivasan, A. (1992) "Are There Cost Savings from Bank Mergers?", *Federal Reserve Bank of Atlanta Economic Review*, March/April, 17–28.

Srinivasan, A. and Wall, L.D. (1992) "Cost Savings Associated with Bank Mergers", Working Paper, Federal Reserve Bank of Atlanta.

Standard & Poor's (2007) "How Systemic Importance Plays a Significant Role in Bank Ratings", *RatingsDirect*, 3 July.

Stern, G.H. (2008) "Too Big to Fail: The Way Forward", Speech at Winton State University, Minnesota, 13 November. Available at www.minneapolisfed.org/publications_papers/studies/tbtf/index.cfm.

Stern, G.H. (2009a) "Banking Policies and Too Big to Fail", Speech at the Economic Club of Minnesota, 26 March. Available at www.minneapolisfed.org/publications_papers/studies/tbtf/index.cfm.

Stern, G.H. (2009b) "Better Late than Never: Addressing Too-Big-To-Fail", Speech at the Brookings Institution, Washington DC. Available at www.minneapolisfed.org/publications_papers/studies/tbtf/index.cfm.

Stern, G.H. and Feldman, L.J. (2004) *Too Big to Fail: The Hazards of Bank Bailouts*, Washington: Brookings Institution Press.

Stern, G.H. and Feldman, R.J. (2009) "Addressing TBTF by Shrinking Financial Institutions: An Initial Assessment". Available at www.minneapolisfed.org/publications_papers/studies/tbtf/index.cfm.

Stiglitz, J. (2008) "Commentary: How to Prevent the Next Wall Street Crisis". Available at http://www.cnn.com/2008/POLITICS/09/17/stiglitz.crisis/index.html.

Stiglitz, J. (2009) "Capitalist Fools", *Vanity Fair*, January.

Stiroh, K.J. and Rumble, A. (2006) "The Dark Side of Diversification: The Case of US Financial Holding Companies", *Journal of Banking and Finance*, 30, 2131–2161.

Story, L., Thomas, L. and Schwartz, N. (2010) "Wall Street Helped Debt Fueling Europe's Crisis", *New York Times*, 14 February.

Summers, L., Greenspan, A., Levitt, A. and Rainer, W. (1999) *Over the Counter Derivatives Markets and the Commodity Exchange Act: Report of the President's*

Working Group on Financial Markets. Available at www.ustreas.gov/press/releases/reports/otcact.pdf.

Taleb, N.N. (2008) *The Black Swan*, London: Penguin Books.

Taleb, N.N. and Triana, P. (2008) "Bystanders to This Financial Crime were Many", *Financial Times*, 7 December.

Tarullo, D.K. (2008) "Banking on Basel: The Future of International Financial Regulation", Washington DC: Peterson Institute for International Economics.

Taylor, J.B. (2009) *Getting off Track: How Government Actions and Interventions Caused, Prolonged and Worsened the Financial Crisis*, Stanford: Hoover Institution Press.

Teather, D. (2008) "The Woman Who Built a Financial 'Weapon of Mass Destruction'", *The Guardian*, 20 September.

Tett, G. (2009) *Fool's Gold*, London: Little Brown.

The Baseline Scenario (2010) "The Obama Financial Tax is a Start, Not the End". Available at http://baselinescenario.com/2010/01/14/the-obama-financial-tax-is-a-start-not-the-end/.

The Economist (1997) "In the Land of Milk and Honey", 16 August, 54.

The Economist (2008a) "Paradise Lost", 17 May 2008 (Special Report on International Banking), 3–6.

The Economist (2008b) "Make Them Pay", 17 May (Special Report on International Banking), 16–17.

The Economist (2008c) "Tightrope Artists", 17 May (Special Report on International Banking), 17–19.

The Economist (2008d) "Joseph and the Amazing Technicalities", 26 April, 16–18.

The Economist (2008e) "Professionally Gloomy: Risk Mangers Take a Hard Look at Themselves (Special Report on International Banking)", 17 May, 11–13.

The Economist (2009a) "Desperate Measures", 14 November, 61.

The Economist (2009b) "Goodbye or See You Again?", 19 December, 113.

The Economist (2009c) "Scapegoat Millionaire", 7 March, 18.

The Economist (2009d) "Bearing All", 7 March, 81.

The Economist (2009e) "Too Big for its Gucci Boots", 12 September, 71.

The Economist (2009f) "Dilute or Die", 16 May, 81.

The Economist (2009g) "How Efficient Market Theory has been Proved both Wrong and Right", 7 March, 73.

The Economist (2009h) "Efficiency and Beyond", 18 July.

The Economist (2009i) "The Other-Worldly Philosophers", 18 July, 58–60.

The Economist (2009j) "What If?", 12 September, 74.

The Economist (2009k) "Systems Failure", 28 November, 82.

The Economist (2009m) "Rearranging the Towers of Gold", 12 September, 66–68.

The Economist (2009n) "Over the Counter, Out of Sight", 14 November, 74–76.

Thomson, J. (2009) "On Systematically Important Financial Institutions and Progressive Systemic Mitigation", Federal Reserve Bank of Cleveland, Policy Discussion Papers, No 27, August.

Time (2009) "25 People to Blame for the Financial Crisis", 13 February. Available at www.time.com/time/specials/packages/article/0,28804,1877351_1877350,00.html.

Tobin, J. (1969) "A General Equilibrium Approach to Monetary Theory", *Journal of Money, Credit and Banking*, 1, 15–29.

Todd, W.F. and Thomson, J.B. (1990) "An Insider's View of the Political Economy of the Too Big to Fail Doctrine", Federal Reserve Bank of Cleveland, Working Paper 9017.

Topping, S. (2008) "Reassessing Basel II", Source+, October.

Trigaux, R. (1989) "Isaac Reassesses Continental Bailout", American Banker, 31 July, 6.

Tryhorn, C. and Inman, P. (2009) "Fred Goodwin to Hand Back More than £200,000 a Year of His Pension", The Guardian, 18 June.

Turner, L.E. (2009) "The Systemic Dismantling of the System", The CPA Journal, May, 16.

US Fed News Service (2009) "No Financial Institution is Too Big to Fail", Mahoney Tells Congress, 24 July.

Vadum, M. (2008) "Liberalism Never Sleeps", The American Spectator (Special Report), 25 November.

van Rixtel, A., Wiwattanakantang, Y., Souma, T. and Suzuki, K. (2004) "Banking in Japan: Will Too Big to Fail Prevail?", in Gup, B.E. (ed.) Too Big to Fail: Policies and Practices in Government Bailouts, West Port (CT): Praeger.

Volz, M. and Wedow, M. (2009) "Does Banks' Size Distort Market Prices? Evidence for Too-Big-to-Fail in the CDs Market", Deutsche Bundesbank, Discussion Papers, No 06/2009.

Wall Street Letter (2010) "BNY Mellon: Bank Tax Equals Bad Policy". Available at http://www.emii.com/Articles/2383386/Banking–Brokerage/Top-Stories/BNY-Mellon-Bank-Tax-Equals-Bad-Policy.aspx.

Walter, J.R. (2004) "Closing Troubled Banks: How the Process Works", Federal Reserve Bank of Richmond Economic Review, 90, 51–68.

Washington's Blog (2009) "Why Consolidation in the Banking Industry Threatens Our Economy". Available at http://georgewashington2.blogspot.com/2009/09/why-consolidation-in-banking-industry.html.

Watson, P.J. and Watson, S. (2009) "Obama Regulatory Reform Plan Officially Establishes Banking Dictatorship in the United States", Prison Planet.com, 18 June.

Wellink, N. (2008) "Basel II Might Have Prevented Crunch". Available at www.Bobsguide.com/cgi-bin/guide/newsExtras.

Wihlborg, C. (2005) "Basel II and the Need for Bank Distress Resolution Procedures", Financial Markets, Institutions and Instruments, 14, 359–369.

Wilmarth, A.E. (2004) "Does Financial Liberalization Increase the Likelihood of a Systemic Banking Crisis? Evidence from the Past Three Decades and the Great Depression:, in Gup, B.E. (ed.) Too Big to Fail: Policies and Practices in Government Bailouts, West Port (CT): Praeger.

Wolf, M. (2009) "The Cautious Approach to Fixing Banks will Not Work", Financial Times, 1 June.

Wood, D. (2008) "A Model Model?", OpRisk & Compliance, March, 35–37.

Word Press (2008) "What Does Too Big to Fail Mean?" Available at http://servant-enterprenuer.wordpress.com/2008/11/30/what-does-too-big-to-fail-mean/. Check Chap 7.

Wyplosz, C. (2009) "The ICMB-CEPR Geneva Report: 'The Future of Financial Regulation'", Vox, 27 January.

Zuckerman, G., Craig, S. and Ng, S. (2010) "Goldman Sachs Charged with Fraud", Wall Street Journal, 17 April.

Index